Buddhist Responses to Religious Diversity

Buddhist Responses to Religious Diversity: Theravāda and Tibetan Perspectives

Edited by
Douglas Duckworth, Abraham Vélez de Cea,
and Elizabeth J. Harris

equinox

SHEFFIELD UK BRISTOL CT

Published by Equinox Publishing Ltd.
UK: Office 415, The Workstation, 15 Paternoster Row, Sheffield, South Yorkshire S1 2BX
USA: ISD, 70 Enterprise Drive, Bristol, CT 06010

www.equinoxpub.com

Chapters 5, 6, 8, 9, 12, 13, and also parts of the Introduction were first published in Volume 4 Issue 1 of the journal *Interreligious Studies and Intercultural Theology*

First published in book form 2020

British Library Cataloguing-in-Publication Data

A catalogue record for this book is available from the British Library.

ISBN-13 978 1 78179 904 8 (hardback)
978 1 78179 905 5 (paperback)
978 1 78179 906 2 (ePDF)

Library of Congress Cataloging-in-Publication Data

Names: Duckworth, Douglas S., 1971- editor. | Vélez de Cea, J. Abraham, editor. | Harris, Elizabeth J. (Elizabeth June), 1950- editor.
Title: Buddhist responses to religious diversity : Theravāda and Tibetan perspectives / edited by Douglas Duckworth, Abraham Vélez de Cea and Elizabeth J Harris.
Description: Bristol, CT: Equinox Publishing Ltd, 2020. | Includes bibliographical references and index. | Summary: "This volume discusses contemporary Buddhist responses to religious diversity from Theravādin and Tibetan Buddhist perspectives. Buddhist attitudes toward other religious traditions (and its own) are unquestionably diverse, and have undergone changes throughout historical eras and geographic spaces, as Buddhists, and traditions Buddhists have encountered, continue to change (after all, all conditioned things are impermanent). The present time is a particularly dynamic moment to take stock of Buddhist attitudes toward religious others, as Buddhist identities are being renegotiated in unprecedented ways in our increasingly globalized age. Is it true that Buddhists are tolerant of other religions? To what extent are Buddhists tolerant? Is nirvana held to be attainable through Buddhism alone? If so, through which Buddhist tradition? This volume approaches these questions and others from perspectives representing Theravādin and Tibetan traditions of Buddhism. The chapters herein bring together a spectrum of views that are not often found side-by-side in a single volume or in a meaningful dialogue with each other, needless to mention with other religions. This volume seeks to remedy this situation, and break new ground to enable further dialogue, understanding, and constructive encounters across Buddhist traditions and between other religious traditions and Buddhists"-- Provided by publisher.
Identifiers: LCCN 2019034461 (print) | LCCN 2019034462 (ebook) | ISBN 9781781799048 (hardback) | ISBN 9781781799055 (paperback) | ISBN 9781781799062 (ePDF)
Subjects: LCSH: Buddhism--Relations. | Cultural pluralism.
Classification: LCC BQ4600 .B83 2020 (print) | LCC BQ4600 (ebook) | DDC 294.3/35--dc23

LC record available at https://lccn.loc.gov/2019034461
LC ebook record available at https://lccn.loc.gov/2019034462

Typeset by CAUFIELD COPYEDITING AND TYPESETTING

Table of Contents

Acknowledgements

To bring this volume, and the vision behind it, to fruition has taken several years. The editors would like to thank all those who have supported the project during this journey. Particular thanks must go to the contributors for their willingness to revise their chapters during the editorial process and to stay with the project, through its initial setbacks.

One aim of the project was to bring together, in one place, Buddhist perspectives on religious diversity that otherwise might only have been accessible in other languages, other countries or other academic contexts. Five of the articles fall into this category. Earlier versions of "Was the Buddha an Exclusivist?" by Abraham Vélez de Cea and "Paths of Liberation? Theravāda Buddhist Approaches to Religious Diversity" by Perry Schmidt-Leukel were published respectively as "The Buddha and Religious Diversity Today" and "Theravāda Buddhist Approaches to Religious Diversity: An Overview" in *Buddhist and Christian Attitudes to Religious Diversity,* edited by Hans-Peter Grosshans, Samuel Ngun Ling and Perry Schmidt Leukel, published by Ling's Family Publication in Yangon, Myanmar in 2017. Carola Roloff's article, "Openness towards the Religious Other in Buddhism" was published in German by Waxmann with permission, at the time of publication, for there to be a translation in another language. John Makransky's paper, "Thoughts on Why, How and What Buddhists can Learn from Christian Theologians" was published in *Buddhist-Christian Studies* Volume 31, 2011 (University of Hawai'i Press). Douglas Duckworth's paper, "How Nonsectarian is 'Nonsectarian'?: Jorge Ferrer's Pluralist Alternative to Tibetan Buddhist Inclusivism" was published in *Sophia* Volume 53 Issue 3, September 2014. We are grateful that the publishers of these articles have granted us permission to re-print these articles, sometimes in a revised form or in translation.

We are also grateful to Equinox Publishing for their willingness to support this project and for their meticulous help in the publishing process.

Abbreviations

A	Aṅguttara-nikāya
Ap	Apadāna
As	Atthasālinī
D	Dīgha-nikāya
Dhp	Dhammapada
Dhp=a	Dhammapada-aṭṭhakathā
It	Itivuttaka
M	Majjhima-nikāya
Mvu	Mahāvastu
Mv	Mahāvyutpatti
P	Pāli
Patis	*Paṭisambhidāmagga*
Pp	Puggala-paññatti
S	Saṃyutta-nikāya
Skt	Sanskrit
Tib	Tibetan
Ud	Udāna
Vibh	Vibhaṅga

Introduction

Douglas Duckworth, Abraham Vélez de Cea, and Elizabeth J. Harris

Temple University; Eastern Kentucky University; Birmingham University

---

Douglas Duckworth is Professor at Temple University and the Director of Graduate Studies in the Department of Religion. He is the author of Mipam on *Buddha-Nature: The Ground of the Nyingma Tradition* (State University of New York 2008) and *Jamgön Mipam: His Life and Teachings* (Shambhala 2011). He also introduced and translated *Distinguishing the Views and Philosophies: Illuminating Emptiness in a Twentieth-Century Tibetan Buddhist Classic by Bötrül* (State University of New York 2011). His latest works include *Tibetan Buddhist Philosophy of Mind and Nature* (Oxford University Press 2019) and a translation of an overview of the Wisdom Chapter of the *Way of the Bodhisattva* by Künzang Sönam, entitled *The Profound Reality of Interdependence* (Oxford University Press 2019).

Born in Saragossa, Spain, Dr. **J. Abraham Vélez de Cea** is professor of Buddhism and World Religions at Eastern Kentucky University (EKU). He came to the US in 2002. Before joining EKU in 2006, he taught Buddhism, Buddhist Ethics, and Buddhist-Christian Mysticism in the department of theology at Georgetown University. He is the author of *The Buddha and Religious Diversity* (Routledge, 2013), which discusses the Buddha's attitude towards religious diversity in conversation with Christian theology of religions.

Elizabeth Harris is an Honorary Senior Research Fellow within the Cadbury Centre for the Public Understanding of Religion, University of Birmingham, UK. Before this, she was an Associate Professor at Liverpool Hope University. She specializes in Buddhist Studies and inter-faith studies, and has published widely in both disciplines. Her publications include: *What Buddhists Believe* (Oneworld 1998); *Theravada Buddhism and the British Encounter: Religious, Missionary and Colonial Experience in Nineteenth Century Sri Lanka* (Routledge 2006); *Buddhism for a Violent World: A Christian Reflection* (Epworth 2010/now published by SCM).

This volume discusses contemporary Buddhist responses to religious diversity from Theravādin and Tibetan Buddhist perspectives. Buddhist attitudes toward other religious traditions (and its own) are unquestionably diverse, and have undergone changes throughout historical eras and geographic spaces, as Buddhists, and traditions Buddhists have encountered, continue to change (after all, all conditioned things are impermanent). The present time is a particularly dynamic moment to take stock of Buddhist attitudes toward religious others, as Buddhist identities are being renegotiated in unprecedented ways in our increasingly globalized age.

Is it true that Buddhists are tolerant of other religions? To what extent are Buddhists tolerant? Is *Nirvāṇa* held to be attainable through Buddhism alone? If so, through which Buddhist tradition or which religious others? This volume approaches these questions and others from perspectives representing the Theravādin and Tibetan traditions of Buddhism. The chapters herein bring together a spectrum of views that are not often found side-by-side in a single volume or in a meaningful dialogue with each other, needless to mention with other religions. This volume seeks to remedy this situation, and break new ground to enable further dialogue, understanding and constructive encounters across Buddhist traditions and between other religious traditions and Buddhists.

The volume brings together leading scholars in the areas of Buddhist Studies, ethics and interreligious dialogue, who have examined the meaning of Buddhist identity in the contemporary age, and the ongoing challenges and opportunities that encounters with religious diversity present. They engage a range of critical and historical methods that both describe and constructively reflect upon the ways that contemporary Buddhist traditions, across Asia, Europe and America, engage with other traditions, Buddhist and otherwise. The result is a collection that offers insights on Buddhist perspectives to religious diversity both historically and in the contemporary age.

Much scholarly literature to date on interreligious encounters has taken the lead from dialogue initiated by and for a Christian tradition. This has been a noble legacy, but the aim of this volume is to provide a counterbalance to how the script of these conversations on diversity has typically been framed. It does so by giving voice to a Buddhist perspective on attitudes toward religious diversity. Yet like the Buddhist traditions that are represented in this volume, the contributors do not assume a unified voice, nor claim to represent the entire scope of the Buddhist tradition. Rather, this volume itself represents some of the internal diversity within Buddhism, and aims to shape and move forward a conversation that will contribute a small step toward mutual understanding across traditions.

This book gives special attention to contemporary developments and innovative attempts to transform traditional Buddhist attitudes. It includes descriptive case studies, new interpretations of Buddhist texts and doctrines, and constructive proposals to foster more fruitful dialogue among Buddhists, and between Buddhists and other religions. The volume is divided into three parts, which correspond to the past, the present and the future of Buddhist responses to religious diversity. The first part introduces the variety of Buddhist responses throughout history, as well as the question of whether such responses are best understood in terms of exclusivism, inclusivism or pluralism. The second part examines recent instances of exclusivism in Theravāda countries (Sri Lanka, Myanmar) and current pluralistic proposals to counteract sectarianism among Tibetan Buddhists ('nonsectarian movement', H. H. the Dalai Lama). The third part explores possible directions for future interactions between Buddhists and other traditions inside and outside Buddhism.

In order to clarify the complexity and variety of Buddhist responses to religious diversity, the book uses three main categories: exclusivism, inclusivism and pluralism. Although these categories are common among Christian theologians, this book presupposes a cross-cultural and interreligious interpretation of each category, thus seeking to avoid an unreflective methodology of intellectual colonialism that uncritically imports culturally specific ideas as the normative, 'unmarked case' (e.g., 'interfaith' dialogue in unstated Christian terms).

The goals of this volume are threefold. The first is to provide an accurate and charitable survey of Theravāda and Tibetan Buddhist attitudes towards other traditions, both in the past and in the present. In order to achieve this goal, the chapters lay out different ways in which Buddhists have responded and are responding to religious diversity. The second goal is to ask normative questions about whether Theravāda and Tibetan traditions could be more open to interreligious dialogue and cross-cultural learning. In order to achieve this second goal, the book proposes new readings of Buddhist texts and doctrines in dialogue with traditional readings. The third goal is to demonstrate that there is a substantial difference between the ways that Buddhist responses to religious diversity have been constructed in popular imagination, and the ways in which specific Theravāda and Tibetan communities actually respond to other traditions. In order to achieve this goal, the chapters in the volume provide information that challenges idealized views of Buddhism, which, rather than being pluralistic in its approach to other religions, often display exclusivist and at times condescending traits.

Popular views of Buddhism as a tolerant religion tend to portray Buddhists as people who accept other religions as long as they help to cultivate ethical conduct and spiritual qualities such as love, compassion, tolerance and generosity. What this conception of Buddhism neglects, however, is that Theravāda and Tibetan Buddhists actually consider the highest stages of spiritual development as exclusive to their own school of Buddhism. Idealized views of Buddhism also overlook the fact that Theravāda and Tibetan Buddhist schools have persecuted and discriminated against members of other schools in order to protect what they thought was the most authentic form of Buddhism.

Our focus on Indo-Tibetan and South and Southeast Asian Buddhism is partly due to practical reasons. Firstly, the editors' fields of expertise begin with Buddhism in India and its iterations in Theravāda and Tibetan traditions. Secondly, it would have been impossible to encompass the entire variety of Buddhist responses to religious diversity in a single volume. Several volumes would be necessary to discuss, for instance, Chinese, Korean and Japanese responses to other traditions. Furthermore, while Theravāda and Tibetan Buddhist traditions are rarely paired in a single volume, their importance cannot be underestimated. Theravāda Buddhism has preserved the Pāli Canon, which contains some of the earliest Buddhist texts available, and arguably allows for a plausible reconstruction of what the historical Buddha may have taught. Theravāda Buddhism is also significant because it is the form of Buddhism that prevails in South and Southeast Asia, with more than one hundred and fifty million followers. Tibetan Buddhism, on the other hand, contains the largest canon of Buddhist texts from India in translation. The Tibetan canon preserves many texts from the mature period of Indian Buddhism (fifth to eleventh centuries) that are no longer available in any other language. Furthermore, Buddhism in Tibet is also an active, living tradition, and notably one that did not emerge into modernity in reaction to European colonialism. Thus, unlike what we see with the history of modern Theravāda, it has a distinctive flavour that is not inflected by the values of the European enlightenment.

In our current globalized age, Buddhists from around the globe have encountered religious diversity in unprecedented ways, both outside and inside of the Buddhist world. We feel that now it is more important than ever to acknowledge and try to understand the impact and implications of religious diversity. We also feel that Buddhist traditions can offer fresh perspectives and valuable insights on this topic, relevant to Buddhists and non-Buddhists. We hope that this volume will help move a cross-cultural conversation around religious diversity forward in new directions and productive ways.

1

The Buddha and the Diversity of Spiritual Paths

Bhikkhu Bodhi

Chuang Yen Monastery

Bhikkhu Bodhi is an American Buddhist monk, scholar and translator of Buddhist texts. After completing a PhD degree in philosophy at Claremont Graduate University (1972), he travelled to Sri Lanka, where he received novice ordination in 1972 and full ordination in 1973. He studied Pāli and Buddhism under Ven. Balangoda Ānanda Maitreya, Mahānāyaka Thera, and the German elder, Ven. Nyanaponika Mahāthera. He lived in Asia for twenty-four years, mostly in Sri Lanka. From 1984 to 2002 he was editor for the Buddhist Publication Society in Kandy. Ven. Bodhi has translated extensively from the Pāli Canon and its commentaries. His published works include *The Middle Length Discourses of the Buddha* (*Majjhima-nikāya* 1995), *The Connected Discourses of the Buddha* (*Saṃyutta-nikāya* 2000), *The Numerical Discourses of the Buddha* (*Aṅguttara-nikāya* 2012), and *The Suttanipāta* (2017), all published by Wisdom.

Introduction

One of the most attractive features of Buddhism is its refreshingly tolerant attitude toward other faiths. Buddhism has no history of forced conversions, makes no demands for exclusive allegiance and does not condemn the followers of other religions to eternal damnation. Prominent Buddhist leaders like the Dalai Lama speak with appreciation of other faiths and propose that all religions recognize compassion and peace as core values. Such tolerance and openness have contributed to a common belief that the Buddha was a religious pluralist who held that all religions share the same ultimate goal. On this view, the Buddha believed that different spiritual paths were merely different means to this one unitary goal and that his own path was only one way "up the mountain to the moonlight at the top."

Such a belief, however, as attractive as it may be in times of interreligious conflict, is belied by the canonical texts of Early Buddhism, as represented by the Pāli *Nikāya*s and their parallels from other Early Buddhist schools. These texts, as I intend to show, offer a dual perspective on the diversity of spiritual paths. On the one hand, they plainly assert that the world-transcending path made known by the Buddha offers the sole means to *the final goal* of the spiritual life, *Nibbāna*, release from the beginningless cycle of repeated birth and death. At the same time, however, Early Buddhist cosmology allows for a more accommodative stance according to which the *provisional goal* of the spiritual life, the achievement of a happy rebirth, is not exclusive to the Buddha's teaching. Rather, Early Buddhism recognizes that the "mundane path" of wholesome conduct and contemplation leading to rebirth in super-human realms can be found in other belief systems, articulated with varying degrees of precision. This dual attitude enables Buddhists to approve of those faiths that promote practices conducive to the provisional goal without considering them sufficient means to the ultimate goal.

I want to state at the outset that in making this case, I am not necessarily expressing my own viewpoint on this issue. On this I have to adopt an agnostic position. I simply do not know where different spiritual paths ultimately lead. Rather, I am trying to extract from the texts the position of Early Buddhism. Further, I am not closing doors to more flexible ways of understanding the relation of Buddhism to other religions. It may be possible for a Buddhist to interpret the *Dhamma* in ways that recognize the capacity of different paths to culminate in the supreme good. This could be achieved, for example, by downplaying the doctrine of rebirth and conceiving the ultimate goal as "awakening to the here and now," as the realization of nondual awareness, or as the unfolding of the heart's capacity for wisdom and compassion.

Such an approach, however, would be an exercise in interpretation, a project launched with a modernist agenda in the background. In this paper I am not concerned with building bridges, however desirable they may be, but with determining the position the texts of Early Buddhism take on this vital issue. These texts, as I read them, unequivocally consider the ultimate goal of the religious life to be a world-transcendent state of liberation that can be reached only through the specific principles and practices promulgated by the Buddha's teaching. This position, so far as I can judge, was not an innovation of Buddhaghosa's commentaries, as is sometimes alleged, but is already evident in the *Nikāya*s.

The Buddha's declaration to Subhadda[1]

The Buddha's conception of the goal of the spiritual life, as found in the Pāli Canon, derives its meaning from the underlying cosmology. It

1. I refer to suttas by their number within the *Nikāya* when this is sufficient; otherwise references are to volume and page number of the Pali Text Society editions.

is rooted in the view of sentient beings as migrating in a beginningless cycle of repeated birth and death, held in bondage by their own ignorance and craving. Since existence in all realms, whether good or bad, is impermanent, contingent and bound to be followed by rebirth elsewhere, the ultimate goal for the Buddha is the eradication of ignorance and craving, and release from the repetitive cycle of birth and death. This is what is known as *Nibbāna*, and those who have reached the goal are called *Arahants*.

In a number of discourses the Buddha surveyed the systems of his contemporaries and found them deficient (see, for example, D 1, D 2, M 60, M 76, M 102, A 3:61, etc.). It is striking that he nowhere affirms the presence of *Arahants* in systems other than his own. However, the question I will be addressing here is a broader one: whether the Buddha held that it was in principle impossible for any spiritual path other than his own to lead to release from the round of birth and death. The answer I arrive at is a principled negation of such a possibility.

The *locus classicus* for this "exclusivist" perspective on the Buddhist path is the Buddha's discussion with the wanderer Subhadda on the eve of his *Parinibbāna*. The discussion occurs in the *Mahāparinibbāna Sutta* (D 16, at D II 151–52). Subhadda was a wandering ascetic who was perplexed by the question whether any of the rival teachers contemporary with the Buddha had attained supreme knowledge as they had claimed.[2] When he approached the Buddha and posed his problem, the Buddha dismissed the question and said instead:

> let it be, Subhadda, whether all these have attained supreme knowledge as they have claimed, or whether none have so attained, or whether some have attained and others not attained supreme knowledge as they have claimed. I will teach you the *Dhamma* [...]. In whatever *Dhamma* and discipline, Subhadda, the Noble Eightfold Path is not found, there the [first] ascetic is not found, the second ascetic is not found, the third ascetic is not found, the fourth ascetic is not found. In whatever *Dhamma* and discipline the Noble Eightfold Path is found, there the [first] ascetic is found, the second ascetic is found, the third ascetic is found, the fourth ascetic is found. In this *Dhamma* and discipline, the Noble Eightfold Path is found. Just here (*idh'eva*), Subhadda, the [first] ascetic is found, here the second ascetic is found, here the third ascetic is found, here the fourth ascetic is found. The doctrinal systems of others

2. The six were named Pūraṇa Kassapa, Makkhali Gosāla, Ajita Kesakambala, Pakudha Kaccāyana, Sañjaya Belaṭṭhaputta, and Nigaṇṭha Nāthaputta. An account of their teachings, as understood by the compilers of the Early Buddhist texts, can be found at D I 52–59.

> (*parappavādā*) are empty of ascetics. And if these monks dwell properly, the world will not be empty of *Arahants*. (D II 151)[3]

The four ascetics referred to here are noble disciples at the four stages of realization – stream-entry, once-returning, non-returning, and Arahantship – the first three stages being stepping stones to the last. Thus the Buddha is proposing that the presence of the Noble Eightfold Path in a spiritual system is a prerequisite for the arising of *Arahants*, those who have eradicated all ignorance and craving and thereby attained final liberation. His teaching contains the eightfold path, therefore it can engender *Arahants*. Other systems lack the eightfold path and thus are devoid of *Arahants*.

As stated so far, there are two apparent supports for an exclusivistic reading of the statement. One is the use of the term *idh'eva*; the other is the assertion that other systems are devoid of *Arahants*. In a recent book, Abraham Vélez de Cea has challenged this exclusivistic interpretation (Vélez de Cea 2013, esp. Part II). As he points out, the expression *idh'eva* is ambiguous. Depending on how the particle *eva* is construed, *idh'eva* can mean either "here indeed" or "here only." There is no way to determine from this sentence alone exactly what is intended. I have tried to avoid biasing the issue by rendering it "just here." Contrary to my position, the dismissal of other spiritual systems can also be seen merely as a repudiation of the systems contemporary with the Buddha, not a principled rejection of all other spiritual systems.

Nevertheless, while I agree with Vélez de Cea that the text merely posits a general conditional relationship between the Noble Eightfold Path and the existence of the four types of ascetics, the fact that the eightfold path is historically and doctrinally specific to the Buddha's teaching immediately establishes an exclusivistic limiting condition on the prospects for attaining the final goal of the spiritual life. That is, the realization of Arahantship requires a path historically and doctrinally unique to the *Dhamma* expounded by the Buddha. The *Nikāya*s, to be sure, do not regard the Noble Eightfold Path as exclusive to the teaching of the *historical* Buddha Gotama. If that were the case, the path to liberation would have become available only once in all of beginningless and endless cosmic time. This, however, flies in the face of the texts themselves.

Early Buddhism operates with a cyclic view of human and cosmic history, according to which fully enlightened beings, known as *Sammā-sambuddha*s, repeatedly arise at rare intervals and proclaim the liberating *Dhamma*. Although they never arise simultaneously in one and the same

3. A similar claim is made at M I 64, followed by a fuller explanation.

world system (as stated at M III 65), the course of cosmic history is punctuated by the appearance of these extraordinary beings who awaken to the same essential liberating *Dhamma* and reveal it to the world, leading countless beings to the deathless bliss of *Nibbāna*. During the periods when they arise, the *Dhamma* will flourish, but over time the teaching will gradually fade until all traces of it have vanished. Thereafter, after a long period of spiritual darkness, at some point a being will arise who rediscovers the "ancient path" and opens it up for countless others (S II 105–7). These are the *Sammā-sambuddha*s, each of whom establishes a *S*āsana, a codified expression of the *Dhamma* institutionally embodied in the *Saṅgha*, an order of monks and nuns. Thousands of people enter the path under the Buddha's guidance and win the fruits of liberation. Then, once again, the *Dhamma* gradually declines and the path vanishes until a new Buddha arises, rediscovers it and reveals it to the world.[4] While each Buddha will adapt their teachings to accord with the proclivities of their disciples, so that the fine details of their teachings may vary,[5] at the core of every Buddha's teaching is the Four Noble Truths and the Noble Eightfold Path. These are the trademarks of their teaching that distinguish it from all other forms of human spirituality.

The Buddha's statement to Subhadda gains its meaning against this cosmic background. It is not an affirmation of religious pluralism in regard to the final goal, an assertion that other spiritual systems can include the Noble Eightfold Path, but an implicit indication that all Buddhas teach the Noble Eightfold Path and thus give rise to *Arahants*. If the eightfold path were to be found in systems other than the Buddha's at the time he made his declaration to Subhadda, it would either have already been present in those systems before he attained enlightenment or it would have been freshly proclaimed by another spiritual teacher at some point during his teaching career. From the internal perspective of the *Nikāya*s, however, neither of these alternatives is tenable. The first alternative is ruled out by the special function the *Nikāya*s ascribe to a Buddha, which is to "open the doors to the deathless" (*apārutā amatassa dvārā*; M I 169), that is, to discover and reveal to the world the Four Noble Truths and the Noble Eightfold Path. The Buddha says (S V 442–43) that just as, when the sun and moon have not arisen in the world, a mass of darkness prevails, so until a *Sammā-sambuddha* arises there is "no manifestation of great light

4. The most ancient texts speak of seven Buddhas, among whom Gotama is the sixth; still later texts increase the number exponentially.

5. Thus at Vin III 9 the Buddha explains how some Buddhas teach abundantly while others teach more sparingly, how some lay down a code of monastic rules while others do not lay down such a code.

and radiance" but only a mass of darkness. It is only when a perfectly enlightened Buddha arises that there is "the explaining, teaching, and elucidating of the Four Noble Truths." Likewise in regard to the Noble Eightfold Path, it is said:

> the Tathāgata, the *Arahant*, the Perfectly Enlightened One is the originator of the path not arisen before, the creator of the path not created before, the teacher of the path not taught before; he is the knower of the path, the finder of the path, the one skilled in the path. His disciples presently live following the path and acquire it afterwards. (S III 66)

Now if the eightfold path had been in circulation in the world before the arising of the Buddha, he could not be described as "the originator of the path not arisen before." Rather, he would have been teaching a path already known and taught by his contemporaries.

On the other hand, if the Noble Eightfold Path were taught by his contemporaries *after his enlightenment*, but during the course of his teaching career, the system that proclaimed the path would have been able to engender *Arahants*. In that case, we would expect to find suttas in which the Buddha praises those systems and declares some of their practitioners to be *Arahants*. Yet there are no such suttas at all, nor any recognition of such a possibility in the doctrinal treatises of the Early Buddhist schools. The concept of an *Arahant* was not unique to the Buddha's teaching but was a term of general usage to designate one who had attained liberation from the cycle of rebirths. In the suttas we see other ascetics claim the status of *Arahant* or its equivalents for themselves or their teachers. However, rather than endorse their claims, the Buddha pointedly rejects them and admits *Arahants* only in his own system.[6]

One might maintain that the Noble Eightfold Path can, *in principle* if not in fact, be found in spiritual systems outside the Buddha's teaching and thus that other systems are in principle capable of bringing forth *Arahants*. If this were the case, however, those other systems would have to meet the following criteria. (1) They would have to share the Buddhist view that human beings are bound to an oppressive cycle of repeated birth and death. (2) They would have to regard ignorance and craving as the drivers of the process of rebirth, whose specific forms are determined by

6. The *Vinaya Mahāvagga*, in its narrative of the Buddha's early teaching career, categorically affirms the presence of *Arahants* only in his system. Thus, after the first five disciples attain Arahantship, Vin I 14 states: "then there were six *Arahants* in the world," the Buddha and the five disciples. After sixty had attained Arahantship, Vin I 20 says: "then there were sixty-one *Arahants* in the world." These figures are clearly intended as restrictive.

the operation of *kamma*. (3) They would have to posit the ultimate goal to be the eradication of defilements and liberation from the cycle of rebirths. And (4) they would have to teach the tenets that the Buddha considers central to winning liberation.

It seems impossible that those who do not accept these premises would aspire for the ultimate goal that the Buddha posited for his followers. After all, if a spiritual system does not accept the idea of rebirth, or acknowledge that we are bound to a potentially endless cycle of becoming, it would have no reason to take liberation from the cycle as its ultimate goal. And if the ultimate goal the followers of this alternative system seek is different from the ultimate goal of the Buddha's teaching, it seems impossible for them to adopt in full the Noble Eightfold Path, which is intended to facilitate attainment of the ultimate goal of the Buddha's teaching. If they did accept these premises, and followed the Noble Eightfold Path – along with the Four Noble Truths, which form the content of right view – the teaching to which they adhere would in essence be virtually indistinguishable from the *Dhamma* of the Buddha. In that case, the question would arise how they could arrive at these principles without dependence on a fully enlightened Buddha. From the standpoint of the *Nikāya*s, that would not be possible.

This problem becomes even more acute when we consider the specific constituents of the path. It may be the case that other spiritual systems include, at least in some measure, the path factors of right intention (2), the three morality factors (3–5), right effort (6), and even the four *jhāna*s that constitute right concentration (8). But *right view*, defined in the suttas as the understanding of the Four Noble Truths, and *right mindfulness*, defined as the practice of the four establishments of mindfulness, are in their completeness quite distinctive of the Buddha's teaching. If any other system expounded the Noble Eightfold Path – the prerequisite for possessing ascetics of the four stages – its doctrinal exposition would have to centre around the Four Noble Truths and its meditative practice around the four establishments of mindfulness.[7] In effect, this means that in both doctrine and practice it would be identical with the *Dhamma* of the Buddha and thus would lose its distinct identity. To the extent that its core vision differed from the Four Noble Truths and its practice did not revolve around the four establishments of mindfulness, it would not include the Noble Eightfold Path and thus would be incapable of producing the four types of ascetics as understood by the texts of Early Buddhism, namely, as

7. In view of the current spread of mindfulness throughout American popular culture, I would have to emphasize that *all four* establishments of mindfulness must be present, ending in the realization of the Four Noble Truths, the culmination of the whole process of cultivation.

the four grades of noble ones from stream-entry to Arahantship.

Nevertheless, the *Nikāyas* are quite categorical that the factors that make up the Noble Eightfold Path are found in their purity and perfection only in the teaching of a *Sammā-sambuddha*. Thus a series of suttas (S 45:14–17, V 14–15) states that "these eight things, developed and cultivated, when unarisen do not arise apart from the appearance of a *Tathāgata*, an *Arahant*, a Perfectly Enlightened One." The eight things are the eight path factors. The same is said about the eight path factors as "purified, cleansed, flawless, free from corruptions;" they too do not arise apart from the appearance in the world of a perfectly enlightened Buddha. Similar assertions are made about the seven factors of enlightenment (S 46:9–10, V 77) and the five spiritual faculties (S 48:59–60, V 235), alternative ways of arranging the path factors and their concomitants.

The *Cūlasīhanāda Sutta* (M 11, at I 64) gives us some indication of the reason for this. At the beginning of the discourse, the Buddha makes the same claim that he makes to Subhadda, and in an imaginary dialogue between his own disciples and the wanderers of other sects, he specifies why: his system alone makes known "the full understanding of all kinds of clinging," especially the clinging to a doctrine of self (*attavādupādāna*). This locates the ground of exclusivity in the Buddha's distinctive teaching that all the factors of existence are not-self (*sabbe dhammā anattā*; see Dhp 279).

Further evidence for exclusivism

That the Buddha did not recognize the possibility of enlightened ascetics arising in systems other than his own is reinforced by the last line of the verse that follows his declaration to Subhadda: *ito bahiddhā samaṇopi natthi*, "outside here there is no ascetic," that is, apart from his own system there is no ascetic who has reached any of the four stages of realization. The expression *ito bahiddhā* occurs elsewhere in the *Nikāyas* in other contexts that support this exclusivist reading of the Subhadda passage. Thus, among the six kinds of knowledge possessed by a noble disciple, knowledges described as "noble, world-transcending, not shared by worldlings" (*ariyaṃ lokuttaraṃ asādhāraṇaṃ puthujjanehi*), we find the following (M I 324): "he understands thus: 'there is no other ascetic or brahmin outside here who possesses such a view as I possess' (*natthi ito bahiddhā añño samaṇo vā brāhmaṇo vā tathārūpāya diṭṭhiyā samannāgato*)." The view referred to is the view of the Four Noble Truths, which is "noble and emancipating, and leads one who acts upon it to the complete destruction of suffering" (*ariyā niyyānikā niyyāti takkarassa sammā dukkhakkhayāya*). Again, among the reflections on the basis of which a trainee (*sekha*, one irreversibly on the way to Arahantship) can confirm that he or she is a trainee is the understanding: "there is no other ascetic or brahmin outside here who teaches a *Dhamma* so real, true, and genuine as the Blessed One" (S V 229–30).

A series of suttas in the *Sacca-saṃyutta* puts the Four Noble Truths at the centre of the liberative project. Thus S 56:3 states that those who have rightly gone forth into homelessness all do so in order to realize the Four Noble Truths. S 56:4 says that those who realize things as they really are all realize the Four Noble Truths as they really are. S 56:5 says that those ascetics or brahmins who have awakened to things as they really are all awakened to the Four Noble Truths as they really are. And S 56:21 states that it is only when the Four Noble Truths have been penetrated that craving will be eradicated and the wandering in the round of rebirths be brought to an end.

A similar claim is made about dependent origination in the *Mahānidāna Sutta* (D 15 at II 55), where the Buddha tells Ānanda: "it is because of not understanding and not penetrating this principle [of dependent origination] that this population has become like a tangled skein [...] and does not escape *saṃsāra* with its plane of misery, bad destinations, and lower realms." Thus any teaching that leads to release from *saṃsāra* must reveal the dependent origination of the cycle of rebirths and the cessation of the cycle by eliminating its conditions, mainly ignorance, craving and clinging. Since dependent origination is said to be the transformative discovery of all perfectly enlightened Buddhas (see S 12:4–10 and S 12:65), from the perspective of the texts, it follows that the prospect for final liberation must lie solely in the domain of their teaching.

Again, the Buddha declares that "without directly knowing and fully understanding the all, without developing dispassion toward it and abandoning it, one is incapable of eradicating suffering" (S IV 17–18). The "all" (*sabbaṃ*) spoken of here, as the sutta explains, refers to the six sense bases, their objects and the corresponding types of consciousness. Thus for a spiritual teaching to lead to release from the suffering of *saṃsāra*, the round of repeated existence, it must articulate the "all" and explain how to "directly know" and "fully understand" it. Yet this, it seems, is quite unique to the Buddha's teaching.

How the "all" is to be contemplated and known is set out in another sutta (M 64), where the Buddha explains to Ānanda the way to sever the five lower fetters, that is, to reach the stage of a non-returner or an *Arahant*. The method is to enter one or another of the seven meditative absorptions (the eighth being too subtle for analysis) and then to contemplate its factors as "impermanent, suffering, a disease, a boil, a dart, etc., as empty, as not self." He says: "just as it is impossible to cut out the heartwood of a tree without cutting through its bark and sapwood, so it is impossible to sever the five lower fetters without relying on this method" (M I 434–35). Again, this is a method that relies entirely on the Buddha's presentation of the path of serenity and insight meditation.

Finally, there is a sutta in which a wanderer named Uttiya asks the Buddha whether the whole world will attain emancipation. When the Buddha remains silent, Ānanda, apprehensive that Uttiya would think the Buddha incapable of answering, tells him:

> Uttiya, the Tathāgata has no concern whether the entire world will be emancipated, or half the world, or a third of the world. But he can be sure that all those who are emancipated from the world first abandon the five hindrances, those corruptions of the mind that weaken wisdom, and then, with their minds well established in the four establishments of mindfulness, develop correctly the seven factors of enlightenment. (A V 95)

Ānanda compares this to a walled city with a single gate, such that a prudent gatekeeper would know that whoever enters or leaves the city must enter or leave through this gate. While ascetics outside the Buddha's teaching who practise tranquility meditation (*samatha*) would naturally succeed in temporarily overcoming the five hindrances, the practice of the four establishments of mindfulness and the correct development of the seven factors of enlightenment are features specific to the Buddha's teaching.[8] Read in the light of the simile, this again implies that for the texts, "emancipation from the world" is available only through the Buddha's teaching.

While it is true, as Vélez de Cea says, that the Buddha lays down objective criteria for distinguishing between teachings that are truly liberating and those that at best lead to lesser goals, without claiming them triumphantly for "Buddhism," what is striking about these criteria is that they are all exclusive to the Buddha's own teaching. One can argue (as Vélez de Cea does) that the path to liberation should not be equated with Buddhism as

8. In S 46:52, the wanderers of other sects are shown protesting to the Buddhist monks that they too 'correctly develop the seven factors of enlightenment' and teach them to their disciples. The passage is strange, for nowhere else are the seven enlightenment factors ascribed to non-Buddhist ascetics. In any case, the Buddha hardly considers this a reason for congratulating the wanderers; rather he explains a mode of analyzing the seven factors that would bewilder anyone but "the Tathāgata or his disciple or one who has heard it from them." The implication seems to be that the wanderers are parroting the seven factors they have learned from the Buddhists.

a historically emergent religion, and thus one can contend that liberation does not depend on "Buddhism" as a specific tradition. But that is a fairly trivial point, a matter mainly of terminology. The crucial point is that those principles that, according to the texts of Early Buddhism, are definitive of any programme of practice that culminates in final liberation (the four truths, the eightfold path, dependent origination, the teaching of non-self, the full understanding of sensory experience) are not found among other religious traditions but only in religious systems that embody the Buddha's teaching. In their completeness, they are not found among the Buddha's contemporaries nor among any subsequent historical systems of religious thought and practice, whether in India or elsewhere. Hence their import if not their description is exclusivistic, closing off the possibility that the *Nikāya*s might recognize religious systems that lack these factors as capable of leading to the final goal of the spiritual life.

The criteria of a liberating teaching are not, however, the only factors that mark the Buddha's teaching as exclusivistic. More personal and tradition-specific features are involved. One is the "four factors of stream-entry" (*sotāpattiyaṅga*), the factors acquired by a disciple at the first stage of awakening. These are unwavering confidence in the Buddha, the *Dhamma* and the *Saṅgha*, along with adherence to the "virtues dear to the noble ones" (see, for example, S V 342). The first three clearly anchor the stream-enterer in the "Three Jewels" as the only objects worthy of ultimate trust. If one following another faith commitment were somehow to become a stream-enterer, by the logic of these texts that person would acquire unwavering confidence in the Buddha, the *Dhamma* and the *Saṅgha*. That would be a rather strange situation. Still another personal factor is the statement of the six things that cannot be done by a "person endowed with view" (*diṭṭhisampanna puggala*), that is, one who is at minimum a stream-enterer. Here the last thing that cannot be done is to acknowledge someone other than the Buddha as a supreme spiritual guide.[9] Thus the Noble Eightfold Path and its subsidiary practices are not tradition-neutral criteria. From the perspective of the *Nikāya*s, they are firmly connected to personal faith in the Buddha as the supreme guide and in the *Saṅgha*, the community of noble disciples, as the "unsurpassed field of merit for the world" (*anuttaraṃ puññakkhettaṃ lokassa*).

9. A I 27, M III 65, and Vibh 336. The gravity of this is suggested by its inclusion with the first five: matricide, patricide, killing an *Arahant*, injuring the Buddha, and causing schism in the *Saṅgha*.

The *Paccekabuddha*

Since, according to the *Nikāyas*, Gotama was not the only Perfectly Enlightened One ever to appear during the long course of cosmic time, the prospects for final liberation are not limited to the duration of his own teaching. The teachings of other *Sammā-sambuddhas* are likewise capable of bringing forth disciples who attain Arahantship and pass away into "the element of *Nibbāna* without residue" (*anupādisesā nibbānadhātu*; see It 38). But what is never recognized in the *Nikāyas* is the possibility of reaching the final goal of the spiritual life through a system other than and different from that of a Perfectly Enlightened One.

This does not mean, however, that all who gain liberation do so directly through the instrumentality of the teaching of a *Sammā-sambuddha*. The texts of Early Buddhism speak of an exceptional type of person who attains enlightenment independently, without direct reliance on the system of a Perfectly Enlightened One. This is the figure known as the *Paccekabuddha* (Skt *pratyekabuddha*).[10] The word "*paccekabuddha*" literally means "one individually enlightened." Since the concept of such a figure is also found in Jainism, K.R. Norman conjectures that both Early Buddhism and Jainism learned of a category of enlightened beings from another sect and incorporated them into their own systems (Norman 1991, 233–248). That hypothesis is purely speculative, since the idea of the *Paccekabuddha* could have arisen in one of these two systems and then been borrowed by the other. However, even if the concept of the *Paccekabuddha* did originate elsewhere, in discussing the place of this figure in the Buddhist scheme of liberation, we are not concerned with the origins of this concept but with how the *Paccekabuddha* was construed by Early Buddhism.

Just as the idea of the *Arahant* predated Buddhism but was incorporated into the Buddha's teaching with a highly specific meaning, this may also have been the case with the *Paccekabuddha*. We are, in other words, not inquiring whether there were people who actually achieved final liberation through some system of belief and practice other than the Buddha's (a fact we can never know), but whether the texts of Early Buddhism recognize such a possibility. And the answer is unambiguously negative. Though the *Paccekabuddha* attains enlightenment independently of the Buddha's teaching, the crucial point in relation to the theme of this inquiry is that he does not do so *through some system of spiritual thought and practice*

---

10. Except when quoting Sanskrit sources, for consistency I will use the Pāli form, *paccekabuddha*.

different from that of a *Sammā-sambuddha*.[11] Rather, as we will see, the *Paccekabuddha* attains enlightenment independently of any established religious structure but on the firm ground of principles integral to the Buddha's *Dhamma*.

The four *Nikāya*s are hardly sufficient as a basis for reaching categorical conclusions about the *Paccekabuddha*, for what they say about this figure can literally be compressed into a single paragraph. He is said, obviously, to be a *buddha* (A I 77). The *Isigala Sutta* (M 116) merely states the names and epithets of a number of *Paccekabuddha*s who arose "in ancient times" (*bhūtapubbaṃ*), that is, long before the Buddha Gotama. The epithets applied to them are exactly those that might be ascribed to an *Arahant*: quenched, released, dispassionate and so forth. In terms of worthiness to receive gifts, they are placed below a *Sammā-sambuddha* but above disciples who are *Arahants* (M III 254; A IV 394–95). Along with Buddhas and disciples who are *Arahants*, they are worthy of a *stūpa* (D II 142). On two occasions, situated hundreds of thousands of years in the past, two men who separately offended against a *Paccekabuddha* named Tagarasikhī are said to have undergone painful karmic retribution as a result (Ud 50; S I 92). And that is pretty much all that is said about them in the *Nikāya*s.

For more illuminating information about *Paccekabuddha*s, we are dependent entirely on texts of later provenance. Since texts from different schools are in remarkable agreement on *Paccekabuddha*s, it is likely they reflect older perspectives not articulated in the *Nikāya*s but taken for granted. A treatise in the *Abhidhamma Piṭaka*, the *Puggala-paññatti*, defines a *Paccekabuddha* as one who "on his own becomes enlightened to the truths, but does not attain all-knowledge with respect to them or mastery over the powers."[12] In this text, the *Paccekabuddha* is contrasted with the *Sammā-sambuddha*, who attains all-knowledge with respect to the truths and mastery over the powers.

Various early Buddhist traditions ascribe the "Verses on the Rhinoceros Horn" to *Paccekabuddha*s.[13] In the Pāli Canon, these verses comprise the *Khaggavisāṇa Sutta*, "The Discourse on the Rhinoceros's Horn."[14] The

---

11. I use masculine pronouns in relation to the *Paccekabuddha* because, in all the textual traditions of Early Buddhism, they are depicted as exclusively male.

12. *Idh'ekacco puggalo pubbe ananussutesu dhammesu sāmaṃ saccāni abhisambujjhati; na ca tattha sabbaññutaṃ pāpuṇāti, na ca balesu vasībhāvaṃ, ayaṃ vuccati puggalo paccekasambuddho* (14).

13. For source citations from the various traditions, see Salomon 2000, 8–9.

14. For a translation of this sutta along with its commentary and excerpts from the *Cūḷaniddesa*, see Bodhi 2017, 162–167, 401–496.

verses shine a light on the character of this formidable figure. We learn from the verses that *Paccekabuddha*s lead rigorous ascetic lives, incline to seclusion and are averse to worldly entanglements. The commentaries depict some *Paccekabuddha*s as solitary and others as dwelling in small groups. Contrary to a common stereotype, *Paccekabuddha*s are not entirely silent, nor do they entirely refrain from teaching others. They give other aspirants the going forth into the homeless life, instruct them in the ascetic practices, and teach ethics and mental cultivation, stressing the dangers of sensual pleasures and the benefits of renunciation. What *Paccekabuddha*s do not do, unlike the *Sammā-sambuddha*s, is establish a *Sāsana*, a systematized version of the path to liberation, preserved and transmitted by an institutional structure, a *Saṅgha*.

The *Cūḷaniddesa* is a canonical expository work stemming from an early period that comments on the *Khaggavisāṇa Sutta*. This work explains that *Paccekabuddha*s awaken to the 'three characteristics' of impermanence, suffering and non-self, the twelve factors of dependent origination and the Four Noble Truths.[15] These are exactly the things that a *Sammā-sambuddha* awakens to. The difference between them is primarily that the *Paccekabuddha* does not attempt to convey his realization to others and guide them to liberation, while that is precisely the task of a *Sammā-sambuddha*.

Vélez de Cea argues that the recognition of the *Paccekabuddha* proves that for the Buddha realization of the highest goal is not tied to the Buddhist tradition. In a sense this is true: the *Paccekabuddha* does not profess faith in the religion known as Buddhism and does not carve out a space for himself in any institutions associated with Buddhism as a historical form. However, while the *Paccekabuddha* attains liberation outside the institutional structure established by a *Sammā-sambuddha*, there are no indications in the texts that the *Paccekabuddha* follows *some other tradition*, professes faith in *some other religion*, and it is the latter point that would have to be established to refute an exclusivistic conception of the path to final liberation.

The only tradition the *Paccekabuddha* can be said to follow is the ancient Indian culture of ascetic renunciation and solitary contemplation. While, historically, enlightened beings may have arisen in other traditions prior to or contemporary with the Buddha – for example among the sages of the Upanishads or the Sāṃkhya system – these are not acknowledged by Early Buddhism. The question we are concerned with is not the factual

15. For a translation of the passage, which is at Nidd II 210–12 (of the VRI ed.), see Bodhi 2017, 420–422.

question whether enlightened beings can arise outside the Buddhist fold, but the hermeneutical question whether the texts of Early Buddhism recognize such a possibility. All the sources at our disposal – the Pāli Canon, its commentaries and texts from other Early Buddhist schools – situate the *Paccekabuddha* squarely in the Buddhist fold. This is so, not in the sense that *Paccekabuddha*s pledge allegiance to a Buddhist religious system, but in the sense that the path of practice they follow and the truths they realize are respectively identical with the Buddhist path and the principles enunciated by the Buddha.

The content of their realization, as the *Puggala-paññātti* and the *Cūḷaniddesa* show, is exactly the same as that of a *Sammā-sambuddha.* The practices by which they achieve their realization fall within the parameters of the Noble Eightfold Path. They observe strict moral discipline, practise the meditations of serenity and insight, comprehend dependent origination and discern the three characteristics: impermanence, suffering and non-self. Their breakthrough is marked by realization of the Four Noble Truths. Admittedly, this information comes from later sources, not from the *Nikāya*s, and thus we cannot know for certain how the latter might have construed the path of a *Paccekabuddha.* But from these passages it is clear that *Paccekabuddha*s do not adhere to a doctrine and discipline different from that taught by a *Sammā-sambuddha.* They only follow the path to liberation outside the institutional heritage of Buddhism. They are, in effect, Buddhist ascetics who discover the path by themselves and travel the path to its goal without adhering to any organized tradition. The path they take, however, and the truths they realize, are, according to these Early Buddhist texts, exactly the same as those distinctive of the teaching of the *Sammā-sambuddha*s.

A few further facts about the *Paccekabuddha* as appropriated by the Early Buddhist tradition are worth mentioning. Texts of diverse schools are in complete accord on these, which testifies to their early origins. *Paccekabuddha*s never exist simultaneously with a *Sammā-sambuddha.* They arise in the world only at a time when the teaching of a *Sammā-sambuddha* has vanished. In their prior lives, *Paccekabuddha*s may encounter and train under a *Sammā-sambuddha*, yet without attaining any stage of realization. For if a person attains even stream-entry under a *Sammā-sambuddha*, that person would have realized the liberating truth through the teaching of a Buddha and thus could not become a *Paccekabuddha*, who must become enlightened on his own. Even the *Apadāna*, a later text of the Pāli *Sutta Piṭaka*, says (at v. 84) that *Paccekabuddha*s "have done services under past Buddhas but do not gain liberation in the teachings of the Conquerors." The *Mahāvastu*, a text of the Lokottaravādin branch of the Mahāsāṃghika school, says that deeds of merit done to a *Paccekabuddha* ripen in the attainment of enlightenment under a Perfectly Enlightened Buddha.[16] The Perfect Buddhas give others predictions of their future attainment of enlightenment as *Paccekabuddhas*.[17] Pupils of the Buddha occasionally form aspirations to become *Paccekabuddhas*, and the Buddha sometimes gives them predictions of the future success of their aspirations.[18] In at least one *Jātaka* (no. 490), a *Paccekabuddha* gives the *Bodhisatta*, the future Buddha Gotama, a prediction of his future Buddhahood.

All these details demonstrate how the different Buddhist schools, with only slight divergences in details, adopted the obscure figure of the *Paccekabuddha*, whose existence is barely acknowledged in the oldest canonical texts, and bestowed on him a distinctive Buddhist identity. Without these details, the *Paccekabuddha* is virtually a cipher. He is said to be enlightened, reclusive, purified, a field of merits and worthy of a *stūpa*; but everything else about him is an enigma. All this is surely a poor peg on which to hang the assertion that the Buddha held that those following other spiritual traditions can attain the enlightenment and liberation prized by his own *Dhamma*. To the contrary, once we fill in the few strokes of the most ancient canonical texts with the details provided by works of a somewhat later period, the *Paccekabuddha* emerges as a distinctly Buddhist ascetic who attains his individualized type of enlightenment by realizing the same truths of the *Dhamma* as the Buddha Gotama realized and taught, but who does so during a period when institutional Buddhism does not exist.

The way to a fortunate rebirth

Although Early Buddhism holds that the final goal of the spiritual life is accessible only through the principles and path taught by a *Sammā-sambuddha*, it does not assert that a fortunate destiny after death is reserved solely for those who follow the Buddha's teaching. Buddhist cosmology recognizes multiple planes of existence into which beings are reborn in consequence of their karma, their good and bad deeds. The "good destinations" include the human realm, the heavens and higher

16. Mvu III 347–48; trans. at Jones 1956, 3:344–346; Mvu III 414–415, trans. at Jones 1956, 3:414–416.

17. Mvu II 206; trans. at Jones 1952, 2:197; Dhp-a II 46, trans. at Burlingame 1921, 2:126–127.

18. So the *Divyāvadāna*, an ancient collection of Buddhist stories preserved in Sanskrit. Trans. at Rotman 2008, 109, 138, 159, 286, 367.

divine realms, where the life span is much longer than human life, and the residents enjoy much greater happiness, peace and tranquility. This cosmology allows for favourable rebirth by those outside the Buddhist fold and largely accounts for the tolerant attitude Buddhists display toward those following other faiths that advocate moral conduct and meditative practices consistent with their own.

A blessed rebirth is what we might call "the provisional goal of the spiritual life." The minimal determinant of rebirth into the good destinations is moral conduct, as summed up in the "ten courses of wholesome action" (see M I 286–89, A V 263–309): abstaining from taking life, stealing, sexual misconduct, false speech, slander, harsh speech and idle chatter, and developing a mind of contentment, benevolence and right view. The right view comprised in the ten courses of wholesome *kamma* is not the same as the right view within the Noble Eightfold Path. It is the view of the karmic efficacy of action, the conviction that good and bad deeds produce their appropriate fruits.[19]

Those who follow the ten courses of wholesome action, no matter what religion they profess, are able to achieve rebirth into the heavens. However, to go beyond the heavens and achieve rebirth in the higher planes – the blissful divine realms of pure form and the peaceful formless realms recognized by Buddhist cosmology – more than moral conduct is needed. What is required is the development of the corresponding meditative attainments that come under the heading of *samādhi*, concentration. The divine realms are to be reached by developing the four *jhāna*s or the four immeasurables, the latter also known as the four divine abodes (*brahmavihāra*): boundless loving-kindness, compassion, altruistic joy and equanimity. The formless realms are to be reached by mastery over the four formless meditations.

These meditation practices are *not unique* to the Buddha's teaching. They were known prior to the arising of the Buddha and the *Nikāya*s confirm that they existed in non-Buddhist systems. The Buddha taught the way to rebirth in the divine realms to those who aspired to them. Thus in several suttas (D 13 and M 99) he teaches young brahmins the four immeasurables as the path to the *Brahma*-world. Elsewhere (D II 185–187 and M II 76) he ascribes these practices to the sages of past eras.

This broad perspective enables Buddhists to celebrate any religious system that inculcates such virtues as non-harming, generosity, patience, truthfulness, kindness, compassion and peace. These form the common core of inter-religious harmony and they also constitute the path leading

19. For a formal definition, see the explanation of right view at M I 288.

to a higher rebirth. Yet a blissful rebirth is not tantamount to *Nibbāna*, and it is the latter that the Buddha declares to be the supreme good (*paramattha*). From the Buddhist perspective, existence in all realms of existence – including the sensual heavens and the pure divine realms – is still impermanent and defective, and the beings who pass away from them are bound to continue their migration in the cycle of birth and death. To bring an end to the whole cycle and win the unshakable bliss of *Nibbāna*, one must acquire the wisdom that realizes the Four Noble Truths. And to gain this realization one must follow the noble path complete in its eight factors.

Conclusion

We thus see that from the standpoint of the *Nikāya*s the indispensable means to liberation is none other than the path discovered and proclaimed anew by each *Sammā-sambuddha*. This path, those texts make plain, is unique to the teaching of the *Sammā-sambuddha*s. Even the *Paccekabuddha*s follow this path, which they discover on their own but do not promulgate at large. According to the *Nikāya*s, the path is not proclaimed in its completeness and purity apart from the arising in the world of a *Sammā-sambuddha*, one perfectly enlightened. It is not found in its completeness and purity outside a Buddha's teaching. This is the clear position of the Pāli Canon, endorsed, so far as we can determine, by all the schools of Early Buddhism.

References

Bodhi, Bhikkhu. 2017. *The Suttanipāta*. Boston: Wisdom.

Burlingame, Eugene Watson, trans. 1921. *Buddhist Legends* (Stories from the Dhammapada Commentary). 3 volumes. Cambridge, MA: Harvard University Press.

Jones, J. J., trans. 1956 [1949, 1952]. *The Mahāvastu*. 3 volumes. London: Luzac.

Norman, K. R. 1991. "The Pratyeka-Buddha in Buddhism and Jainism." In *Collected Papers, II*, 233–249. Oxford: Pali Text Society.

Rotman, Andy, trans. 2008. *Divine Stories: Divyāvadāna, Part I*. Boston: Wisdom.

Salomon, Richard. 2000. *A Gāndhārī Version of the Rhinoceros Sūtra*. Seattle: University of Washington Press.

Vélez de Cea, J. Abraham. 2013. *The Buddha and Religious Diversity*. Abingdon: Routledge. https://doi.org/10.4324/9780203072639

2

Was the Buddha an Exclusivist?

Abraham Vélez de Cea

Eastern Kentucky University

Born in Saragossa, Spain, Dr. **J. Abraham Vélez de Cea** is professor of Buddhism and World Religions at Eastern Kentucky University. He came to the US in 2002. Before joining Eastern Kentucky University in 2006, he taught Buddhism, Buddhist Ethics, and Buddhist-Christian Mysticism in the department of theology at Georgetown University. He is the author of *The Buddha and Religious Diversity* (Routledge 2013), which discusses the Buddha's attitude towards religious diversity in conversation with Christian theology of religions.

The scope of the *Dhamma* and the scope of the Buddha's school

According to Ven. Bhikkhu Bodhi, it is inaccurate to suggest, as I do in my book, that the Buddha was not an exclusivist with regard to liberation and the four highest stages of spiritual development:

> since this is a discussion about the position of the Pāli *Nikāya*s, let's put aside "Buddhism" (a non-canonical construct) and speak only about the "Dhamma and Discipline taught by the Tathāgata." The major question then is whether the Buddha recognizes liberation and attainment of the four stages of holiness outside the scope of his Dhamma and Discipline. I think the texts, viewed as a whole, give a negative answer to this question. (Email correspondence, 3 March, 2015)

I would like to clarify that I agree with Ven. Bhikkhu Bodhi when he says that, for the Buddha, liberation and the four highest stages of spiritual development cannot take place outside the scope of the *Dhamma*. My contention has never been that, for the Buddha, there is liberation outside the scope of the *Dhamma*, but rather that "the Buddha did not claim that liberation and the four highest stages of holiness were exclusive to Buddhism" (Vélez de Cea 2013, 68). It is obvious that the Buddha never used the term "Buddhism," so my contention is simply that the Buddha did not think about the final goal in sectarian terms as being the monopoly of any school. It is precisely because the Buddha did not conflate the

Dhamma and his school that he cannot be considered an exclusivist. By "exclusivist," I mean someone who makes a *universal* claim about the absence of the final goal or the supreme stages of spiritual development, or the most important truth, or the ultimate reality in other philosophical, religious and spiritual traditions.

The Buddha never made an exclusivist claim about all non-Buddhist schools, and therefore, he was not exclusivist in the aforementioned sense of the term. What the Buddha excludes from being paths to liberation and the four highest stages of spiritual development are specific teachings and specific schools incompatible with the *Dhamma* and the Noble Eightfold Path.

It is important to distinguish between "specific exclusivism," and holding a universal "exclusivist view." It is uncontroversial to state that the Buddha excluded specific teachings and specific schools that were incompatible with the *Dhamma* and the Noble Eightfold Path. This is the Buddha's specific exclusivism. However, it is controversial to suggest that the Buddha made a universal claim about the absence of the final goal in all non-Buddhist schools, including those that he did not know or that did not exist in his time and cultural context (Vélez de Cea 2013, 48–49). Thus, a non-exclusivist reading of the Buddha rejects that he held an exclusivist view, not that he considered specific teachings or specific schools incompatible with the *Dhamma* and the Noble Eightfold Path.

If we extrapolate the specific exclusivism of the Buddha to the present, we can conjecture that the Buddha would continue to reject specific teachings and specific schools, not because they are found in non-Buddhist traditions, but rather because they are incompatible with the *Dhamma* and the Eightfold Noble Path. That is, the Buddha's specific exclusivism would not have sectarian borders and would apply not only to non-Buddhist teachings and schools, but also to Buddhist teachings and schools. Suggesting that the Buddha was not an exclusivist in the sense of making a universal claim about the absence of the final goal in non-Buddhist schools does not mean that he was a relativist who accepted a variety of conflicting yet equally valid paths to attain the final goal. A non-exclusivist interpretation of the Buddha is consistent with believing that, for the Buddha, there were non-negotiable standards to analyze critically the paths of other schools and reject the teachings that were incompatible with such standards.

I also agree with Ven. Bhikkhu Bodhi when he states that, for the Buddha, "it was *in principle* impossible for any spiritual path other than his own to lead to release from the round of birth and death" (Bhikkhu

Bodhi 2020, 7). It is obvious that, for the Buddha, the spiritual path that leads to liberation is the Noble Eightfold Path, but this path does not have to be understood in sectarian terms as belonging to any particular school, be it Buddhist or otherwise. Both Ven. Bhikkhu Bodhi and I agree that, for the Buddha, the Noble Eightfold Path and the *Dhamma* are the "locations" where liberation and the four ascetics can be found. Where Ven. Bodhi and I disagree is in the way we understanding such "locations." For Ven. Bodhi, the Buddha thought that the *Dhamma* and the Noble Eightfold Path were exclusive to his particular school, whereas for me, the Buddha did not think about the *Dhamma* and the Noble Eightfold Path in sectarian terms as being the monopoly of any school.

I also agree with Ven. Bodhi when he explains that the Buddha nowhere affirms that other schools of his time and cultural context contain teachings conducive to liberation and the highest levels of spiritual development. However, whereas for Ven. Bhikkhu Bodhi the absence of positive affirmations about other schools presupposes a universal exclusivist claim about non-Buddhist schools past, present and future, for me the lack of positive affirmations about other schools cannot be universalized and extrapolated beyond the Buddha's time and cultural context.

Ven. Bhikkhu Bodhi and I also disagree in the way we understand the scope of the Buddha's school. Ven. Bodhi translates "*dhammavinaya*" as "Dhamma and Discipline." This translation, however, is problematic because it seems to understand the *Dhamma* as being the same thing as the Buddha's school. The compound "*dhammavinaya*" usually refers to particular schools or particular sets of teachings and practices, whereas "*Dhamma*" refers to the law and order of the universe. When "*dhamma*" refers to the teachings or the doctrines of a particular school— and that seems to be the referent of "*dhamma*" in the compound *dhammavinaya*— it is questionable to write it with capital D. The term "*Dhamma*" in the sense of law and order of the universe is singular, whereas the compound "*dhammavinaya*" need not be singular. In fact, there were many schools at the time of the Buddha, all of them with their respective systems of teachings or doctrines (*Dhamma*) and disciplines (*vinaya*). The Buddha is said to have practised in two different "*dhammavinaya*" before his enlightenment, namely, in those of Ālāra Kālāma and Uddaka Rāmaputta (M I 163-166). Yet another reason not to understand the *Dhamma* and the Buddha's *dhammavinaya* as identical is that whereas the Buddha's "*dhammavinaya*" is dependent on the existence of the Buddha, the *Dhamma* exists independently of Buddhas (S II 25).

Ven. Bhikkhu Bodhi suggests that distinguishing between the *Dhamma* and Buddhism, is "a fairly trivial point, a matter mainly of terminology" (2020, 15). I respectfully disagree. Ven. Bhikkhu Bodhi is aware of the distinction between the *Dhamma* and the Buddha's *dhammavinaya*, but he chooses to underplay it by translating "*dhammavinaya*" as "Dhamma and Discipline." In contrast, I choose not to underplay the distinction because the *Dhamma* is never exhausted by the particular set of teachings and disciplines of any school. I prefer to emphasize the distinction between the *Dhamma* and the Buddha's *dhammavinaya*, or between the *Dhamma* and Buddhism in order to prevent three different types of Buddhist exclusivism. First, if we fail to distinguish between the *Dhamma* and the Buddha's *dhammavinaya* as depicted in the Pāli *Nikāya*s, then members of the Theravāda school may feel entitled to exclude other Buddhist schools because they contain other teachings and disciplines. Second, if we fail to distinguish between the *Dhamma* and the teachings and disciplines of any particular Buddhist school, then members of Mahāyāna traditions may feel justified to adopt condescending attitudes toward the "lower" teachings and disciplines of early Buddhists. These supremacist attitudes, often disguised as inclusive, de facto exclude early Buddhist schools and their teachings from being paths toward the final goal and the highest levels of spiritual development, i.e., Buddhahood. Third, if we fail to distinguish between the *Dhamma* and Buddhism in general, then Buddhists may develop sectarian attitudes that exclude non-Buddhist schools and their teachings from the final goal by definition, simply because they are non-Buddhist. Thus, the distinctions between the *Dhamma* and the Buddha's school as depicted in the Pāli *Nikāya*s, or between the *Dhamma* and any particular Buddhist school, or between the *Dhamma* and Buddhism, are key to prevent Theravāda exclusivism, Mahāyāna exclusivism, and Buddhist exclusivism.

The distinction between the *Dhamma* and Buddhist schools is consistent with the teachings of the Buddha in the Pāli *Nikāya*s. For instance, in S V 438 the Buddha distinguishes between what he taught and what he did not teach. This distinction demonstrates that for the Buddha, there is more to the *Dhamma* than what he taught in his particular school. That is, for the Buddha, the particular set of teachings and disciplines of his school do not exhaust the *Dhamma*. If the Buddha of the Pāli *Nikāya*s did not conflate the *Dhamma* and his school, I do not think that Buddhists should conflate the *Dhamma* and their respective schools. I am aware that the Buddha's distinction between what he taught and what he did not teach correlates with teachings that are helpful and teachings that are unhelpful to attain the final goal. However, I think that the Buddha's distinction can also be constructively interpreted as consistent with the distinction between the *Dhamma* (the forest), and the teachings and disciplines of particular schools (bunch of leaves).

It is clear that Buddhist schools felt the need to keep elaborating on the Buddha's teachings and disciplines. Such elaborations would not have been possible if the early teachings and disciplines of the Buddha's school (bunch of leaves) were perceived by Buddhists as the same thing as the *Dhamma* (the forest). The distinction between the *Dhamma* and the Buddha's school can also be interpreted as a foundation for subsequent Buddhist diversity. Without a distinction between the *Dhamma* and the early teachings and disciplines of the Buddha's school, Buddhism would have not evolved, not even Theravāda Buddhism. Besides counteracting diverse types of Buddhist exclusivism and providing a foundation for subsequent Buddhist diversity, the distinction between the *Dhamma* and Buddhist schools may encourage Buddhists to engage in both interreligious and intra-Buddhist dialogue. That is, dialogue with other possible formulations of the *Dhamma* inside and outside Buddhist traditions.

The Buddha's declaration to Subhadda

One text that is often used to justify an exclusivist interpretation of the Buddha is D II 150-2. The text contains a conversation between the Buddha, here called "venerable Gotama," and Subhadda, a spiritual seeker from another school. Subhadda asks the Buddha whether some, all or none of six spiritual leaders of other schools have attained "*paṭiññā*" (realization, direct knowledge), a term that in this context seems to refer to the final goal:

> 'Venerable Gotama, there are ascetics and brahmans who have orders and followings, who are the teachers of those followers, who are well-known, famous, who have made a ford, who are regarded as holy by many people, – for instance, Pūraṇa Kassapa, Makkhali Gosāla, Ajita Kesakambala, Pakudha Kaccāyana, Sañjaya Belaṭṭhaputta, and Nigaṇṭha Nātaputta, – have they all attained realization or have none of them attained it, or have some attained it and some not?'
>
> 'Enough, Subhadda, never mind whether all, or none, or some of them have attained realization. I will teach you the *Dhamma*, Subhadda. Listen, pay close attention, and I will speak.'
>
> 'Yes, venerable sir,' said the wanderer Subhadda to the Blessed One.
>
> The Blessed One said: 'Subhadda, in whatever teaching-and-discipline the Noble Eightfold Path is not found, there [the first highest]

ascetic is not found, there the second [highest] ascetic is not found, there the third [highest] ascetic is not found, there the fourth [highest] ascetic is not found.

Subhadda, in whatever teaching-and-discipline the Noble Eightfold Path is found, there [the first highest] ascetic is found, there the second [highest] ascetic is found, there the third [highest] ascetic is found, there the fourth [highest] ascetic is found.

Subhadda, certainly in this teaching-and-discipline the Noble Eightfold Path is found. [Consequently] here indeed, Subhadda, the [first highest] ascetic exists, here the second [highest] ascetic exists, here the third [highest] ascetic exists, here the fourth highest ascetic exists. However, other incompatible schools [where the Noble Eightfold Path is not found] are empty of [highest] ascetics. But here, Subhadda, if monks lived rightly, the world would not be empty of arahants.' (*Mahāparinibbāna Sutta* D II 150-1)[1]

According to the exclusivist interpretation, the Buddha claims that the four highest ascetics are exclusive to his school/teaching-and-discipline, and that non-Buddhist schools are empty of the four ascetics. According to the non-exclusivist reading, however, the Buddha claims that the four ascetics are found in schools where the Noble Eightfold Path is found, and, consequently, that schools where the Noble Eightfold Path is not found are empty of the four ascetics.

1. ye 'me, bho gotama, samaṇa-brāhmaṇā saṅghino gaṇino gaṇācariyā ñātā yasassino titthakarā sadhu-sammatā bahu-janassa, seyyathidaṃ – Pūraṇo Kassapo, Makkhali Gosālo, Ajito Kesakambalo, Pakudho Kaccāyano, Sañcayo Belaṭṭha-putto, Nigaṇṭho nāṭa-putto, sabbete sakāya paṭiññāya abbhaññiṃsu, sabbe va na abbhaññiṃsu, udāhu ekacce abbhaññiṃsu, ekacce na abbhaññiṃsū"ti? "Alaṃ, Subhadda, tiṭṭhat' etaṃ – 'sabbe te sakāya paṭiññāya abbhaññiṃsu, sabbeva na abbhaññiṃsu, udāhu ekacce abbhaññiṃsu, ekacce na abbhaññiṃsū'ti. Dhammaṃ te, Subhadda, desessāmi; taṃ suṇāhi sādhukaṃ manasikarohi, bhāsissāmī"ti. "Evaṃ, bhante"ti kho subhaddo paribbājako bhagavato paccassosi. Bhagavā etadavoca –"Yasmiṃ kho, Subhadda, dhammavinaye ariyo aṭṭhaṅgiko maggo na upalabbhati, samaṇo pi tattha na upalabbhati. Dutiyo pi tattha samaṇo na upalabbhati. Tatiyo pi tattha samaṇo na upalabbhati. Catuttho pi tattha samaṇo na upalabbhati. Yasmiñca kho, Subhadda, dhammavinaye ariyo aṭṭhaṅgiko maggo upalabbhati, samaṇo pi tattha upalabbhati, dutiyo pi tattha samaṇo upalabbhati, tatiyo pi tattha samaṇo upalabbhati, catuttho pi tattha samaṇo upalabbhati. Imasmiṃ kho, Subhadda, dhammavinaye ariyo aṭṭhaṅgiko maggo upalabbhati, idheva, Subhadda, samaṇo, idha dutiyo samaṇo, idha tatiyo samaṇo, idha catuttho samaṇo, suññā parappavādā samaṇebhi aññe, ime ca Subhadda, bhikkhū sammā vihareyyuṃ, asuñño loko arahantehi assa.

The exclusivist reading of the Buddha's declaration to Subhadda is problematic for several reasons. First, the exclusivist reading fails to appreciate the conditional reasoning underlying the Buddha's teaching to Subhadda. Instead of answering directly to Subhadda whether specific leaders have achieved the final goal, the Buddha says he is going to "teach the *Dhamma,*" an expression that usually refers to explaining a conditional relationship. In this context, the conditional relationship is between the Noble Eightfold Path and the four ascetics: if the Noble Eightfold Path is found, then the four ascetics are found. This seems to be a particular application of the principle of specific conditionality: "when this exists, that comes to be; with the arising of this that arises. When this does not exist, that does not come to be; with the cessation of this, that ceases."[2] Right after establishing a conditional relationship between the Noble Eightfold Path and the four ascetics, the Buddha further applies this principle to his school: the Noble Eightfold Path exists in the Buddha's teaching-and-discipline, consequently the four ascetics exist here. What logically follows from this conditional reasoning is not that the four ascetics are exclusive to the Buddha's school (exclusivist reading), but rather that schools where the Noble Eightfold Path is not found are empty of ascetics (non-exclusivist reading). From the fact that the Noble Eightfold Path and the four ascetics certainly exist in the Buddha's school, it does not logically follow that all non-Buddhist schools must be empty of ascetics.

Second, in order to be logically sound, the exclusivist reading must translate the expressions "*imasmiṃ kho dhammavinaye*" and "*idheva*" as necessarily implying a universal exclusivist claim. However, these expressions are ambiguous because they can be interpreted in both exclusivist and non-exclusivist terms. That is, they do not have to be translated in exclusivist terms as "only in this teaching-and-discipline" and as "only/just here." They can also be translated as "certainly in this teaching-and-discipline" and "here indeed."

I do not deny that "*idheva*" is best translated as "only here" in other parts of the Pāli *Nikāya*s, for instance, when people from other schools make universal exclusivist claims in Sn 824 and Sn 892. What is remarkable is that the Buddha rejects the universal exclusivist claims of those who believe that only their school or teaching leads to liberation (literally "*visudhi,*" purification). The Buddha not only rejects such universal exclusivist claims, but also associates them with disputes and attachment to views.

2. Dhammaṃ te desessāmi: "imasmiṃ sati idaṃ hoti, imassuppādā idaṃ uppajjati, imasmiṃ asati idaṃ na hoti, imassa nirodhā imaṃ nirujjhatī'ti (M II 32).

If the Buddha associates universal exclusivist claims with disputes and attachments to views, it makes little sense to attribute a similar universal exclusivist claim to the Buddha, who is free from attachment to views and avoids disputes derived from attachment to views. One can always say that whereas the Buddha's exclusivist claim is free from attachment to views, the exclusivist claims of others are not, but I prefer to interpret the Buddha consistently as avoiding exclusivist claims in both contexts.

Ven. Bhikkhu Bodhi interprets "*idheva*" in exclusivist terms as "just here," and translates the phrase "*suññā parappavādā samaṇehi aññe*" as "the doctrinal systems of others are empty of ascetics" (Bhikkhu Bodhi 2020, 7–8). Another problem with these translations is that then the Buddha makes a universal claim about schools that he did not know because they did not exist in his time and cultural context. But the Buddha was critical of those who made universal claims about things that they did not know by themselves. For instance, the Buddha objects to Sāriputta's claim about past, present and future Buddhas, whom he did not know directly (D II 82). It would be hermeneutically inconsistent to present the Buddha criticizing Sāriputta for making a universal claim about Buddhas that he did not know, and later in the same text present the Buddha making a universal claim about non-Buddhist schools that he did not know. That is why I prefer to interpret the phrase "*suññā parappavādā samaṇehi aññe,*" not as implying a universal exclusivist claim but rather as an instance of specific exclusivism. The Buddha seems to be referring to specific teachings or specific schools that are incompatible with the *Dhamma*, or where the Noble Eightfold Path is not found. I am not the first one to favour a non-exclusivist translation. For instance, Rupert Gethin translates the same phrase as "other contrary systems are empty of ascetics" (Gethin 2008, 86).

It is true that the prefix "*para*" usually means "of others" and that is why Ven. Bhikkhu Bodhi translates "*parappavādā*" as "doctrinal systems of others." However, "*para*" may also connote the idea of opposition, as for instance in the compound "*parabhūmi,*" which is not best translated as "land of others" but rather as "hostile territory."[3] Even if the only possible translation of "*para*" in "*parappavāda*" were "of others," and "*para*" in this context did not connote the idea of opposition, it could still be possible to derive such an idea of opposition from "*pavādā.*" Reading "*pavādā*" as connoting the idea of opposition seems to be justified by several dictionaries. For instance, the PTS dictionary defines "*pavāda*" as follows: "[pa+vad, cp. Epic Sk. *pravāda* talk, saying] talk,

3. I am indebted to Rupert Gethin for this point about the less common usage of "*para.*"

disputation, discussion" Rhys Davids and Stede, 1921, 443). Similarly, among the possible meanings of "*pravādḥ,*" Apte's Sanskrit dictionary mentions "litigious language, words of challenge, mutual defiance" (Apte 1890, 1107). Likewise, Monier-Williams gives a variety of meanings for *pravāda*, including "mutual defiance, words of challenge (prior to combat)" (Monier Williams 1899, 690). In sum, whatever way we decide to interpret "*para*" and "*pavādā,*" it seems plausible to translate the compound "*parappavādā*" as "incompatible schools" or "contrary systems." And if translating "*parappavādā*" as "incompatible schools" or "contrary systems" is plausible, then the exclusivist rendering of the phrase is at least unnecessary.

A third reason against the exclusivist reading of the Buddha's declaration to Subhadda is that it clashes with what the Buddha says he is going to do at the beginning of the text. Instead of answering Subhadda's question, the Buddha says he is going to teach the *Dhamma*. That is, the Buddha avoids making a polemical claim about other masters at the beginning of the conversation. Instead of making such a claim, the Buddha decides to teach the *Dhamma*, that is, to teach a conditional relationship between the Noble Eightfold Path and the four ascetics. In my reading, the Buddha avoids a polemical claim about non-Buddhists both at the beginning and at the end of the conversation with Subhadda. In contrast, the exclusivist reading portrays the Buddha as avoiding a polemical claim about non-Buddhist masters at the beginning, and as making a polemical exclusivist claim about non-Buddhists schools at the end.

Fourth, the exclusivist reading does less justice to the context of the text. The conversation with Subhadda begins with a question about specific leaders of specific schools of the Buddha's time and cultural context. In my reading, the conversation also concludes with an answer about specific schools incompatible with the *Dhamma*, or schools where the Noble Eightfold Path is not found. Subhadda mentions the names of six masters whose teachings are incompatible with the *Dhamma* and the Noble Eightfold Path. The six masters are Pūraṇa Kassapa, Makkhali Gosāla, Ajita Kesakambala, Pakudha Kaccāyana, Sañjaya Belaṭṭhaputta and Nigaṇṭha Nātaputta. The teachings of these six masters are rejected in the *Discourse on the Fruits of Spiritual Practice* (D I 52–9). Given that the specific teachings of the six masters mentioned by Subhadda are incompatible with the *Dhamma* and the Noble Eightfold Path, it seems more consistent with the text to interpret the expression "*parappavāda*" as referring to specific schools or specific teachings that are also incompatible with the *Dhamma* and the Noble Eightfold Path.

Fifth, the exclusivist reading seems to contradict the Buddha's explicit refusal to make a universal exclusivist claim at Sn 1082. Instead of stating that all ascetics and brahmins do not attain liberation, the Buddha limits himself to teaching the *Dhamma*, that is, establishing a conditional relationship:

> 'I do not say, Nanda,' said the Blessed one, 'that all ascetics and brahmins are shrouded in birth and death. Whoever has renounced here [attachment to] what is seen, heard or thought, and has renounced [attachment to] all rules and rituals, and has renounced [attachment to] all diversification of forms, fully comprehending craving, without taints, them indeed I call "stream-crossers."' (Sn 1082. My translation)

The Buddha rejects a universal exclusivist claim about ascetics and brahmins. Instead of making such a claim, the Buddha teaches the *Dhamma*, i.e., provides a conditional relationship: if someone abandons all kinds of attachment, fully understands craving, and is without taints, then she or he can be considered a "stream-crosser," i.e., a liberated being.

Avoiding a universal exclusivist claim at Sn 1082 is consistent with avoiding a universal exclusivist claim in the conversation with Subhadda. Claiming that "in whatever teaching-and-discipline the Noble Eightfold Path is found, the four highest ascetics are found," is consistent with claiming that whomsoever renounces attachment, fully understands craving and lacks taints, is a "stream-crosser." If the Buddha does not say in reference to non-Buddhists "that all ascetics and brahmins are shrouded in birth and death" (Sn 1082), then he cannot say without contradiction that all the schools of others are empty of ascetics (D II 151). Interpreting the Buddha as avoiding universal exclusivist claims about other schools in D II 15 and Sn 1082 is also consistent with Sn 824 and Sn 892, where the Buddha rejects the universal exclusivist claims of other masters.

Sixth, the exclusivist reading of the phrase "*suññā parappavādā samaṇehi aññe,*" contradicts the way this phrase is understood in the commentary to A II 238. Ven. Bhikkhu Bodhi translates the phrase in A II 238 as "the other sects are empty of ascetics." According to the commentary, the phrase refers specifically to the proponents of the sixty-two views.[4] That is, according to the Theravāda school, when the Buddha says "*suññā parappavādā samaṇehi aññe,*" he is not making a universal exclusivist claim about all possible non-Buddhist schools past, present and future, but rather making a more specific claim about the proponents of

4. Ven. Bhikkhu Bodhi writes: "Mp says that 'other sects' are the proponents of the sixty-two views" (2012, 1720).

the sixty-two views.[5] Some people may try to interpret the sixty-two views as encompassing all possible views in the universe. However, I prefer to interpret the sixty-two views as reflecting the specific doctrines of specific schools found in the Buddha's time and cultural context.

In conclusion, according to the non-exclusivist reading, the Buddha's declaration to Subhadda teaches that there is a conditional relationship between the Noble Eightfold Path and the four ascetics, and that the four ascetics are indeed found in the Buddha's school/teaching-and-discipline. Similarly, keeping in mind the aforementioned conditional relationship, the Buddha teaches that schools where the Noble Eightfold Path is not found are empty of ascetics. The Buddha does not teach that only members of his school attain the levels of the four ascetics, nor that all possible non-Buddhist schools are empty of ascetics.

Paccekabuddhas

The early Buddhist concept of *Paccekabuddha* is a symbol for the existence of liberation and the highest stages of spiritual development outside the Buddha's school. I am not the first scholar who has seen the implications of the early Buddhist concept of *Paccekabuddha*. For instance, K.N. Jayatilleke suggests that the concept of *Paccekabuddha* demonstrates that, just like the Buddha, people from other religions may discover for themselves not only aspects of the truth, but also the whole truth. In his words:

> the concept of the Buddha as one who discovers the truth rather than as one who has the monopoly of the truth is clearly a source of tolerance. It leaves open the possibility for others to discover aspects of the truth or even the whole truth for themselves. The Buddhist acceptance of Pacceka-Buddhas, who discover the truth for themselves, is a clear admission of this fact. (Jayatilleke 1966, 13)

Similarly, Y. Karunadasa addresses the question of whether there can be emancipation or salvation outside Buddhism in these terms:

> the Buddha is one who discovers the truth but does not have a monopoly on the truth. This leaves open the possibility for others to discover truth. The Buddhist idea of an "individual Buddha" (pacceka-buddha), one who discovers the truth for oneself, is a clear admission of this fact. (Karunadasa 2018, 181)

Like Jayatilleke and Karunadasa, I believe that the early Buddhist concept of *Paccekabuddha* allows for the existence of liberation and the highest

5. The most comprehensive account of the sixty-two views appears in the *Brahmajāla Sutta* D I 1-46.

stages of spiritual development outside Buddhist traditions. If the Buddha did not feel the need to deny the existence of self-enlightened beings outside his school, why should contemporary Buddhists deny the possible existence of other enlightened beings outside Buddhist traditions?

Buddhist exclusivism seems to be a later scholastic development. Scholastic interpreters realized at some point in the history of Buddhism that there was a tension between the cosmic significance of the Buddha and the existence of self-enlightened beings outside his school. The scholastic solution was to say that *Paccekabuddha*s can arise only in a universe where the influence of Buddhas and their schools no longer exist. Buddhist scholasticism also assimilated *Paccekabuddha*s into Buddhism transforming them into anonymous Buddhists: they can attain the final goal outside Buddhist traditions, but after having studied Buddhist teachings in previous lives and by following exactly the same path as Buddhists do.

The crucial question, however, is not how Buddhist scholasticism reinterpreted the early concept of *Paccekabuddha*, but rather how the Buddha responded to the existence of self-enlightened beings outside his school. What I find remarkable is that the Buddha did not send *Paccekabuddha*s to another universe where the influence of Buddhas and their schools no longer existed, nor said anything about *Paccekabuddha*s being trained by past Buddhas, nor suggested that they must follow exactly the same path as his disciples. Rather, the Buddha acknowledged the existence of *Paccekabuddha*s and encouraged others to show them respect. Neither the acknowledgment of *Paccekabuddha*s nor the advice to respect them would make much sense if they were not real historical beings existing in the same universe as Buddhas and Buddhists. Most probably, for the Buddha, *Paccekabuddha*s did not live in his time and cultural context, but this did not mean that they lived in a different universe. The textual evidence does not support the scholastic interpretation, the Pāli *Nikāya*s speak about *Paccekabuddha*s of ancient times (M III 68-71), and about the impossibility of two Buddhas existing in the same universe (M III 65, A I 27-8, and D II 225), but they say nothing about the impossibility of *Paccekabuddha*s and Buddhas living in the same universe.

It is true that for the Buddha of the Pāli *Nikāya*s, *Paccekabuddha*s, like any other enlightened being, must realize the Four Noble Truths, fulfil the Noble Eightfold Path, completely uproot greed, hatred and delusion, fully understand Dependent Origination and so on. But this does not need to mean that the teachings of their schools were identical to the teachings of the Buddha's school. I could not agree more with Ven. Bodhi when he affirms that "the four *Nikāya*s are hardly sufficient as a basis for reaching categorical conclusions about the *Paccekabuddha*" (2020, 17). It is precisely because the Pāli *Nikāya*s do not provide sufficient information about *Paccekabuddha*s that we cannot categorically conclude what later Buddhist scholasticism concluded about them!

One can understand the scholastic exclusivist rationale for "converting" *Paccekabuddha*s to Buddhism and "expelling" them from a universe inhabited by Buddhas and Buddhists. If there is no liberation outside Buddhism, then *Paccekabuddha*s must be anonymous Buddhists, and if the cosmological role of Buddhas is unique, then *Paccekabuddha*s must dwell in a different universe. However, these exclusivist moves are not required by the Buddha of the Pāli *Nikāya*s, who did not understand the *Dhamma* in sectarian terms as being the monopoly of any school.

Ven. Bhikkhu Bodhi rightly affirms that the Buddha of the Pāli *Nikāya*s nowhere states that *Paccekabuddha*s attain liberation and highest holiness through a system of teachings other than the teachings of his school (2020, 16). I obviously agree, but this does not need to mean that *Paccekabuddha*s follow exactly the same teachings in exactly the same manner as the members of the Buddha's school. Only if we conflate the *Dhamma* with the Buddha's school, and only if we believe that formulations of the *Dhamma* do not change over time, can someone assimilate *Paccekabuddha*s to the Buddhism of the Pāli *Nikāya*s. But the Buddha of the Pāli *Nikāya*s did not conflate the *Dhamma* and his school, and the history of Buddhism demonstrates that the multiple formulations of the *Dhamma* found in Buddhist traditions are neither identical to the Buddhism of the Pāli *Nikāya*s nor expression of a universal doctrinal essence. We cannot claim that *Paccekabuddha*s follow exactly the same teachings in exactly the same manner as members of Buddhist traditions because Buddhist traditions lack a universal doctrinal essence. Even if *Paccekabuddha*s were anonymous Buddhists, it would not be possible to identify which specific set of teachings and disciplines they practised.

My contention is more subtle. The multiple formulations of the *Dhamma* found inside and outside Buddhism need be interpreted neither as identical nor as totally different from each other; they just need to be compatible with the *Dhamma* and the Noble Eightfold Path. The early Buddhist concept of *Paccekabuddha* demonstrates that for the Buddha there can be formulations of the *Dhamma* outside his school where it is possible to attain liberation and find the four highest ascetics. Whatever were the schools of *Paccekabuddha*s, something that we can never know (as Ven. Bodhi rightly points out), such schools had to contain teachings compatible with the *Dhamma* and the Noble Eightfold Path. This is a middle way position between claiming that *Paccekabuddhas* must follow the same teachings as Buddhists or claiming that they must follow totally different teachings.

Some people may object to this middle way interpretation that if self-enlightened beings outside Buddhism realize the *same* Four Noble Truths, that is, the *same Dhamma* and the *same* Noble Eightfold Path, then they must be anonymous Buddhists. I respectfully disagree because that would amount to conceiving the *Dhamma* in essentialist terms as having a permanent identity that persists throughout the centuries and across Buddhist schools. The *Dhamma* may not change and remain stable over the eons, but the formulations of the *Dhamma* in particular and historically conditioned schools have indeed changed, as the history of Buddhism demonstrates.

The intrinsic diversity of Buddhism and the multiple formulations of the *Dhamma* does not have to be inconsistent with the Buddha's teachings in the Pāli *Nikāyas*. In fact, the Buddha suggests in S V 430 that the Four Noble Truths possess innumerable nuances (*aparimāṇā vaṇṇā*), innumerable aspects (*aparimāṇā vyañjanā*, and innumerable implications (*aparimāṇā saṅkāsanā*). If the Four Noble Truths have so many nuances, aspects and implications, they need to be elucidated, and that may require diverse formulations at different times and in different cultural contexts. The diversity of formulations of the *Dhamma* is already visible in the Pāli *Nikāyas*, so it should not come as a surprise to find many more formulations in later Buddhist schools. And if there are multiple formulations of the *Dhamma* inside Buddhist schools due to the innumerable nuances, aspects and implications of the Four Noble Truths, it is possible to conjecture that there could have been further diversity of formulations of the *Dhamma* in the non-Buddhist schools of *Paccekabuddhas*. And if it is not illogical to assume that there could have been diverse formulations of the *Dhamma* in the non-Buddhist schools of *Paccekabuddhas* in the past, it is not illogical to assume that there might be other formulations of the *Dhamma* outside Buddhist traditions today.

In sum, the exclusivist reading of the Buddha domesticates the early Buddhist concept of *Paccekabuddha* by saying that the Pāli *Nikāyas* provide little information about them; by setting them aside as legendary, non-historical figures; by assimilating them to Buddhist traditions and transforming them into anonymous Buddhists. In contrast, the non-exclusivist interpretation of the Buddha takes the early Buddhist concept of *Paccekabuddha* seriously, and infers from such concept the possible existence of liberation and the highest levels of spiritual development outside the scope of Buddhist traditions, although not outside the scope of the *Dhamma* and the Noble Eightfold Path.

Further arguments in favour of exclusivism

Ven. Bhikkhu Boddhi deploys another four arguments against a non-exclusivist reading of the Buddha. For the sake of simplicity, I will call these arguments the "outside here" argument, the "Buddhist doctrines" argument, the "faith of stream-enterers" argument, and the "cosmological uniqueness" argument.

The "outside here" argument suggests that the Buddha often uses the expression "*ito bahiddhā*" (outside here) in reference to his school. For instance, when the Buddha states in the verse section after his declaration to Subhadda that "outside here there is no ascetic" (*ito bahiddhā samaṇo pi n'atthi*), the Buddha would be referring to his school:

> I was twenty-nine years old, Subhadda
>
> When I became a wanderer to seek the wholesome
>
> Now it has been more than fifty years
>
> Since I became a wanderer, Subhadda
>
> Dwelling in the scope of the Right Method (*ñāyassa*), of the *Dhamma* (*dhammassa*)
>
> Outside here (*ito bahiddhā*) there is no [first highest] ascetic
> Nor second, nor third, nor fourth ascetic
>
> Other incompatible schools [where the Noble Eightfold Path is not found] are empty of ascetics
>
> But Subhadda, [in this teaching-and-discipline where the Noble Eightfold Path is found] if these monks lived rightly
>
> The world would not be empty of Arahants.
> (*Mahāparinibbāna Sutta* D II 151-2)6

In my reading, however, the phrase "*ito bahiddhā samaṇo pi n'atthi*" (Outside here there is no [first highest] ascetic) does not support the exclusivist interpretation. The phrase is immediately preceded by the

6. Ekūnatiṃso vayasā Subhadda,
Yaṃ pabbajiṃ kiṃ-kusalānuesī.
Vassāni paññāsasamādhikāni
Yato ahaṃ pabbajito Subhadda,
Ñāyassa dhammassa padesa-vattī,
Ito bahiddhā samaṇo pi n'atthi,
dutiyopi samaṇo n'atthi. Tatiyo pi samaṇo n'atthi, catuttho pi samaṇo n'atthi. Suññā parappavādā samaṇehi aññe, ime ca, Subhadda, bhikkhū sammā vihareyyuṃ, asuñño loko arahantehi assā ti.

phrase "*ñāyassa dhammassa padesa-vattī*" (dwelling in the scope of the Right Method, of the *Dhamma*). If the Buddha says "*ito bahiddhā samaṇo pi n'atthi*" after stating that "*ñāyassa dhammassa padesa-vattī,*" it seems most appropriate to interpret the referent of "outside here" not in sectarian terms as referring to his school, but rather in non-sectarian terms as referring to the scope of the *Dhamma* and the scope of the Right Path. That is, according to the non-exclusivist reading, the Buddha simply suggests that outside the scope of the *Dhamma* and the Right Path, the four ascetics cannot be found.

The non-exclusivist reading keeps consistent the prose and the verse sections. The term "ñāya» (Right Method) seems to be another designation for the "Noble Eightfold Path." That is, the scope of the Right Method or the scope of Noble Eightfold Path is the scope of the *Dhamma*. The prose section contends that wherever the Noble Eightfold Path is found, the four ascetics are found. Similarly, the verse section suggests that outside the Right Method, outside the *Dhamma*, there can be no ascetics. The Buddha reiterates with a slightly different terminology the main point of the prose section. In the verse section, the Buddha establishes a conditional relationship between the Noble Eightfold Path and the four ascetics. In the verse section, there is a conditional relationship between the four ascetics and the "Right Method," the "*Dhamma*." Neither the prose nor the verse sections make a universal exclusivist claim about all possible non-Buddhist schools. Rather, both sections teach the *Dhamma*, that is, both establish a conditional relationship: between the four ascetics and the Noble Eightfold Path in the prose section, and between the four ascetics and the Right Method of the *Dhamma* in the verse section.

Another text with the expression "*ito bahiddhā*" that could be interpreted as supporting an exclusivist reading is M I 324. There, it is said that "he understands thus: 'there is no other ascetic or brahmin outside here who possesses such a view as I possess (*natthi ito bahiddhā añño samaṇo vā brāhmaṇo vā tathārūpāya diṭṭhiyā samannāgato*).'" The text is talking about the supramundane knowledges of a Noble Disciple, and the view referred to is the view of the Four Noble Truths. The Noble Disciple says a few lines before that his mind is disposed towards awakening to the Truths. These Truths are directly realized in the mind of a Noble Person, that is, a person who has begun to develop in his mind the Noble Eightfold Path. The first factor of the Noble Eightfold Path is right view, and supramandane right view involves direct realization of the Four Noble Truths. Thus, the expression "*ito bahiddhā*" in this context seems to refer to the Noble Eightfold Path as found in the mind of a Noble Person. Another possibility would be that *ito bahiddhā* refers to the community of Noble

Persons, who are those who actualize in their minds the Noble Eightfold Path. But again, it would be inconsistent with the Buddha's teachings to conflate the community of Noble Persons and the Buddha's school, which contains many types of disciples at different levels of training, not just Noble Disciples. I interpret the text as suggesting that only in the mind of Noble Persons are the factors of the Noble Eightfold Path fully present, and only when the Noble Eightfold Path is fully present can ascetics and brahmins be said to possess such a direct view of the Four Noble Truths. Consequently, outside the Noble Eightfold Path and outside the community of Noble Persons, other ascetics and brahmins do not possess such a view of the Four Noble Truths. Nothing in the context of M I 324 seems to indicate that a Noble Disciple realizing the Four Noble Truths is thinking in sectarian terms about the Buddha's school. It just does not fit the context to interpret the expression "*ito bahiddhā*" as referring to the Buddha's school. It makes much more sense to understand the referent of "here" in "outside here' (*ito bahiddhā*) as the Noble Eightfold Path as actualized by the community of Noble Persons. This reading of *ito bahiddhā* as referring to the Noble Eightfold Path would be consistent with the reading of the same expression at D II 152, which also relates the Noble Eightfold Path to Noble Persons, namely the four ascetics.

Yet another text with the expression "*ito bahiddhā*" that could be interpreted as supporting an exclusivist view is S V 229–230. The text is talking about a "trainee" (*sekha*) who has just realized the Four Noble Truths. That is, the text is talking about someone who has become a Noble Disciple, possesses the factors of the Noble Eightfold Path and has direct knowledge of the Four Noble Truths. Only at this level of spiritual development can a Noble Person acquire insight into the Buddha's teachings and only at this level can someone rightly affirm that "there is no other ascetic or brahmin outside here who teaches a *dhamma* so real, true, and genuine as the Blessed One." In my reading, the expression "outside here" refers to those who fulfil the Noble Eightfold Noble Path or the members of the community of Noble Persons, not necessarily the Buddha's school and his members.

We cannot analyze here all the texts with the expression "outside here" in the *Nikāya*s. Suffice to say that such texts need not be interpreted in sectarian terms as referring to the Buddha's school. Rather, such texts can be interpreted as referring to the *Dhamma* or to doctrinal expressions of the *Dhamma*: the Noble Eightfold Path, the Four Noble Truths, Dependent Origination. This leads us to the second argument or the "Buddhist doctrines" argument.

According to the "Buddhist doctrines" argument, (1) certain doctrines are necessary to attain the final goal; (2) such doctrines are characteristic of the Buddha's school and the traditions derived from it; consequently, (3) the Buddha and Buddhist traditions are best interpreted in exclusivist terms. In Ven. Bhikkhu Bodhi's words:

> the crucial point is that those principles that, according to the texts of Early Buddhism, are definitive of any programme of practice that culminates in final liberation (the four truths, the eightfold path, dependent origination, the teaching of non-self, the full understanding of sensory experience) are not found among other religious traditions but only in religious systems that embody the Buddha's teaching. In their completeness, they are not found among the Buddha's contemporaries nor among any subsequent historical systems of religious thought and practice, whether in India or elsewhere. Hence their import if not their description is exclusivistic, closing off the possibility that the Nikāyas might recognize religious systems that lack these factors as capable of leading to the final goal of the spiritual life. (2020, 15)

This way of reasoning seems to me problematic. From the fact that certain doctrines are necessary to attain the final goal, and from the fact that such doctrines are characteristic of the Buddha's school and the traditions derived from it, it does not logically follow that such doctrines are exclusively Buddhist and that only Buddhists can attain the final goal. It is true that in the Pāli *Nikāya*s awakening is related to the realization or the full understanding of the Four Noble Truths (S V 452; S V 415; S V 416), Dependent Origination (S II 14-15; S II 45-46; S II 58), Impermanence, Suffering and Non-self (S II 110-111) and the Noble Eightfold Path (S II 105-107). However, none of these texts state that only members of the Buddha's school attain such realization or full understanding. These texts establish a conditional relationship between realizing certain teachings and attaining the final goal, but they never suggest that such realization is the monopoly of any school.

Another problem with the "Buddhist doctrines" argument is that it presupposes a too literal understanding of "Buddhist doctrines," and a quite limited knowledge of the doctrines of non-Buddhist traditions. It is obvious that non-Buddhist traditions do not speak with the same language as Buddhist traditions. This, however, does not mean that non-Buddhist traditions lack doctrines that relate to the arising and the cessation of suffering (Four Noble Truths), the diverse aspects of the spiritual path (Noble Eightfold Path), the conditionality of ignorance, desire, attachments and evil actions (Dependent Origination) or the importance of overcoming the ideas of "self" "I" and "mine" (Non-self).

Non-Buddhist ascetical and mystical traditions may not speak exactly like Buddhists schools do, but they say many things about suffering and its cessation, the spiritual path, the causality of wholesome and unwholesome character traits, the eradication of the ego and selfishness. Yet another problem with the "Buddhist doctrines" argument is that we can find holy people and analogous stages of spiritual development in non-Buddhist traditions. This seems to indicate that other spiritual traditions besides Buddhism contain teachings conducive to the transcendence of the ego and selfishness, critiques of the ideas of "self", "I" and "mine," causal explanations of negative and positive mental states, and methods to eradicate greed, hatred and delusion. There are two main options to explain the existence of teachings conducive to analogous levels of spiritual development outside Buddhist traditions. One option is to accept that there are other doctrines besides the Buddhist doctrines conducive to the final goal; doctrines that would be different to some extent from the Buddha's doctrines yet compatible with the *Dhamma* and the Noble Eightfold Path. Another option is to assume that there are doctrines in non-Buddhist traditions somewhat similar to Buddhist doctrines. The exclusivist reading of the Buddha does not allow for either of these two options because non-Buddhist schools are by definition empty of ascetics and, therefore, they cannot contain any doctrines conducive to the highest levels of spiritual development and liberation. In contrast, the non-exclusivist reading of the Buddha allows for both options.[7]

The third argument contends that practising the Noble Eightfold Path is firmly connected to faith in the Triple Gem (Buddha, *Dhamma*, *Saṅgha*). In Ven. Bhikkhu Bodhi's words: "the eightfold path and its subsidiary practices are not tradition-neutral criteria. From the perspective of the *Nikāya*s, they are firmly connected to faith in the Buddha as the supreme guide and in the *Saṅgha*, the community of holy disciples" (2020, 15). This argument seems to entail that only disciples with faith in the Triple Gem can attain the level of stream-enterer (*sotāpanna*), the first highest level of spiritual development.

It is true that several texts in the Pāli *Nikāya*s consider faith in the Triple Gem a factor of stream-entry.[8] It is also true that some texts in the Pāli *Nikāya*s state that a person accomplished in view, i.e., the stream-

7. In my book I conjecture that the Buddha today would be open not only to similar representations of the *Dhamma* (inclusivism), but also to different representations of the *Dhamma* as long as they were compatible with the representation found in the Pāli *Nikāya*s (pluralistic-inclusivism).

8. See for instance A III 211-2; A IV 406–407; S V 347; S V 403.

enterer, cannot acknowledge someone other than the Buddha as teacher.[9] However, these texts are insufficient to conclude that only Buddhists are able to become stream-enterers.

The Pāli *Nikāya*s speak about different types of stream-enterers. Some types of stream-enterers are described in terms of faith, but others are not described in terms of faith. For instance, there are stream-enterers who are faith-followers and others who are *Dhamma*-followers. Whereas the faith-follower is a person who cultivates the Noble Path with faith as the dominant faculty, the *Dhamma*-follower cultivates the Noble Path with wisdom as the dominant faculty. Even if we admit that all stream-enterers must have some degree of faith, such faith is not always understood as faith in the Triple Gem. For instance, S III 225-8 describes faith-followers, *Dhamma*-followers and stream-enterers as having faith in certain teachings:

> the eye is impermanent, changing, becoming otherwise. The ear… the nose […] the tongue […] the body […] the mind […] (the twelve sense spheres, the six forms of consciousness, the six contacts, the six feelings, the six perceptions, the six volitions, the six forms of craving, the six elements, the five aggregates) is impermanent, changing, becoming otherwise. One who places faith in these teachings and resolves on them thus is called a faith-follower, one who has entered the fixed course of rightness, entered the plane of superior persons, transcended the plane of the worldlings […] [the same is repeated of *Dhamma*-followers and stream-enterers]

Thus, the "faith of stream-enterers" argument is problematic because not all the texts of the Pāli *Nikāya*s discussing the faith of stream-enterers understand such faith in sectarian, exclusivist terms as faith in the Triple Gem. The "faith of stream-enterers" argument is also problematic because there are texts in the Pāli *Nikāya*s that describe stream-enterers without mentioning faith. For instance, S V 348 describes stream-enterers as those who are endowed with the Noble Eightfold Path. Likewise, S V 193-4 describes stream-enterers as those who understand as they really are the gratification, the danger and the escape in the case of the five faculties; S V 205 describes stream-enterers in a similar manner as those who understand such things about the six senses, and S III 160-1 about the five aggregates.

What seems to define stream-enterers is not faith in the Triple Gem but rather acquiring the vision of the *Dhamma*, abandoning perplexity with regard to the Four Noble Truths, insight into the dependent arising

9. See for instance A I.27; M III 65.

and cessation of suffering, abandoning the first three lower fetters of personality-view, doubt, and attachment to rules and ceremonies. By overcoming doubt, stream-enterers gain insight into the *Dhamma* and that may reinforce their faculty of faith, but this is not necessarily devotional faith in the Triple Gem. Some texts suggests that the reinforced faith is devotional faith in the Triple Gem, but other texts indicate that the reinforced faith is cognitive faith in certain teachings.

It is interesting to point out that later Buddhist scholasticism tends to understand faith in sectarian terms as a faculty exclusive to Buddhists,[10] but this is not the only possible interpretation of the Pāli *Nikāya*s. In sum, only a limited selection of texts from the Pāli *Nikāya*s, or only the projection of later scholastic assumptions about the faith of stream-enterers may lead someone to conclude that, for the Buddha, the Noble Eightfold Path is only accessible to Buddhists, namely stream-enterers with faith in the Triple Gem.

The fourth argument relates to the "cosmological uniqueness" of the Buddha. The main assumption of this argument is that the existence of liberation and the highest levels of spiritual development outside the Buddha's school would contradict early Buddhist cosmological assumptions. Early Buddhist texts understand the Buddha as having a unique role in the universe as the person who originates the teaching of the *Dhamma*, as the one who opens the door to the Deathless, and as the one who rediscovers and restores an ancient path and ancient city. If it is the case that the Buddha performs such a unique role in the universe, then there cannot be other enlightened beings in the universe except those belonging to Buddhist traditions.

My response to the "cosmological uniqueness" argument is that it depends on a later scholastic interpretation of *Paccekabuddha*s. Another reason is that Mahāyāna Buddhists rejected the cosmological uniqueness of the Buddha Gotama when they introduced the belief in countless Buddhas in the same universe and that did not undermine his cosmic significance. If introducing countless Buddhas in the same universe did not erode the cosmic significance of the Buddha Gotama, then accepting the possible existence of other enlightened beings outside Buddhist traditions need not undermine his cosmic significance either. Not being unique is compatible with being uniquely relevant, and the Buddha's contribution to the universe continues to be uniquely relevant today despite the Mahāyāna belief in countless Buddhas. We can infer that the Buddha's cosmic significance will remain unaltered by the belief in the possible existence of enlightened

10. See for instance As 249–250.

beings outside Buddhist traditions.

Yet another reason against the "cosmological uniqueness" argument is that it is based on a cosmology that is scientifically outdated, at least in some regards. The same cosmology that considers the Buddha the soteriological centre of the universe considers Mount Sumeru and the Indian subcontinent as the physical centre of the universe. If assuming that Mount Sumeru and Jambudīpa are the centre of the universe seems questionable today, it seems arbitrary to consider unquestionable other assumptions of the same cosmology such as the uniqueness of the Buddha. The final reason against the "cosmological uniqueness" argument is that it seems unnecessary for Buddhist practice today. We can practise the *Dhamma* and the Noble Eightfold Path without having to believe in scientifically outdated cosmological assumptions that are not necessary to preserve the core of the Buddha's teachings. The core of the Buddha's teachings is not the cosmological uniqueness of the Buddha but rather the Four Noble Truths and the Dependent Origination of suffering, i.e., specific conditionality. The truth of the Buddha's teachings does not depend on the truth of early cosmological assumptions. A literal understanding of early Buddhist cosmology leads to Buddhist exclusivism and the belief in Mount Sumeru and Jambudvīpa as the centre of the universe. However, the core of the Buddha's teachings does not need to be practised with the cosmological assumptions of Buddhist exclusivism. Teaching the *Dhamma* simply requires that we teach the specific conditionality of suffering, not Buddhist exclusivism with its scientifically outdated and soteriologically unnecessary cosmological assumptions.

Acknowledgements

A shorter and substantially different version was previously published in 2017 as "The Buddha and Religious DiversityToday." In *Buddhist and Christian Attitudes to Religious Diversity*,edited by Hans-Peter Grosshans, Samuel Ngun Ling and Perry Schmidt Leukel, 77–106. Yangon, Myanmar: Ling Family.

References

Apte, V.S. 1890. *The Practical Sanskrit-English Dictionary*. Poone: Shiralkar.

Bodhi, Bhikkhu. 2012. *The Numerical Discourses of the Buddha: A Translation of the Aṅguttara Nikāya*. Somerville, MA: Wisdom.

———. 2020. "The Buddha and the Diversity of Spiritual Paths." *Buddhist Responses to Religious Diversity: Theravāda and Tibetan Perspectives*. Sheffield: Equinox.

Gethin, Rupert. 2008. *Sayings of the Buddha*. Oxford: Oxford University Press.

Jayatilleke, K.N. 1966. *The Buddhist Attitude to Other Religions*. Ceylon: Department of the Public Trustee.

Karunadasa, Y. 2018. *Early Buddhist Teachings*. Somerville, MA: Wisdom.

Monier-Williams, Monier. 1899. *A Sanskrit-English Dictionary*. Oxford: Clarendon.

Rhys Davids, T.W. and W Stede. 1921. *Pali Text Society's Pali-English Dictionary*. London: Pali Text Society.

Vélez de Cea, Abraham. 2013. *The Buddha and Religious Diversity*. Abingdon: Routledge. https://doi.org/10.4324/9780203072639

3

Paths of Liberation? Theravāda Buddhist Attitudes to Religious Diversity

Perry Schmidt-Leukel

University of Münster

Perry Schmidt-Leukel is Professor of Religious Studies and Intercultural Theology at the University of Münster and one of the Principal Investigators of Münster University's Cluster of Excellence "Religion and Politics." Previous to this, he taught at the universities of Munich, Innsbruck, Salzburg and Glasgow. Schmidt-Leukel is known as one of the leading proponents of a pluralist theology of religions. His main research interests are in the fields of Buddhist-Christian dialogue, theologies of religions in the various religious traditions and interreligious theology. He has published more than thirty books in German and English. Among his more recent publications in English are: *Understanding Buddhism* (2006); *Buddhist Attitudes to Other Religions* (ed.) (2008); *Transformation by Integration: How Inter-faith Encounter Changes Christianity* (2009); *Buddhism and Religious Diversity*, four volumes (2013); *Religious Diversity in Chinese Thought* edited with Joachim Gentz (2013); *God Beyond Boundaries. A Christian and Pluralist Theology of Religions* (2017); *Buddha Mind – Christ Mind: A Christian Commentary on the Bodhicaryāvatāra* (2019). In 2015 he gave the renowned Gifford Lectures, published as *Religious Pluralism and Interreligious Theology* (2017).

Introduction

When speaking about religious attitudes to religious diversity it is important to distinguish between tolerance and appreciation. I take "tolerance" in the original meaning of the European Enlightenment where it signifies an attitude of enduring what one does not like. The key idea is to tolerate, as much as possible, the fact that there are people who have ideas and do things which oneself deems to be wrong. In contrast, "appreciation" signifies that one can fully agree with ideas and practices of other people, even if they are somewhat different from one's own (Schmidt-Leukel 2009, 30–45). In this chapter I am not dealing with the question of whether Theravāda Buddhists can tolerate people of other faiths. This question would be easier to answer in the affirmative. In what follows, I will address the more difficult issue of whether, and to what extent, Theravāda teachings may allow an appreciation of other faiths as paths of liberation.[1]

Doctrinal foundations

In an important nevertheless often neglected saying of the Buddha it is stated:

> there is, bhikkhus, a not-born (*ajātaṃ*), a not-brought-to-being (*abhūtaṃ*), a not-made (*akataṃ*), a not-conditioned (*asaṅkhataṃ*). If, bhikkhus, there were no not-born, not-brought-to-being, not-made, not-conditioned, no escape would be discerned from what is born, brought-to-being, made, conditioned. But since there is a not-born, a not-brought-to-being, a not-made, a not-conditioned, therefore an escape is discerned from what is born, brought-to-being, made, conditioned. (Ireland 1997, 103, 180)

This statement is found twice in the Pāli *Tipiṭaka* (*Udāna* 8:3; *Itivuttaka* 43) and it is remarkable in two respects. *First*, *Nirvāṇa* (P. *Nibbāna*) is clearly presented as a transcendent reality,[2] essentially different from *saṃsāra*. In this samsaric world everything is marked by being conditioned. That is, everything exists because of certain causes and conditions. Therefore everything in *saṃsāra* is transitory, since it is a general Buddhist premise that everything which has a conditioned existence is also subject to decay.[3] In contrast, *Nibbāna* is completely unconditioned. Because of being unconditioned it is imperishable. Hence, it is totally different from *saṃsāra*: it is "the deathless" (*amata*).

The *second* important aspect of the statement is that *Nibbāna* is presented as the foundation of ultimate liberation/salvation (*vimutti*). That is, without the existence of *Nibbāna* "no escape would be discerned." This implies that according to Theravāda Buddhism, *Nibbāna* must not be misunderstood as merely a mental state, that is, as the mental state of the enlightened person. Two highly authoritative texts from the Theravāda tradition, the *Milindapañha* (4:7:13–17) and Buddhaghosa's *Visuddhimagga*

---

1. For an overview of Buddhist attitudes to other religions see Schmidt-Leukel 2008 & 2020 and Harris 2013. An extensive discussion of Buddhist inclusivism is offered by Kiblinger 2005 and of a possible Theravāda pluralism by Veléz de Cea 2013. A large anthology of relevant essays is Schmidt-Leukel 2013, volumes 1–4.
2. Even the term "transcendence" has a more or less exact equivalent: While "transcendence" derives from the Latin word "*transcendere*" = "going beyond," *Nibbāna* is said to be *lokuttara* "beyond the world" (*loka* = world + *uttara* = beyond).
3. See *Mahāvagga* (of the *Vinayapiṭaka*) 1:23:5: "Whatsoever is subject to the condition of origination is subject also to the condition of cessation" (Rhys Davids and Oldenberg 1996, 146).

(16: 67–74) make this point unambiguously clear. Both texts present the same argument: if *Nibbāna* were the state of the enlightened person, it would be conditioned by the successful completion of the Noble Eightfold Path. But as a conditioned reality *Nibbāna* would itself be transitory and not be the deathless reality that it is said to be. Therefore *Nibbāna* cannot be identified with enlightenment. Enlightenment, or better, awakening (*bodhi*), is rather the first full experience of *Nibbāna*, the "plunging into *Nibbāna*" as it is sometimes phrased.[4] Or as Buddhaghosa puts it: *Nibbāna* "is only reachable, not arousable by the path; that is why it is uncreated. It is because it is uncreated that it is free from aging and death" (Ñāṇamoli 1999, 516). Being uncreated, *nibbāna* has no first beginning (Ñāṇamoli 1999, 516). It exists without beginning or end, independently of whether someone reaches it or not.

Thus, in contrast to some forms of modernist Theravāda Buddhism, traditional Theravāda clearly presents *Nibbāna* as an ultimate transcendent reality.[5] Being itself unconditioned, *Nibbāna* is the *first and foremost condition* that makes awakening and liberation possible. Without the existence of *Nibbāna* "no escape would be discerned," as the canonical statement says. But enlightenment and liberation also depend on a *second condition*. This is the existence of a path leading towards enlightenment, that is, a path leading towards the experience of *Nibbāna*. This path is part of the *Dharma* (P. *Dhamma*), the eternal metaphysical truth/law. The path has been discovered, or better, re-discovered, and taught by the Buddha. On a traditional understanding the path is not the Buddha's invention. And this implies a *third condition*: there must be some kind of inner relationship between the human mind and *Nibbāna*, for otherwise it would be neither possible for a human mind to discover nor to follow the path leading to *Nibbāna*. The Theravāda tradition has specified this inner relationship in two ways: (1) in terms of an existential inclination towards *Nibbāna* and (2) in terms of the original purity of the mind. According to *Majjhima-nikāya Sutta* 26 (*Ariyapariyesanā Sutta*), all transitory things of

4. E.g. *Aṅguttara-nikāya* 5:107. See also *Sutta Nipāta* 228 and *Khuddaka Pāṭho* 6:7.

5. For the differentiation of two conceptions of *Nibbāna* (*Nirvāṇa*), a "naturalist" conception in terms of a mental state (which Tilakaratne prefers) and a "metaphysical" interpretation as an unconditioned, transcendent reality, see Tilakaratne 2016. Implicitly, Tilakaratne admits that the "metaphysical" understanding is the one affirmed in the abhidhammical and commentarial tradition. For a thorough investigation of early Buddhist and Theravāda conceptions of *Nirvāṇa*/*Nibbāna*, see: Chandrkaew 1982; Pandit 1993, 254–339; Collins 1998; 2010; Gowans 2003, 50–54, 148–157; Harvey 2004, 180245. The two eminent Pāli-scholars and Theravāda monks, Nyanaponika Mahāthera and Bhikkhu Bodhi have both unambiguously defended the traditional idea of *Nibbāna* as a transcendent reality. See Nyanaponika 2008; Bodhi (n. d.).

the world are unfit to provide lasting peace and satisfaction to the human mind. Such peace can only be gained from *Nibbāna*, the deathless reality. Our deepest longing, the "noble search," is therefore for *Nibbāna*. But if we misdirect this longing in turning towards the transitory things of the world, we will inevitably end up in suffering and frustration.[6] This inner inclination towards *Nibbāna* is further understood as entailing that the true nature of our mind is "pure," that is, the mind is somehow *Nibbāna*-affine. The defilements (*kilesa*), greed, hate and delusion, do not constitute the mind's essence. Instead they are literally "defilements" or "stains." They are of an exterior nature, alien to the true, originally pure nature of the mind.[7] The experience of *Nibbāna* is thus in a sense an experience of the fulfilment of our mind's deepest longing and of its true nature.

These three conditions of awakening as taught in Theravāda Buddhism: ([1] the existence of an unconditioned reality; [2] the revelation of a path leading to it; and [3] an inner relationship between ultimate reality and the human mind), allow for three different types of awakened persons. *Firstly* there are the *Paccekabuddha*s (solitary Buddhas). According to the Theravāda tradition, *Paccekabuddha*s found the path towards awakening on their own, that is, without being instructed by a Buddha, at least not in their present (i.e. last) life. However, in contrast to a *Sammā-sambuddha*, a "Buddha in the full sense," a *Paccekabuddha* does not lead others to awakening; that is, he does not establish a *Saṅgha*, a community which includes all four stages of saintliness, including enlightened *Arahant*s. It is often said in textbooks that *Paccekabuddha*s do not teach at all. But this is incorrect. There are various traditional Buddhist texts which report of teaching *Paccekabuddha*s. However, *Paccekabuddha*s do not teach the whole path but only some parts of it, in particular *sīla* (morality).[8] They are therefore unable to establish a *Saṅgha*. The *second* type of awakened persons are the *Sammā-sambuddha*s, the perfect Buddhas. Like a *Paccekabuddha*, the *Sammā-sambuddha* has also found awakening on his own. But in contrast to a *Paccekabuddha*, a *Sammā-sambuddha* teaches the whole *Dhamma*, leads other people to awakening and thus establishes a *Saṅgha*. According to the Theravāda school, there can be – and in fact are – many more than just one Buddha in the full sense, but not at the

6. For my interpretation of the Four Noble Truths in the light of the *Ariyapiyesanā Sutta* see Schmidt-Leukel 2006, 30–36.

7. See A 1:10-11. See also Harvey 2004, 166–179, and Gowans 2003, 154–156.

8. E.g. *Jātaka* 378, 408, 424, 459, 496, etc. The Theravāda manual *Sārasaṅgaho* explicitly states that *Paccekabuddha*s only teach spiritual and moral duties but not the essential *Dhamma*.

same time (!) – a clause which, as I will show, is of huge significance for the Theravāda assessment of other religions. The *third* type of awakened persons are finally the *Arahants*, that is those who attain awakening under the influence of the *Dhamma*, the Buddhist teaching, as they have learned it from a full Buddha or through the *Saṅgha* established by such a Buddha.

Classification of attitudes

With these doctrinal presuppositions and distinctions in mind, let me now pursue the question of how Theravāda Buddhists assess other religions. In the first place, this is a question of whether or not Theravādins can acknowledge that people may achieve liberation (*vimutti*) or awakening (*bodhi*) by following the doctrines and practices taught by other faiths. Or, to put the question in a more precise way: Will the teachings of other religions lead their adherents to that transcendent reality which is known in Theravāda as *Nibbāna*?[9]

Basically, there are three possible answers. The *first* possible answer would simply be: "no." This is what I call the *exclusivist* position. A *second* possible answer could be: "Yes, but only in an incomplete and fragmentary way." This might mean that some other religions may lead their followers to the experience of the reality known in Theravāda as *Nibbāna*, but they do so in less efficient ways; or they might lead them at least some steps closer to *Nibbāna*, but not to the full attainment of it. This is what I call the *inclusivist* position. Finally, a *third* possible answer would be: "Yes, at least some may indeed lead them to *Nibbāna* and they do so in as good a way as Theravāda, while their ways are somewhat different or look different and their perception of the transcendent reality is differently shaped." This can be called a *pluralist* position in as much as it combines the assessment of liberative equality with the recognition of diversity. In what follows, I will discuss these three possible answers in more detail.[10] But note that I use the terms "exclusivism," "inclusivism"

9. Hence I do not contest Vélez de Cea's (2013, 14–21) suggestion to use, as he calls it, "OTMIX (our tradition most important X)" as a starting point for a classification of tradition-specific approaches to religious diversity. Yet unlike Vélez de Cea, I think that the Theravāda-Buddhist understanding of *Nibbāna* can legitimately be interpreted (in accordance with John Hick) as one particular manifestation of "the Real" in human thought and experience (*cf.* Hick 1989, 283–287) and in fact has to be interpreted in this way if one adopts a Theravādin pluralist position.

10. The answer that other religions lead to some other goals but not to *Nibbāna* would not constitute a further option. For either these other goals are just irrelevant or even opposed to the attainment of *Nibbāna*, which would be the exclusivist option, or they are intermediary goals on the way to *Nibbāna*, which would be in line with the inclusivist position.

and "pluralism" throughout this discussion only in the sense in which I have just introduced them.[11]

Discussion

The exclusivist position

According to the canonical scriptures of the *Tipiṭaka* (D 16:5:26), the Buddha himself, on the very last day of his life, was asked the following question about other religious persuasions by an ascetic called Subhadda:

> 'Venerable Gotama, all those ascetics and Brahmins who have orders and followings, who are teachers [...], have they all realized the truth as they all make out, or have none of them realized it, or have some realized it and some not?'

In his reply, the Buddha explains:

> In whatever Dhamma and discipline the Noble Eightfold Path is not found, no ascetic is found of the first, the second, the third or the fourth grade. But such ascetics can be found [...] in a Dhamma and discipline where the Noble Eightfold Path is found. Now, Subhadda, in this Dhamma and discipline the Noble Eightfold Path *is* found, and in it are to be found ascetics of the first, second, third and fourth grade. Those of other schools are devoid of (true) ascetics. (D 16; Walshe 1995, 268)[12]

As a result of this conversation, Subhadda became a follower of the Buddha and attained awakening within a short time.

The point of the story is exclusivist: there is only one path leading to the liberating experience of transcendent reality, the Noble Eightfold Path, which is exclusively taught by the Buddha. Quite similarly the canonical *Dhammapada* (v. 274) says about the Eightfold Path: "Just this path, there is no other for purity of vision" (Carter and Palihawadana 2000, 49). The same message is given in the Buddhist version of the famous story of the blind-born men and the elephant. While the Buddha is in the position of the king who with his healthy eyes sees the elephant as it really is, the rival teachers of his time are likened to the blind-born men who have only a very limited insight and understanding of the elephant's nature. Their views are unable to lead to liberation and hence they remain caught in *saṃsāra* (*cf. Udāna* 8:4–6). Compared to the Buddha, their light is like that of glow worms in relation to the sun:

---

11. For a broader discussion that also includes Mahāyāna perspectives, see Schmidt-Leukel 2017, 71–89 and Schmidt-Leukel 2020.

12. Similarly *Majjhima-nikāya* 11 (*Cūḷasīhanāda Sutta*).

> the glow worm shines as long as the sun has not risen, but when that illuminant arises, the glow worm's light is quenched and shines no more. [...] These thinkers are not purified nor yet their disciples, for those of perverse views are not released from suffering. (*Udāna* 6:10; Ireland 1997, 93)

Despite these fairly clear statements, one may still discuss whether the exclusivist position as documented in the Theravāda *Tipiṭaka* is inevitable. When the Buddha teaches in the *Mahāparinibbāna Sutta* (D 16) that ascetics of all four degrees of saintliness, including that of enlightened *Arahants*, are found "in a Dhamma and discipline where the Noble Eightfold Path is found" (see above), this seems to allow, at least in principle, for the possibility of an inclusivist or even pluralist position in relation to other religions. Perhaps, so one may speculate, the actually negative assessment of other religious persuasions as found in this text needs to be confined to the rival schools at the time of the Buddha, but does not apply to all non-Buddhist religions.

However, there are two further doctrines making such a conclusion difficult. As I said before, according to the presuppositions of traditional Theravāda, the Noble Eightfold Path is taught only by a *Sammā-sambuddha* and transmitted by a *Saṅgha,* which such a Buddha had established. If the Noble Eightfold Path were taught by another religious teacher and be transmitted in his community, this teacher, by definition, would also have to count as a *Sammā-sambuddha* and his community as a *Saṅgha.* However, the problem is that *first,* according to Theravāda Buddhism, the life of each full Buddha always follows the very same pattern. And *second,* according to the Theravāda school, there cannot be more than one Buddha at a time. The latter is claimed in a number of canonical places (see for example *Bahudhātuka Sutta* M 115)*;* A 1:15:10; *Mahāgovinda Sutta* D 19). In one such place, Sakka, the king of the gods, praises Buddha Gotama by the words:

> as regards the way in which the Lord has striven for the welfare of the many, for the happiness of the many, out of compassion for the world, for the welfare and happiness of devas and humans – we can find no teacher endowed with such qualities, whether we consider the past or the present, other than the lord.

In response to this, some of the gods considered that it would be even better for the world if there were not just one fully enlightened Buddha but several, to which Sakka replied:

> it is impossible, gentlemen, it cannot happen that two fully-enlightened Buddhas should arise simultaneously in a single world-sys-

tem. (*Mahāgovinda Sutta* D 19: 5 and 14; Walshe 1995, 301–303)

The question of why there cannot be more than one Buddha at a time is discussed at considerable length in the *Milindapañha*. This discussion provides a fuller understanding of the implications of this teaching. Among the arguments given in defence of this doctrine we find the following (see *Milindapañha* 4:6:4–10): *first*, there can be only one Buddha because the Buddha is a uniquely supreme being; *second*, the teaching of only one Buddha at a time is based on the authority of the scripture; and *third*, a plurality of Buddhas might easily lead to religious strife and rivalry among their followers, each claiming that their own Buddha is the most supreme being. Particularly the latter argument sheds light on how to understand the phrase: not more than one "at the same time." Apparently this refers to the idea that there cannot be more than one valid *Saṅgha*. Within one world-system, several Buddhas can only coexist successively, not simultaneously, and they can succeed each other only *after* the *Saṅgha* of the previous Buddha has fully disappeared, that is, after the *Dhamma* has been completely forgotten. For, as stated above, a "Buddha" is defined as someone who rediscovers the *Dhamma* in a world, in which the knowledge of the *Dhamma* has completely vanished, and who through his teaching establishes a *Saṅgha* anew. This implies that other religious communities, which exist simultaneously to the Buddhist *Saṅgha*, cannot have been established by a fully awakened being, a Buddha, and hence cannot be regarded as salvific communities at all.

Given these doctrinal foundations, it appears that traditional Theravāda is as exclusivist as some of the most fundamentalist forms of Christianity.[13] Yet there is more to say.

---

13. This comparison necessitates highlighting at least one important difference: In Christianity, radical exclusivists believe that all non-Christians go to hell, which according to their understanding is an eternal, irredeemable state of suffering. In contrast, exclusivists within Theravāda Buddhism believe that all those who do not follow the Noble Eightfold Path will remain caught in *saṃsāra*. Yet life in *saṃsāra* is only potentially everlasting, not necessarily and irreversibly so. At some stage one may again find human rebirth under those favourable conditions that include learning the *Dhamma*. And while the *saṃsāra* also contains a number of different hells, existence in the Buddhist hells, though extremely long, is never everlasting. Thus, at the end of the day, Buddhist exclusivism is comparatively more optimistic than radical forms of Christian exclusivism. On the other hand, there are Christian exclusivists who maintain that, although non-Christian religions have no salvific value, ultimately all human beings will be saved by the grace of Christ alone (a position often ascribed to Karl Barth).

The inclusivist position

As far as I can see, in the past, Theravāda Buddhism usually took an exclusivist stance in relation to other religions, beginning with the sharp rejection of the different schools of Hinduism (Schmidt-Leukel 2008; 2013; 2020). Other branches of Buddhism were usually branded as heresies, while Mahāyāna Buddhism in particular was criticized as the product of too much Hindu influence and as a tool in the hands of the evil deity Māra (see for example Rahula 1993, 89; see also Kim 2013, 197). In fact, Mahāyāna Buddhist schools, despite their former strong presence, disappeared entirely from the now Theravāda-Buddhist countries, in several cases as a result of violent suppression.[14]

A new discussion over the Theravāda attitude to other religions was started in 1966, when Kalatissa Nanda Jayatilleke (1920–1970), the renowned Theravāda Buddhist philosopher from Sri Lanka, presented an inclusivist perspective on non-Buddhist religions.[15] In his tract "The Buddhist Attitude to Other Religions" he interprets the traditional doctrine on *Paccekabuddha*s as entailing "the possibility for others to discover aspects of the truth or even the whole truth for themselves" (Jayatilleke 1975, 20), that is, outside of a Buddhist context. As further evidence, he cites *Sutta Nipāta* (v. 1082) where the Buddha is reported to say: "I do not declare that all these religious men[16] are sunk in repeated birth and decay" (Jayatilleke 1975, 21). In addition, he draws on the traditional distinction between "false religions" (*abrahmacariya-vāsā* – views leading to an unwholesome conduct) and "unsatisfactory" religions (*anassāsikaṃ* – unconsoling) (*cf. Sandaka Sutta* (M 76). Although unsatisfactory religions are not on a par with Buddhism, they may nevertheless be of some limited spiritual value to their followers, that is, they may take them closer to the ultimate goal. Jayatilleke seems to go even further in suggesting that the first limb of the Noble Eightfold Path, the "right view" (*sammā diṭṭhi*),

---

14. In Sri Lanka the fight against Mahāyāna Buddhism involved the assassination of their religious leaders, burning of their scriptures and large-scale suppression (see Mudiyanse 1967, 1–11). According to the Burmese chronicles, the "Ari" (apparently a form of Mahāyāna with Tantric elements) existed in the kingdom of Bagan for "thirty generations." The chronicles further report that in the eleventh century, under the influence of the Theravādin, Dhammadassi (or Shin Arahan), King Anawrahta persecuted the Ari and tried to replace them by Theravāda. He is reported of having defrocked sixty thousand Ari monks, forcing them to serve in his army or as scavengers (see U Pe Maung Tin Luce 2008, 39, 44–45).

15. K. N. Jayatilleke 1975 (reprinted in *Dialogue N.S.* 13 and 14, 1986–1987, 11–39, and in Schmidt-Leukel 2013, vol. 4, 88-108). The text is based on a lecture which K. N. Jayatilleke gave on 4 April 1966, at the University of Sri Lanka.

16. Literally: "samanas and brahmanas" (*samaṇābrahmaṇāse*).

"comprehends the basic beliefs and values of the higher religions" (1975, 24). He specifies these as belief in a transcendent reality, life after death, moral responsibility and in the teaching of a "good life" (Jayatilleke 1975, 25). Thus in relation to theistic religions Jayatilleke claims that "on pragmatic grounds the belief in a Personal God is not discouraged in so far as it is not a hindrance but an incentive for moral and spiritual development" (Jayatilleke 1975, 29).

Nevertheless Jayatilleke's deliberations remain somewhat ambiguous on the question of whether other religions might lead their adherents only closer to the goal or whether they might lead them right to the end. The first position would be easier to harmonize with the canonical texts. For this is exactly what *Paccekabuddha*s are said to do (See also *Mahāgovinda Sutta* D 19). They teach others certain fragments of the path and hence cause some spiritual progress in them but do not lead them all the way towards *Nibbāna*. The difficulty, however, is that according to the Theravāda tradition, *Paccekabuddha*s were not expected to live in a world and at a time when the *Dhamma* is available through the teaching of a full Buddha and/or his *Saṅgha* (De Silva 1988, 98). Therefore the status of a *Paccekabuddha* would hardly be applicable to the teachers of other religions. Yet despite that difficulty, Lily de Silva, a scholar of Theravāda Buddhism at the Peradeniya University of Sri Lanka, supported Jayatilleke in an article from 1985 holding "that Buddhism does not completely rule out the possibility of the presence of emancipated beings in other religious traditions" (De Silva 1988, 98), although she does not specify why this is so. Perhaps de Silva was led to her position by the recognition that central values of the Noble Eightfold Path are actually realized in other faiths. Referring for example to Jesus' prayer on the cross that God may forgive his tormentors, she concludes that from a Buddhist perspective "this is undisputable evidence that Jesus had developed liberation of the mind through loving-kindness (*mettā-cetovimutti*)" (De Silva 1992, 7). Thus, according to Lily de Silva, another religion can be regarded as true "to the extent it incorporates aspects of the Noble Eightfold Path," that is, that it contributes to the cultivation of the three principles of the path, morality (*sīla*), contemplation (*samādhi*) and wisdom (*pañña*) (De Silva 1988, 93, 98).

The ambiguity in Jayatilleke's position was pointed out in a critical response given by the monk scholar, Venerable Yatadolawatte Dhammavisuddhi in 1986. Jayatilleke, says Dhammavisuddhi, "does not clarify whether or not other religious men could attain nibbāna while remaining within their own religious frameworks." If Jayatilleke had intended to affirm this possibility this would seem "irreconcilable with corresponding utterances of the Buddha found elsewhere in the canon" (Dhammavisuddhi 1986–1987, 41). To substantiate his position Dhammavisuddhi refers to the canonical tradition according to which neither the Noble Eightfold Path nor any degree of liberation are found in the teachings and disciplines of other schools. Not even the lowest degree of saintliness, the "Entering into the Stream" (*sotāpanna*), would thus be something that other religions could foster. Somewhat cynically Dhammavisuddhi concludes that he does not deny the possibility of liberation for adherents of other religions. But in order to achieve liberation such a person would have "to cut off his affiliation to the disciplinary system to which he belonged" (1986–1987, 47).

Thus in general Theravādins agree that there is only one path of salvation, the Noble Eightfold Path. But they disagree over the question of whether and to what extent this path is also found in other religions. Behind this question stands the belief in the uniqueness of the Buddha and his *Saṅgha*, which by implication seems to rule out any alternative to a Theravāda exclusivism or, at best, allows only a very cautious type of inclusivism. However, at least[17] one prominent Theravādin has attempted to give a pluralist answer, the Thai Buddhist reformer Bhikkhu Buddhadāsa (1906–1993), and to him I will now turn.

The pluralist position

If Theravādins study other religions carefully, they may find it hard to deny that significant elements of the Noble Eightfold Path are also found in other faiths. This creates a major challenge to the traditional belief that the path to liberation is exclusively taught by the Buddha and exclusively transmitted by the Buddhist *Saṅgha*. Buddhadāsa took up this challenge and replied to it with a radical dismissal of a literalist understanding of the canonical texts. He replaced such literalism by a spiritual hermeneutics which clearly displays Mahāyāna, especially Zen-Buddhist, influence.[18]

Buddhadāsa argues that the three fundamental principles of the Noble Eightfold Path, morality, contemplation and wisdom, are actually present in Christianity, Islam, Hinduism and Buddhism, though with different emphases and in different forms, which Buddhadāsa explains by their

17. Another prominent contemporary Theravādin who, during the last years of her life, apparently moved in the direction of a pluralist position was Ayya Khema. I am grateful to Elizabeth Harris who pointed this out to me. Ayya Khema's views are based on the understanding that the leading spiritual exemplars of the major religions had recognised the original purity of the mind and its inclination towards the ultimate (see Ayya Khema 1995, 55).

18. On the Mahāyāna influence on Buddhadāsa see Jackson 2003 and Ito 2012.

exposure to different cultural influences (Buddhadasa 1967, 24f, 38f). He thus retains the idea that only the Noble Eightfold Path will lead to salvation, but assumes that this path is taught in several religions, although in different forms. That is, there are different legitimate centres of practice: Buddhist practice is focused on wisdom, Christian practice on confidence/ trust (*saddhā*), Muslim practice on will-power (*viriya*) (Buddhadasa 1967, 12ff). According to Buddhadāsa, all three foci are complementary and "each religion comprises all the three ways" (Buddhadasa 1967, 13). To him, the central aspect of the path to liberation is the realization of complete selflessness. This, says Buddhadāsa, is clearly identifiable in each of the different forms that the one path takes in the various religions. He thus concludes: "The goal of all religions is salvation, and throughout history all religions have shown the way to salvation" (Swearer 1989, 169). In relation to Christianity, Buddhadāsa holds that even "the few pages of the Sermon on the Mount" are "far more than enough and complete for practice to attain emancipation" (Buddhadāsa 1967, 29). Accordingly, Buddhadāsa refers to Jesus as a Buddha.[19]

Thus Buddhadāsa implicitly denies the teaching that there can be only one Buddha at a time. What enables him to do so is his specific religious hermeneutics being a variant of the two-truths teaching. According to Buddhadāsa, Buddhist terms have an ordinary meaning and an ultimate meaning. In the ultimate sense, the word "Buddha" refers not to a particular human being but to the highest truth of the *Dhamma*. Only through the realization of this truth does someone become a Buddha. Hence, by implication, everybody who realizes the highest truth and teaches it, is a Buddha in the ultimate sense (Swearer 1989, 129*ff*.; see also Buddhadāsa 1967, 105*ff*.). Buddhadāsa applies the same hermeneutics to other religions as well. He holds that the term "son of God" refers, in the ultimate sense, "to those who can lead the world to perfect understanding of the dhamma" (Buddhadāsa 1967, 106). Thus Jesus is a Buddha and Gotama a "son of God." In a similar way Buddhadāsa relativizes the uniqueness of the *Saṅgha*. In the highest sense, the word "*Saṅgha*" does not refer to the Buddhist community but to those spiritual qualities which have been realized by the members of the *Ariya-Saṅgha*, that is, by those who have achieved one of the four degrees of saintliness (Buddhadāsa in Swearer 1989, 129). Given that according to Buddhadāsa these qualities can be realized in each of the major religions, the term *Saṅgha* loses its exclusivist connotations. If properly understood, notions such as *Dhamma* or *Nibbāna* refer to the same reality as the theistic term "God" (*cf.*

19. Buddhadasa 1967, 105ff. See also 1967, 98, where he speaks of Jesus as a "victor" (*jina*) that is, using one of the titles of a Buddha.

Buddhadasa 1967). The ultimate criterion of whether transcendence has been reached is the full liberation from the ego: "The mind which is free from the feeling of self or ego is the mind which has reached God or Dhamma in the highest sense" (Buddhadāsa 1967, 43). This shows that the ultimate basis of Buddhadāsa's pluralism is the ancient Theravāda doctrine of an inner affinity between mind and *Nibbāna*. According to Buddhadāsa, the attainment of *Nibbāna* is possible because greed, hate and delusion are not the mind's true nature. Thus, as Peter Jackson summarizes, in Buddhadāsa's view, "the human mind is fundamentally pure and undefiled" (Jackson 2003. 135). And because this is true of *every* human mind, *Nibbāna* is in principle universally available. It is what each one of us is deeply longing for: "The blessed nibbāna is the destination point of every person."[20] Or, as he says in using Christian words: "if God is not everywhere then he is not God"(Buddhadāsa 1967, 77).

Conclusion

Why does it matter whether Theravāda Buddhists adopt an exclusivist, inclusivist or pluralist approach? I suggest that, at least, two important issues are involved. *First*, the exclusivist position makes it impossible for Theravādins to recognize and appreciate the existence of what is true, ethically good and "holy" (*ariya*), that is, *Nibbāṇa*-bound, in other religious traditions. The inclusivist position allows for such recognition but makes it impossible to appreciate that whatever is true, good and holy in other religions may be equally liberative despite its appearance in different religious forms and contexts. And this leads to a *second* important observation: neither exclusivism nor inclusivism can support a genuine appreciation of religious diversity. Exclusivism regards other religions as false because they differ from one's own religion while inclusivism sees them as false to the extent they differ. In both cases difference, and thus diversity, is seen as problematic. Exclusivists regard their own religion as uniquely true and inclusivists regard it as uniquely superior. From both perspectives it appears as ideal if all false religions and all inferior religions would disappear so that all human beings could be in the happy position of joining the uniquely true or uniquely superior faith. This, however, implies that religious diversity is at best to be tolerated as a perhaps inevitable evil. But it is not appreciated as a genuine value. In contrast, pluralist approaches, as developed within the different religious

20. Buddhadāsa, *Nipphan phon samai pai laeo rue?*, Samut Prakan 1965, 25; quoted after Jackson 2003, 142.

traditions,[21] attempt to combine plurality with equality and hence enable a religious appreciation of at least some religions as different but equally meaningful and efficient "vehicles" (*yānāni*) towards liberation.

However, Buddhist belief in rebirth may modify and soften the logic of this argument to some extent because of the underlying assumption that spiritual maturation may stretch over the course of several lives. As in various Hindu and Mahāyāna teachings, Theravādins too can interpret the actual diversity of religions as reflecting different degrees of spiritual development. That is, those who are spiritually underdeveloped will be satisfied with lower forms of religion. Those who are spiritually more advanced will feel at home in higher forms of faith. But those who are most advanced in their spiritual development will join the uniquely superior religion. In the course of many lives, people may belong to many different religions depending on, and reflecting, their spiritual state. From this perspective it may even be seen as good that there exists a diversity of different religions because they satisfy a diversity of spiritual needs. But people are situated in different religions because they are on different spiritual levels. That is, the diversity of religions is good to some extent, but it is not a diversity of equally valid and liberative religions. It is a hierarchically ordered diversity of higher and lower traditions. Yet this still raises a critical question: would it not be far more realistic to see spiritual maturation as a process that is possible *within each* of the major religious traditions? Are all followers of Theravāda Buddhism on the same spiritual level? Certainly not. So why should it be excluded, *a priori*, that the highest level of spiritual perfection can be achieved – although in different forms – in each of the major faiths? Exclusivism and inclusivism are dogmatic cages which hinder people from seriously reckoning with this possibility. At this stage of the argument, defenders of Theravāda superiority usually point to the uniqueness of the Theravāda doctrines as clear evidence that the highest form of insight is only found in Theravāda. Yet this again raises a question: Is insight (*paññā*), which is certainly of capital importance to Buddhism, perhaps confused with dogmatism?[22]

Acknowledgements

A previous version was published in 2017 as "Theravāda Buddhist Approaches to Religious Diversity: An Overview." In *Buddhist and*

21. For an overview of pluralist positions in different religious traditions see Schmidt-Leukel 2017, 15–106.

22. For a similar warning against dogmatism and a plea for non-dogmatic openness see Vélez de Cea 2013, 148–156.

Christian Attitudes to Religious Diversity, edited by Hans-Peter Grosshans, Samuel Ngun Ling and Perry Schmidt Leukel, 59–75. Yangon, Myanmar: Ling Family.

References

Ayya Khema. 1995. *Das Größte ist die Liebe. Die Bergpredigt und das Hohelied der Liebe aus buddhistischer Sicht*, Uttenbühl: Jhana.

Bodhi, Bhikkhu (n. d.). "Nibbana." http://www.dhammatalks.net/Books16/Bhikkhu_Bodhi-Nibbana.pdf

Buddhadāsa Indapañño Bhikku. 1967. *Christianity and Buddhism*. Sinclaire Thompson Memorial Lecture. Bangkok: Fifth Series.

Carter, John Ross, Mahinda Palihawadana trans. 2000. *The Dhammapada*. Oxford: Oxford University Press.

Chandrkaew, Chinda. 1982. *Nibbāna. The Ultimate Truth of Buddhism*. Bangkok: Mahachula Buddhist University.

Collins, Steven. 1998. *Nirvana and Other Buddhist Felicities*. Cambridge: Cambridge University Press. https://doi.org/10.1017/CBO9780511520655

———. 2010, *Nirvana. Concept, Imagery, Narrative*. Cambridge: Cambridge University Press.

De Silva, Lily. 1988. "The Buddha, the Eightfold Path and the other Religions." *Dialogue N.S.* 15: 84–100.

De Silva, Lily. 1992. *The Buddha and Christ as Religious Teachers*. The Wheel Publication 380. Kandy, Sri Lanka: Buddhist Publication Society.

Dhammavisuddhi, Yatadolawatte. 1986–1987. "Does Buddhism Recognize Liberation from Samsara Outside Its Own Dispensation?" *Dialogue N.S.* 13/14: 40–51.

Gowans, Christopher. 2003. *Philosophy of the Buddha*. Abingdon: Routledge. https://doi.org/10.4324/9780203480793

Harris, Elizabeth. 2013. "Buddhism and the Religious Other." In *Understanding Interreligious Relations*, edited by David Cheetham, Douglas Pratt and David Thomas, 88–119. Oxford: Oxford University Press.

Harvey, Peter. 2004. *The Selfless Mind. Personality, Consciousness and Nirvāṇa in Early Buddhism*. London: RoutledgeCurzon.

Hick, John. 1989. *An Interpretation of Religion. Human Responses to the Transcendent*. Basingstoke: MacMillan.

Ireland, John, trans. 1997. *The Udāna. Inspired Utterances of the Buddha & The Itivuttaka. The Buddha's Sayings*. Kandy, Sri Lanka: BPS.

Ito, Tomoni. 2012. *Modern Thai Buddhism and Buddhadāsa Bhikkhu. A Social History*. Singapore: National University of Singapore Press. https://doi.org/10.2307/j.ctv1ntgk6

Jackson, Peter A. 2003. *Buddhadāsa. Theravada Buddhism and Modernist Reform in Thailand.* Chiang Mai: Silkworm.

Jayatilleke, Kalatissa Nanda. 1975. *The Buddhist Attitude to Other Religions*. The Wheel Publications 216. Kandy, Sri Lanka: Buddhist Publication Society.

Kiblinger, Kristin Beise. 2005. *Buddhist Inclusivism. Attitudes Towards Religious Others*. Aldershot: Ashgate.

Kim, Yong-pyo. 2013. "An Intra-Buddhist Dialogue Between Theravāda and Mahāyāna." In *Buddhism and Religious Diversity*, Volume 1, edited by Perry Schmidt-Leukel, 188–205. Abingdon: Routledge.

Mudiyanse, Nandasena. 1967. *Mahayana Monuments in Ceylon*. Colombo: M.D. Gunasena.

Ñāṇamoli Bhikkhu, transl. 1999. *The Path of Purification* (*Visuddhimagga*) by Bhadantācariya Buddhaghosa. Seatle: BPS Pariyatti.

Nyanaponika Mahāthera. 2008. "Anattā and Nibbāna." In *Collected Wheel Publications*, 239–264. Kandy, Sri Lanka: Buddhist Publication Society.

Pandit, Moti Lal. 1993. *Being as Becoming. Studies in Early Buddhism*. New Delhi: Intercultural.

Rahula, Walpola. 1993. *History of Buddhism in Ceylon. The Anuradhapura Period. Third Century BC – Tenth Century AC*. Third Edition. Dehiwale: Buddhist Cultural Centre.

Rhys Davids, T.W., Hermann Oldenberg transl. 1996 [1985]. *Vinaya Texts*. Part I. SBE 13. Delhi: Motilal Banarsidass.

Schmidt-Leukel, Perry. 2006. *Understanding Buddhism*. Edinburgh: Dunedin Academic Press.

———. 2009. *Transformation by Integration. How Inter-faith Encounter Changes Christianity*. London: SCM.

———. 2017. *Religious Pluralism and Interreligious Theology. The Gifford Lectures – An Extended Edition*. Maryknoll: Orbis.

———. 2020. "Buddhist Accounts of Religious Diversity." In *The Wiley-Blackwell Companion to Religious Diversity*, edited by Kevin Schilbrack. New York: Wiley-Blackwell.

Schmidt-Leukel, Perry, ed. 2008. *Buddhist Attitudes to Other Religions*. St. Ottilien: EOS.

———, ed. 2013. *Buddhism and Religious Diversity*. Four volumes. Abingdon: Routledge.

Swearer, Donald, ed. 1989. *Me and Mine. Selected Essays of Bhikkhu Buddhadāsa*. New York: State University of New York.

Tilakaratne, Asanga. 2016. "The Ultimate Buddhist Religious Goal, Nirvana and its Implications for Buddhist-Christian Dual Belonging." In *Buddhist-Christian Dual Belonging. Affirmations, Objections, Explorations*, edited by G. D'Costa and R. Thompson, 89–106. Farnham: Ashgate. https://doi.org/10.4324/9781315562735-6

U Pe Maung Tin and Gordon Hanninton Luce, eds. 2008. *The Glass Palace Chronicle of the Kings of Myanmar*. Yangon: Unity.

Vélez de Cea, J. Abraham. 2013. *The Buddha and Religious Diversity*. Abingdon: Routledge. https://doi.org/10.4324/9780203072639

Walshe, Maurice, transl. 1995. *The Long Discourses of the Buddha. A Translation of the Dīgha Nikāya*. Boston: Wisdom.

4

Openness towards the Religious Other in Buddhism

Carola Roloff (Bhikṣuṇī Jampa Tsedroen)

University of Hamburg

Dr. phil. **Carola Roloff** (monastic name: Bhikṣuṇī Jampa Tsedroen) is a Visiting Professor for "Buddhism in Dialogue with Contemporary Societies" at the Academy of World Religions, University of Hamburg (foundation lectureship 2018–2025). She was a post-Doctoral and Senior Research Fellow for the European research project "Religion and Dialogue in Modern Societies" (2013–2018), Forum Humanum Visiting Professor at the Academy of World Religions (2012), and Principal Investigator on Buddhist nuns' ordination in the Tibetan canon (DFG project) at the University of Hamburg (2010–2017). Her current research foci include: Buddhism and dialogue, contextual dialogical theology, Buddhist nuns' ordination, and research on gender theories.

Challenges and chances

Nowadays the question of peaceful co-existence of different religious traditions is more important than ever. Since the beginning of this century we have been confronted with a growing number of ostensibly religiously-motivated terror attacks and conflicts, with oppression, expulsion and discrimination, with violence and hatred. All religions are involved, they are no longer limited to one area or another; all religious traditions are increasingly practised everywhere. Therefore, we need to understand diversity and we need mutual respect and confidence. Openness towards the religious other plays a major role in this process. How open is Buddhism in this regard?

Buddhism is widely regarded as *the* tolerant religion. But is this fact or fiction? How tolerant is Buddhism? How open is Buddhism towards religious others? And what does openness actually mean in this context? Mutual tolerance and respect, or even mutual appreciation? Renunciation of the claim to sole representation and proselytizing? And how far should tolerance go? Are there limits to openness? Does openness require us to grant that other religions are *equal* or *equally valid*, despite their differences? Does openness in the final analysis refer to ultimate truth?

For Abrahamic religions truth is about God and revelation. Buddhism is a non-theist/a-theist religion. Supposing the religious other's understanding of ultimate reality differs from mine, do I need to accept it as equally valid? Does such a kind of openness require a pluralistic attitude that avoids exclusivism and inclusivism as defined by John Hick? He says:

> by exclusivism I mean the view that one particular mode of religious thought and experience (namely one's own) is alone valid, all others being false. By inclusivism I mean the view [...] that one's own tradition alone has the whole truth but that this truth is nevertheless partially reflected in other traditions. [...] And by pluralism I mean the view [...] that the great world faiths embody different perceptions and conceptions of, and correspondingly different responses to, the Real or the Ultimate. (Hick 1983, 487)

The Christian tripolar typology (Schmidt-Leukel 2005) has framed academic discourse about interreligious dialogue for more than 30 years now.[1] The challenge of religious pluralism "amounts to the question of whether to abandon traditional claims to the exclusive or inclusive superiority of one's own tradition, thus rejecting the idea that, ideally, all should become members of one's own faith" (Schmidt-Leukel 2013, 1).

Schmidt-Leukel (2009, 5–6) discusses the necessity of a Universal Theology, which he characterizes as a search for truth, for a better, wider, deeper understanding of it. His vision of intercultural theology (2011, 9) proceeds from the positive assumption that theologically relevant truths are to be found not only in one's own but also in the other's religious tradition, and that diversity is to be welcomed.

Although I agree that diversity should be welcomed, and accept that relevant truths can be found not only in "my own" Buddhist Prāsaṅgika Mādhyamika tradition, the tripolar typology as far as Buddhism is concerned seems to end in a kind of "meta-inclusivism" (Küster 2015, 100). The readiness to understand, to respect and to appreciate other religious traditions presupposes an open (mental) *attitude*. For a Buddhist this approach can be facilitated by cultivating an attitude of love, compassion, sympathetic joy and equanimity for all sentient beings. Through examples of contemporary leading Buddhist teachers as well as Buddhist texts. I will argue that these teachings, although not explicitly speaking about

---

1. An overview of different approaches in the context of the tripolar typology and how they differ from each other is given by Vélez de Cea (2013, 28–31). He himself builds upon Schmidt-Leukel's reformulation of the tripolar typology (according to Race) (28, 35) and modifies it by introducing a fourth category like Knitter (2002) and Hedges and Race (2008). Vélez terms his category "pluralist inclusivism."

religious others, still have the potential to generate openness towards the religious other.

Current state of research

The Buddha's attitude towards religious others has been of interest to classical Indology, especially Buddhist studies, since the late nineteenth century. Indologists examined "historico-critically" the relation between the Buddha's teachings and the already existing pronouncements by other teachers and their theses (Frauwallner 1956/2010) and asked for the Buddha's opponents (Oldenberg 1881). Buddhism has been part of German culture for almost two hundred years now, counting philosopher Arthur Schopenhauer (1788–1860) among its early adherents (Roloff and Weiße 2015, 7).

Buddhist relations with the religious other

A brief historical summary of the encounter of Buddhists with religious others inside and outside of India, from the time of the historical Buddha (ca. 500 BCE) until today, can be found in Harris (2013). She refers to *The Discourses of the Buddha (Sutta-piṭaka)* in the Pāli Canon which have been transmitted primarily in the form of dialogues engaged in by the Buddha with his monks and nuns, and lay followers from all walks of life. Harris identifies five "faces" or strategies towards the religious other:

> adherence to a code of conduct predicated on respectful, non-violent yet rigorous debate; robust teaching of ideas that opposed or challenged those taught by other groups; ridicule of the practices/beliefs of the 'other;' the demotion or subordination of these practices/beliefs; the appropriation and modification of practices/symbols from the religious 'other.' (Harris 2013, 89)

Summing up, Harris observes a fundamental tension in the Buddhist relation to the religious other. On the one hand, Buddhism teaches that taking one's own view to be the only correct one leads away from enlightenment. On the other hand, there is the conviction that the Buddha's teaching surpasses other systems. In history, this is expressed in different ways, "from absorption of the "other" to supercessionism and polemical defence" (Harris 2013, 117). This goes hand in hand with politeness, respectful coexistence and cooperation. In the light of the tripolar typology, this implies that the discourses of the Buddha as recorded in the Pāli Canon display both exclusivistic and inclusivistic traits: exclusivistic when, for example the Buddha says in the *Cūḷasīhanāda Sutta, The Shorter Discourse on the Lion's Roar*:

> Bhikkhus, only here is there a recluse, only here a second recluse, only here a third recluse, only here a fourth recluse. The doctrines of others are devoid of recluses: that is how you should rightly roar your lion's roar. (M 11)[2]

And incusivist when, for example, central elements of other religious traditions are included like the Indian God Brahmā in the *Ariyapariyesanā Sutta, The Noble Search* (M 26).[3]

Openness towards religious others in terms of pluralism

In his study "How the Buddha dealt with Non-Buddhists," Freiberger (2013) asks how the Buddha (or his direct disciples) behaved towards non-Buddhists and how Buddhist source texts constructed religious others. He discusses the imprecision of the term "tolerance" and distinguishes between "two dimensions: dogmatic tolerance and social or institutional tolerance" (Freiberger 2013, 48). To be dogmatically tolerant would be to integrate other religions' beliefs into one's own framework of religious theory; methodologically, this is either inclusivistic or pluralistic.

To be socially or institutionally tolerant, on the other hand, is to reject the use of force against adherents of other religions. It appears that early Buddhists were not violent towards others, and so Buddhism was at the outset institutionally tolerant in this sense. Freiberger adopts John Hick's framework as a foundation for his definitions (2013, 48; see also Freiberger and Kleine 2011, 442; see also page 63 above). He states that pluralism is not asserted in the Pāli Canon; the two other categories, exclusivism and inclusivism, however, might be helpful for analysis. Freiberger regards "categories such as tolerance, the Buddha's skill-in-means, or inclusivism" as "problematic because they carry an inherent (positive) value judgement that obstructs the analytic view, or they fail to include certain aspects." Instead of using those abstract categories, he suggests an approach that starts with identifying and analysing the actual techniques of dealing with "the other" (2013, 55).

Kiblinger (2008), like Schmidt-Leukel (2009, 51–52), argues that an attitude towards others is exclusivistic when it is assumed that the realization of a transcendent reality that is essential for salvation can only be reached through *one* single religion. At the same time, she emphasizes overlaps between inclusivism and pluralism. She herself favours an

2. Sutta Central, www.suttacentral.net (05 March 2019), >Sutta>Middle>MN11 *Cūḷasīhanāda Sutta* (M I 63): https://suttacentral.net/mn11.
3. Sutta Central, www.suttacentral.net (18 February 2016), >Sutta>Middle>MN 26 *Ariyapariyesanā [Pāsarāsi] Sutta* (M I 160): https://suttacentral.net/mn26.

inclusivistic subtype combined with pluralism (Kiblinger 2008, 35–36, 44) to capture the Buddhist attitude towards religious others, as does Vélez de Cea (2013), who creates the sub-category "pluralist-inclusivism" to characterize Buddhist attitudes.

Rita Gross, on the other hand, suggests that we simply celebrate diversity and learn "from and about each other, rather than trying to find theological validations of such diversity" (Gross 2005a, 76). Nevertheless, she thinks that demographics force us to defend pluralistic theologies in order to allow for the reality of religious diversity. As a Buddhist theologian, she points out that "Buddhism historically has regarded religious diversity as anything except a normal fact of existence" spreading worldwide "without a strong imperative to become the world's sole religion" (Gross 2005a, 79) and suggests to better "center on questions of ethics not metaphysics" (2005a, 82).

Nonetheless, when she proposes "that Buddhist methods of working with words and ideas can help us to a genuine theology of pluralism" she turns out to be either an inclusivist or a pluralistic inclusivist, suggesting that the most useful contribution Buddhists can make is "to push the insight that words, thoughts, ideas, doctrines, teachings, and so forth are only and nothing more than fingers pointing to a moon" (Gross 2005a, 86) and that "we should concern ourselves not with the truth of religious teachings but with their utility, with how well they function as methods to get people from point A to point B" which "one could call (...) ignorance and enlightenment" (2005a, 83).

Volker Küster (2011, 121–139) describes how representatives of the pluralistic theology of religions tried to overcome the inherent dilemma of exclusivism-inclusivism by progressively giving up Christian positions of faith – from Christocentrism through theocentrism to a position beyond theism/non-theism. He distinguishes between three types of interreligious dialogue rather than three kinds of views: dialogue of life, of reason, and of the heart, while the category "dialogue of reason" includes a "shared search for truth"(Küster 2011, 138). Küster describes (vice versa) an "inclusivism-exclusivism dilemma" as follows (the author's English translation):

> In principle each religion is confronted with this inclusivism-exclusivism dilemma. The postmodern pluralistic theology of religions tries to break through this dilemma but ends up in some kind of meta-inclusivism that sees all religions as converging in one point of salvation history. (2015, 100)

Hayes understands "pluralism" as a "celebration of diversity." Like those who celebrate biodiversity, he argues, pluralists think that religious diversity is healthy and desirable because it is a prerequisite for enabling any form of life. He, however, objects that Gross and her followers are wrong to see this pluralism in the Buddhist tradition, and demonstrates that the classical literature of Indian Buddhism does not promote it. For him pluralism is a "modern ideology that, like all ideologies, has evolved to help people deal with the problems of a particular age in history" (1991, 18). Therefore, it would be anachronistic and intellectually dishonest to look for anticipations of a modern kind of thought in traditions like Buddhism, Christianity, or Islam that developed in a completely different social and political environment (Hayes 1991, 19).

In a later paper Hayes (Hayes and Hsin Tao 2014, 124) focuses on "universal friendship" – in his view a notion more common in Buddhist texts and closely related to hospitality, and reflects on religious pluralism in relation to the fulfilment of human potential and the achievement of human flourishing (*eudaimonía*):

> the realization of the human potential is one that requires the combined efforts of all people. Moreover, cooperation is something that requires mental and emotional flexibility and a willingness to learn not only from one's own experiences but also from the experiences of others. From these two considerations, I claim that it follows that the healthiest human community is one that encourages individuals to benefit from the entire collective wisdom and experience of humankind as a whole. [...] So this leads to my third observation, which is that when Buddhist principles are taken to their logical conclusion, they must embody a spirit of religious pluralism and can never be seen from the narrow perspective of the Buddhist tradition alone. (Hayes and Hsin-Tao 2014, 141)

Thus, Hayes does not understand pluralism in the way Hick defines it, but as a "celebration of diversity" in the sense of respect for other convictions. Dealing with religious others one always needs to consider the different perspectives and to take into account one's own subjectivity. This is necessary because it is highly questionable whether somebody from inside a tradition is able – even with the best intent – to develop a truly objective view on things outside and whether religious pluralism is not just an abstract which does not exist in the particular, namely in an ordinary person's mind.

Vélez de Cea (2013, 28–31, 35) extends Schmidt-Leukel's reformulation of the tripolar typology (according to Race) and modifies it by introducing a fourth category: "pluralist inclusivism." According to him, openness manifests in two ways, in views (openness in theory) as well as in attitudes (openness in practice).[4] Theory refers to doctrinal claims, and practice to the attitudes or practical dispositions towards them, for example how one engages in dialogue. He uses the acronym OTMIX (our tradition's most important x): this could be a doctrine, a value, a reality or a goal and may refer to different "referents" like God, ultimate reality, redemption, liberation, perfection of the spiritual path, highest truth, all-encompassing goodness or holiness, namely anything that helps to define one's own position in comparison with those of others. Vélez de Cea himself does not aspire to a unity between religions, but to an acceptance of diversity.

McCagney (1997) chooses a radically different approach by translating the central Buddhist term "emptiness" (Skt. *śūnyatā*) as "openness," arguing that Nāgārjuna's usage of the term "*śūnyatā*" "is inspired by the imagery of the sky or space (Skt. *ākāśa*) in early *prajñāpāramitā* literature" (McCagney 1997, xix). I agree with her idea in so far as indeed the concept of *śūnyatā* makes space for liberation, for inner growing and transformation.

Gross (2005b) claims that the tension between religious identity and openness to the validity of religious others' beliefs has never puzzled her. The answer is easy: "Religions are language systems, and no language is universal and absolute. [...] We also recognize that more than one language could be "valid," whatever that might mean." It is impossible to express the inexpressible. We have to accept the limits of language and thus the limits of the doctrinal systems of religions. For her:

> this is the solution for the problem of coexistence of a strong individual religious identity with openness to the relevance of other religious languages. Other religions, as well as my own, are nothing more than highly relative language systems. (...) It seems to me that copping to the limitations of language, to the inability of language ever to capture truth completely, is completely essential in the pluralistic world we now inhabit. (Gross 2005b, 15–16)

She recommends, for assessing religions, to consider to what extent they transform people away from self-centredness towards more love and compassion. Exclusivistic claims of truth, she argues, are unacceptable for pluralists – not for metaphysical but for ethical reasons. They are not part of any religion because they always imply imperialist and harmful consequences.

4. Views (Tib. *lta ba*, Skt. *dṛṣṭi*), attitudes (Tib. *sems pa*, Skt. *cetanā*) or practice (Tib. *spyod pa*, Skt. *carya*) are common Buddhist categories. Vélez de Cea, however, when using them, is not thinking about Sanskrit terms here. (Personal correspondence 13 January 2016).

To date, most systematic studies on openness towards the religious other do not address Buddhism; they focus instead on the Abrahamic religions. In this paper I will consider a teaching that takes a central position in all three main strands of Buddhism but has so far hardly been mentioned in the context of dialogue and openness (Knitter 2008, 93; Schmidt-Leukel 2008b, 157). According to my own experience, it is helpful to develop openness in practice, although it requires partly a new reading when it comes to openness in theory with regard to ultimate truth.

The body of source material in Buddhism

Unlike the Abrahamic religions, Buddhism has no single holy text or even a single shared canon. Nor is there, like in Hinduism, *one* oldest book like the *Rig-Veda* or *one* especially well-known book like the *Bhagavadgītā*. In Buddhism we rather see ourselves confronted with several voluminous canons (*Tripiṭaka*s) that have been transmitted in different Asian source languages (Sanskrit, Pāli, Chinese, Tibetan). The Chinese and the Tibetan canons are primarily based on texts that have been written in Sanskrit or in other Central Indian languages (Prakrit) like Gāndhārī.[5] Although the Buddha allegedly spoke neither Pāli nor Sanskrit but the Central Indian Magādhī-Prakrit (*Ardhamāgadhī),* Sanskrit and Pāli are still considered the two most important Indian "original languages"; one even speaks of the Sanskrit and Pāli tradition of Buddhism (Dalai Lama XIV and Chodron 2014, xix, 39, 49). Precisely speaking there are:

1) the Pāli Canon of Theravāda in South and South East Asia (Sri Lanka, Myanmar, Thailand, Cambodia, Laos and parts of Vietnam; first century BCE, 48 vols., completely preserved),
2) the Sanskrit and Prakrit "canons" of Indian Buddhism that ended in India with its second spread to Tibet (first century BCE until twelfth century CE, mainly manuscripts),
3) the Chinese canon *Sanzang* of East Asian Buddhism (primarily translated from Sanskrit but also from other languages like Gāndhārī) in China, Vietnam, Korea, Japan, Taiwan, Malaysia and Singapore (including also Zen Buddhism; second to tenth centuries CE, 100 volumes),
4) the Tibetan Buddhist canon "Kangyur" and "Tengyur" (primarily translated from Sanskrit) as it can be found in Central Asia (Tibet, Bhutan, Sikkim, Nepal, the Indian Himalayan region, Mongolia; seventh to fourteenth centuries CE, e.g., Derge edition: 316 vols. more than 300,000 pages).

5. For more on the languages and texts cf. Freiberger and Kleine 2011, 171–195.

Therefore it is not always possible to find Buddhist key texts that, in the canonical collections of all traditions:

1) have the same wording,
2) have a comparably high status, and
3) are suitable as proof texts for the potential and the capability for dialogue or openness of Buddhism.

In the previous section we have considered the current state of research, Buddhist relations with the religious other, and openness towards religious others in terms of pluralism. I have presented some of the criteria according to which openness to the religious other can be judged and given a brief introduction into the body of source material in Buddhism. Next I will indicate where I see a potential for openness or constructing openness towards religious others, and what needs to be considered when Buddhism engages in dialogue with other religions. I will argue that although Buddhist teachings are not intentionally aimed at creating an attitude of openness towards religious others, they have the potential to do so by generating a state of mind that enables the development of this kind of openness.

Being aware of the problem that "the (one) Buddhism" does not exist and that it is therefore not easy to find texts all traditions have in common, I have decided to choose widely popular Buddhist key teachings as well as statements by contemporary leading Buddhists to give an overview that may serve as an introduction to the topic.

Methodological approach

Buddhist doxography divides tenets into two types, those of Outsiders (non-Buddhists), and those of Insiders (Buddhists). An Insider is a person who from the depth of his/her heart "has taken refuge" in the Triple Gem, namely the Buddha, his teaching (*Dharma*) and the Buddhist community (*Saṅgha*). In addition to taking refuge one has to accept a certain Buddhist "doctrine" (Skt. *siddhānta*), literally, "fixed conclusion" or maxim (Sopa and Hopkins 1976, 53–55, 68). That means when I have committed myself to a particular religious tradition the limits of my practice of openness seem to be set by this very tradition. I will therefore ask whether the *capability for pluralism* or at least *openness* towards religious others can be found in Buddhism at all.

From the extensive body of Buddhist source material, I have chosen to draw on:

1) canonical texts from all three mainstream traditions (using scholarly German or English translations with occasional ref-

erence to the source texts in the original languages),
2) works by Buddhist philosophers and Yogis (mystics),
3) texts that are *particular* to one tradition and contemporary texts that are eminent, thus usually not having immediate parallels in all mainstream traditions but rather highlighting the exclusivity of one religious tradition and nevertheless having a high potential for dialogue in the sense of "unity in diversity."

Among the texts *particular* to one tradition, I will consider statements by The Fourteenth Dalai Lama, Tenzin Gyatso, because of his widespread popularity and influence among Buddhists and non-Buddhists alike. This is in line with the goal of the Religious Dialogue in Modern Society (ReDi) project to investigate the complex phenomenon of interreligious dialogue with regard to its scope for the social processes of integration and peace building.

Key texts for openness towards religious others

I have already stated that we cannot speak of "the (one) Buddhism." Instead, I will consider how one can develop openness towards the religious others in practice and in theory:

1) by developing the mental attitude of love, compassion, sympathetic joy and equanimity in the sense of the Four Immeasurables (Skt. *apramāṇa*s);
2) by applying the so-called Skill in Liberative Technique, i.e., the principle of *upāyakauśalya,* also referred to as *skill-in-means* or *skilful means*;
3) by accepting the two levels of truth (Skt. *dvayasatya*), the conventional and the ultimate truth.
4) I will ask whether these approaches are helpful when we engage in interreligious dialogue.

The Four Immeasurables

I begin with the "Four Immeasurables,"[6] also known as the Four Divine States (or Four Foundations of Divinity) or the four *brahmavihāra*s,[7] to see whether these values foster an attitude of openness towards religious others in Buddhism. They have been given this name because they relate to an "immeasurable" number of sentient beings.[8] These Four Immeasurables are:

6. Tib. *tshad med pa bzhi*, Skt. *catvāryapramāṇāni*, Pā. *catasso appamaññāyo.*

7. Skt. *catvāri-brahmavihārāḥ*, Pā. *cattāro brahmavihārā.*

8. As explained in the *Abhidharmakośabhāṣya* by the Buddhist master Vasubandhu (fourth/fifth century CE) (1988–90, volume 4, 1264, VIII 29a).

1) Love, Loving-kindness or Benevolence (Skt. *maitrī*, Pāli *mettā*),
2) Compassion or Care (Skt./Pāli *karuṇā*),
3) Sympathetic Joy (Skt./Pāli *muditā*), the opposite of envy or *schadenfreude*,
4) Equanimity or Lack of egocentricity[9] (Skt. *upekṣā*, Pāli *upekkhā*).

A four-line aspirational prayer[10] from the standard liturgy of Tibetan Buddhism serves as a key text:

> May all sentient beings have happiness and the causes of happiness.
>
> May all sentient beings be free from suffering and the causes of suffering.
>
> May all sentient beings never be separated from the supreme happiness that is free from suffering.
>
> May all sentient beings abide in equanimity, free of attachment to close ones and aversion against those distant to.[11]

In the daily practice of Tibetan Buddhism this verse is recited three times daily in the morning and in the evening along with the threefold refuge to Buddha, his teachings and his community.

---

9. I intentionally avoid the translation as "impartiality" here, because the term implies neutrality. Advocating justice, however, means not to remain impartial but to take the side of those oppressed.

10. Tib. *smon lam*, Skt. *praṇidhāna*, see Mvy 764, 778, 921.

11. From "Skyabs 'gro sems bskyed," in *Zhal 'don phyogs bsdebs* (Varanasi: Dge ldan spyi las khang, 2007), 4: Tib. *sems can thams cad bde ba dang bde ba'i rgyu dang ldan par gyur cig | sems can thams cad sdug bsngal dang sdug bsngal gyi rgyu dang bral bar gyur cig | sems can thams cad sdug bsngal med pa'i bde ba dam pa dang mi 'bral bar gyur cig | sems can thams cad nye ring chags sdang dang bral ba'i btang snyoms la gnas par gyur cig.* See also: Bde chen snying po (1878–1941) *Dge ldan snyan brgyud kyi man ngag las byung ba'i bla ma'i rnal 'byor dga' ldan lha brgya mar grags pa.* Short title: *Bla ma'i rnal 'byor dga' ldan lha brgya ma. Gsung 'bum (Collected Works).* volume 2 (*kha*) 512.4–513.2. TBRC W3834. Lha sa: [s.n.], [199-]. Tib. *sems can thams cad bde ba dang bde ba'i rgyu dang ldan par gyur cig | sdug bsngal dang sdug bsngal gyi rgyu dang bral bar gyur cig | sdug bsngal med pa'i bde ba dam pa dang mi 'bral bar gyur cig | nye ring chags sdang dang bral ba'i btang snyoms tshad med pa la gnas par gyur cig* (May all sentient beings enjoy happiness and the causes of happiness, be free of suffering and the causes of suffering, be never separated from the supreme happiness that is free from suffering and abide in immeasurable equanimity, free of attachment to close ones and aversion against those distant to).

While this quatrain does not originate in the canonical works of Buddhism but in a contemporary Tibetan "prayer book,"[12] Buddhist believers, however, trace it back to the Buddha himself. This doctrine is significant for all three main strands of contemporary Buddhism[13] and can therefore serve as a key text for "Buddhist ecumenism" as well as the basis for the dialogue with other religions – it provides a connecting option both on the theological[14] and on the empirical level.[15]

In Tibetan Buddhism, meditation often starts with the cultivation of equanimity. One first becomes conscious of the state of mind in which we discriminate between those close to and those distant from us. Using contemplation one then lets go of any "stigmatization" as friend or enemy, close or distant. The point is to develop a sense of equal nearness to all sentient beings, thus counteracting the tendency to discriminate between near and distant, familiar and strange, Buddhist or non-Buddhist, man or woman and so on and, building upon that, accustoming the mind to new patterns of thought towards love and compassion, and a respectful, compassionate, loving and appreciative attitude towards others. This meditation puts an end to the habit of seeing oneself as the centre of the moral universe, and allows one to become receptive to the needs of others.

Although, in the past, this meditation has hardly been deployed to encourage practitioners to develop openness towards religious others, in order to include them at eye-level, the teaching has the potential to be cultivated in this direction. Furthermore, it is applied today not only in the

12. *Zhal 'don phyogs bsdebs.*

13. Thich Nhất Hạnh, for example, a leading representative of Vietnamese Buddhism builds upon the Chinese canon. He mentions the "Four Immeasurables" in *Old Path, White Clouds: Walking in the Footsteps of the Buddha* (1991, 321). For the Theravāda, see Nyanatiloka 1952/2002, 108. In the course of the project, for the two other mainstream traditions of Buddhism, corresponding literal parallels for *Sutta* M 83 in the Pāli Canon (*Makhādeva [Maghadeva] Sutta* M II 74-83, About King Makhādeva), could be identified, cf. Sutta Central, www.suttacentral.net (23 February 2016), >Sutta>Middle>MN 83: https://suttacentral.net/mn83.

14. For a trans-traditional study of the Four Immeasurables in the history of the development of ideas, see M. Maithrimurthi 1999. Besides, the doctrine of the Four Immeasurables can also be found in Hinduism, in Patañjali and Dvivedi 1980 [1890], 22, verse 33. Moreover, Patañjali's text is said to have been translated into Arabic by the Muslim scholar al-Biruni (973–1048); *cf.* Berzin 2008, 213, 217.

15. In the ReDi handout "Suggestions for Main questions with adaptations and additions for different respondees," 2 October 2013, T. Knauth, J. Ipgrave, and D. Vieregge suggest for the ReDi project (level of dialogical practice) to ask the following guiding questions for the investigation of various "attitudes": "If you think of the people whom you encounter in everyday life: To whom do you feel close and why? Who rather seems strange to you and why? What role does religion have in this?"

religious but also in the secular sphere as a method for cultivating mindful consciousness as I will show below.

Empathy and respect as expressed, for instance, in the Four Immeasurables are also common in public Dharma teachings. Thus the former spiritual leader of the Tibetan Centre Hamburg, Geshe Thubten Ngawang (1932–2003), led a meditation on the Four Immeasurables – in the presence of a predominantly non-Buddhist audience – during the Deutscher Umwelttag (German Day of the Environment) in Frankfurt 1992 and said:

> I tried to connect the four unlimited mental attitudes with wishes for the environment, especially the four elements. Whoever practices this meditation need not follow a particular religion or world-view; it can be practised by anyone and will certainly unfold its power. The Four Unlimited Mental Attitudes are practised as follows:
>
> You turn confidently towards your object of refuge – God, saints, or higher beings. If you do not belong to any religion, you visualize the good forces in nature like the rays of the sun, the light of the stars, the cooling moonlight. (Ngawang 1995, 79; the author's English translation)

In the following slightly altered verse on sympathetic joy, he wishes all sentient beings to become free of false views and wrong actions, thus achieving wellbeing that continues without interruption. For the insider, "happiness continuing without interruption" is a paraphrase for liberation or *Nirvāṇa*. Thus, on the one hand, Thubten Ngawang remains true to his Buddhist philosophical point of view; but on the other hand he respects the fact that others direct their trust to differing objects of refuge and supports them in this. This means that the attitude is pluralistic, but the view is going beyond that of an inclusivist, because he explicitly refers to the different goals of non-Buddhists too.

Against this background, the third line of the Four Immeasurables is cited here once more. It reads: "May all sentient beings never be separated from the supreme happiness that is free from suffering." In order to use the Four Immeasurables to develop openness towards religious others, this line would need an additional interpretation, that is: in the Buddhist context "supreme happiness" refers to *Nirvāṇa* or the ultimate Buddhist goal(s), but in a non-Buddhist context it may refer to OTMIX or simply to peaceful co-existence in the present world.

Applying the "skill in liberative technique"

In a Buddhist framework, openness towards religious others is also furthered by the Buddhist hermeneutical strategy of the *skill in liberative technique* (Skt. *upāyakauśalya*, P. *upāyakosalla*) (Thurman 1976, 10),[16] also known as *skilful means* or *skill-in-means*. "Since ancient times the Buddha had been famed for his ability to adapt his teaching to the powers of comprehension of the audience" (Frauwallner 1956/2010, 157). With the beginning of the Mahāyāna (first century BCE):

> it was now said that only some of the traditional stras primarily of course the new *sūtra*s, proclaimed the complete truth. The rest are intended for hearers who are not yet capable of grasping the complete truth, and are meant to lead them on the right path. They can therefore not be taken literally, but must rather be interpreted accordingly. (Frauwallner 2010, 157)

This concept, however, does not originate in Mahāyāna. It is already present in the Pāli Canon where it is mentioned in a list in the *Saṅgīti Sutta*[17] as one of three skills and also used in a hierarchical way. Similar to Frauwallner, Bhikkhu Bodhi writes that a special characteristic of the Buddha is "his uncanny ability to reach deep into the hearts of those who come to him for guidance and teach them in the unique way suitable for their characters and situations" (Bodhi 2013, 14).

In the history of Indian Buddhism newly written *sūtra*s were introduced as "Words of the Buddha" by using *skilful means*. This technique made it possible to interpret dissenting views from different Buddhist schools as only "apparent" contradictions and to reconcile them with each other. As Makransky points out:

> The doctrine of skillful means has provided a way within the ahistorical consciousness of Asian Buddhist cultures to grant the legitimacy needed for developments in thought and practice to take fresh expression in new periods and cultures despite the backlash by conservative Buddhist institutions that tended to suppress such developments. (Makransky 2008, 126)

16. In Tibetan translation the term is "associated with a kind of wisdom, […] or pedagogical understanding," while in Chinese it has the connotation of "a mere expedience – something necessary but distasteful" (Garfield 2015, 272).

17. For the *Saṅgīti Sutta, Reciting in Concert* D 33 *cf.*: Sutta Central, www.suttacentral.net (22 January 2015), >Sutta>Long>Dīghanikāya>DN 33: https://suttacentral.net/dn33.

Let me cite the Dalai Lama to show how Buddhist teachers can apply *skilful means* to encourage their students to become open towards the religious other. He says:

> humankind has produced a plurality of different religions and world views. I take this to be very positive; for each religion and tradition shows its own special features, and since very many mental predispositions and tendencies exist among human beings, a plurality of philosophies and religions is exceedingly beneficial. (Dalai Lama XIV 1989, 13)[18]

Thus, although not explicitly referring to it, he reasons in the sense of the *Upāyakauśalya Sūtra* (Tatz 1994, 26–111), the *Discourse on the Skill in Means*, that people with different dispositions need different doctrines, substantiating thereby the benefit of religious plurality. By comparison, Schmidt-Leukel writes: "Equally so, a religious pluralist can accept the equal salvific validity of different religious paths without being obliged to follow all of them" (Schmidt-Leukel 2009, 5).

At the first glance the Dalai Lama's view may appear pluralistic, but Vélez de Cea assumes:

> his individual perspective remains committed to the exclusivist view and the inclusivistic attitude characteristic of the Geluk school, but his social perspective is pluralistic in terms of attitude. This pluralistic attitude and the distinction the Dalai Lama makes between two perspectives goes beyond the traditional approach of his Geluk school. (Vélez de Cea 2013, 111–112)

In contrast to Schmidt-Leukel, what remains unsaid with the Dalai Lama, is whether he accepts that these other religious paths are similarly or equally salvific. In order to answer this from a Buddhist perspective we must clarify what we mean by "equal." Is it a matter of equality in the sense of human rights: "everyone is entitled to all the rights and freedoms […], without distinction of any kind, such as race, color, sex […] religion"?[19] Or rather of uniformity in view of the goal of salvation? Are different paths equally valid when it comes to liberation from suffering or leading towards OTMIX?

18. By comparison, Hayes (1991) remarks as discussed above on page 68 that religious pluralism is an attitude that accepts a plurality of religions as beneficial.

19. See article 2 of the Universal Declaration of Human Rights: United Nations, www.un.org/en/ (12 February 2016), >Documents>Universal Declaration of Human Rights: http://www.un.org/en/universal-declaration-human-rights/

The Dalai Lama XIV does not seem to consider himself an exclusivist but to have been transformed by experience. He suggests a new and different approach, when he says, for example:

> looking back I see that, my crucial learning experience was the shift that took place away from parochial and exclusivist vision of my own faith as unquestionably the best. Such a view is understandable in one who has insufficient experience and exposure, and may even be laudable in demonstrating a deep respect for one's own tradition. But it has elements of self-congratulation and even a kind of arrogance born in ignorance. (2010a, 17)

The Dalai Lama's commitment to interreligious dialogue opens a new way of thinking in the Buddhist world. Although there are clear boundaries between Buddhist and non-Buddhist views, in view of a globalized world in a (post-)modern context, he now attributes positive values even to non-Buddhist views, thus relativizing his own one. In doing so he too makes use of the Buddhist hermeneutic technique, the *skill in means*.[20] Whether he wishes that the followers of other religions may reach their specific goal of salvation or, according to his personal conviction, that they may eventually reach the supreme happiness, *Nirvāṇa* – or both - is yet to be clarified.

For followers of Tibetan Buddhism, *skilful means* seem to be suitable to adopting a pluralistic attitude and practising tolerance when it comes to dealing with differing views. The question is whether this technique – undertaken in an open and unbiased way, namely without hierarchization or proselytizing zeal – would work too when applied to religious beliefs outside Buddhism. *Skilful means* may prove to be a helpful tool to reconstruct a kind of "Buddhist Liberation/Contextual Theology," which provides space for openness towards religious others. Provided that these others express an interest, Buddhists could offer to share elements of their religion with them without, however, trying to missionize.

The concept of *skilful means* already includes the idea that the "Words of the Buddha" and their commentaries need to be understood dependent on context and that different people in different places at different times have different needs for which there is no panacea/ universal remedy. To use this device, however, might also be seen as a kind of inclusivism – that other religions are skilful means to Buddhist goals, a reading I do not agree with, preferring instead Gross's idea that religions are different language

20. On this *cf.* also "A Buddhist Hermeneutical Principle" in Dalai Lama 2010a, 152–156 as well as in the hermeneutics part of the ReDi collection (Sketch of the hermeneutical challenges): Knauth, Roloff, Drechsler, Jäckel and Markowsky 2016, 235–238.

systems none of which is universal or absolute. In my view those Buddhist and non-Buddhist religious doctrines that communicate salvific truth can be understood as different attempts to move closer to truth. Whether any of these assertions is true, can only be judged by those who have an insight into that truth. Thus, I would suggest that everybody should follow the path in which he/she has the greatest confidence, taking always into account and remaining open to the possibility that things could turn out to be completely different.

This leads us to the understanding of Truth in Buddhism and the notion of the Two Truths, which I feel to be another helpful tool to further openness towards religious others from a Buddhist perspective.

The Two Truths

Openness towards religious others in Buddhism is also facilitated and furthered through the doctrine of the two levels of truth (Skt. *dvayasatya*), the conventional and the ultimate truth. Expressed in a simplified way, conventional truth describes the composition of things with their diverse particularities as they present themselves to an ordinary consciousness in everyday life; ultimate truth, in contrast, describes the highest truth, *śūnyatā*. Building upon that, the Dalai Lama, explains in a conversation with the French diplomat, Stéphane Hessel (1917–2013) (the author's English translation):

> From an individual perspective the maxim 'one religion, one truth' is true, but when we consider the whole community of human beings we must always represent the conception of 'several religions, several truths.' (Hessel and Dalai Lama XIV 2012, 15)

It can be assumed that the Dalai Lama here does not mean several ultimate truths but several conventional truths, because as Harvey (2008, 130, as cited in Samuel, 1993) notes, Gelugpas have a "linear, structured, single path" (Skt. *ekayāna*), while followers of Tibetan *Ris med* (non-sectarianism) "have a collection of alternative paths and methods to an ultimate goal that goes beyond any verbal formulation" (Apple 2009, 79, 185–187). Thus it is reasonable to presume that the Dalai Lama from his point of view accepts several conventional truths, but not several ultimate truths. Nevertheless, we cannot exclude that he accepts that there are also different notions or theories on ultimate truth.

The conception that several religions have several truths is easy for him to accept – according to Tibetan doxography the major Indian Buddhist schools (Vaibhāṣika, Sautrāntika, Cittamātra/Yogacāra and Madhyamaka) acknowledge that there are two truths. But these two truths are understood differently – each Buddhist school offering its own definition and not only within Indian or Tibetan Buddhism, but in Chinese Buddhism (Gentz 2008, 196–197; Garfield 2015, 56–90) too where the Two Truths play a central role. I understand the Dalai Lama to be saying that at least on a conventional level all these different truths can be accepted as truths.

As mentioned in the introduction, for Abrahamic religions ultimate truth is about God and revelation. Buddhism is a non-theist/a-theist religion. Thus our understanding of ultimate reality seems not only to differ but to be diametrically opposed. Therefore we have to ask, whether there would be any benefit at all to have a dialogue on ultimate truth.

Before coming back to this question, let us have a look how the Two Truths are explained by the Buddhist Mādhyamika tradition: the two levels of truth are considered to be mutually dependent. Things are empty of intrinsic existence because they are interdependent. Thus Candrakīrti (seventh century) says in verse VI, 80 of the *Madhyamakāvatāra* (the author's English translation): "The conventional reality is the means (*upāya*), and the absolute reality is the goal (*upeya*)" (Tauscher 1995, 3). And Nāgārjuna says in the twenty-fourth chapter of his *Mūlamadhyamakakārikā*:

> (10) Without depending on the conventional truth,
> The meaning of the ultimate cannot be taught.
> Without understanding the meaning of the ultimate,
> Nirvana is not achieved. (Garfield 2015, 64)

Thus, I suggest, we should understand Buddhist and non-Buddhist religious doctrines that communicate salvific truths as different attempts/means (Skt. *upāya*) to move closer to truth.

Irrespective of whether religious others want to achieve *Nirvāṇa* or not in order to develop openness towards religious others, if it is possible to respect other Buddhists and their truth claims on an equal footing, it should also be possible to respect that non-Buddhists have different beliefs about the meaning of the ultimate and that an understanding of this may lead to whatever is most important to them (OTMIX).

The paradox of the Two Truths shows that just because something is true one should not conclude that its negation is *not* true. So, even though Buddhists think that there is no God of the kind that theistic religions posit, we can remain open to the possibility that there is one, even though we think we have arguments against it. This could turn out to be one of those surprising true contradictions.

Perhaps it is precisely this paradoxical identity and non-identity of the

Two Truths that enables Buddhists to encounter on eye-level and with respect and appreciation even those religions that assume a universal essence with regard to the ultimate truth, i.e., God. Garfield elaborates that the Buddhist Madhyamaka view leads to the "insight that the heart of being is deeply paradoxical" and "that a logic that can tolerate contradictions may be a better way to understand an inconsistent formal reality":

> reflection on emptiness may be the best way to come to see that a philosophical perspective that can tolerate contradictions is a better way to understand the inconsistent reality we inhabit. After all, who ever said that a particular, and rather arbitrary, human approach to logic must constrain the nature of the universe? (Garfield 2015, 80, 81)

It should be clear that I do not suggest to avoid talking about the different ultimate truth claims. We should instead deepen our understanding of their different conceptions in various religious doctrines. Starting with the conventional level would make it easier to find out where we might agree – or might disagree. Having established common ground we may find a better starting point to talk about our different views of the ultimate truth. This is how I understand "common search for truth." We may find out that we have more in common than we expected or even learn something beneficial we had never even imagined. Such a dialogue could be a great enrichment, and would also help us to better understand ultimate truth in one's own tradition.

An alternative for those with lesser interest in metaphysics may be the more pragmatic approach suggested by the Dalai Lama XIV (2010a, 160–161). He advises to take "a creative approach" to reconcile the two perspectives – the "one truth, one religion" perspective, which most world religions pertain to, and the "many truths, many religions" perspective, which the reality of the human world demands – by making a distinction between faith and respect. He proposes to reserve faith for one's own religion, while cultivating respect for other religions.

Challenges and chances for openness in contemporary Buddhism

In section three I have analysed three central Buddhist teachings in view of their potential for openness towards religious others in theory and in practice: the Four Immeasurables, the Skill in Liberative Technique and the Two Levels of Truth. In this section I will take up a few points from the previous sections and elaborate on them with reference to modern societies in the twenty-first century.

Firstly I will show that the message of the Four Immeasurables is already widely accepted in contemporary Western societies too. Therefore we can say that it has a global impact. Secondly, taking the secular right of gender equality as an example, I will discuss the challenge the secular poses for Buddhism and how it can be met. Challenges like the problem of how to cope with the Universal Declaration of Human Rights show Buddhism to be a religion that is still relevant nowadays. Thirdly, using the Two Truths debate as an example, I will argue that even in Buddhism itself religious diversity has always been – and still is – a challenge. Fourth: now, under the pressure of globalization, the various Buddhist traditions need to overcome their frictions and cooperate more closely in order to be able to engage in dialogue with other traditions as well as with other religions. Cooperation requires greater mutual acceptance of the religious other, whether Buddhist or non-Buddhist.

Secular impact of the Four Immeasurables

As mentioned above the teaching of the Four Immeasurables is applied today not only in the religious but also in the secular sphere as a method of mindful consciousness. Due to the interest of psychology, medicine and pedagogics in Buddhist meditation methods, traditional Buddhism has opened up for dialogue with natural sciences since the 1980s.[21] Due to this well-established dialogue, the meditation on the Four Immeasurables, as a secularized practice, is widely appreciated by religious others. In Anderssen-Reuster and Meibert we read that *upekkhā*/equanimity is to be understood as "openness and acceptance," and:

> although different strands, schools and cultural accretions have emerged in the different traditions of Buddhism, we can find, as common grounds of all directions, the active work on one's own realization, on a balanced, peaceful state of mind as well as on the development of compassion. (the author's English translation; Anderssen-Reuster and Meibert 2013, 72)

Bhikkhu Anālayo points out that the latest research results from psychology demonstrate that cultivating love (Skt. *maitri*, P. *mettā*) not only reduces anger and negative stress but also diminishes symptoms of schizophrenia and strengthens pro-social behaviour (2015, 18). This

21. The Mind & Life dialogues (USA) started in 1987, the Swiss project Science meets Dharma in 2001, and in 2003 the Santa Barbara Institute for Consciousness Studies was founded. One of the starting points may have been the conference "Geist und Natur' (Mind and Nature) in Hanover, Germany 1988. The first exchanges between the Dalai Lama and the German physicist and philosopher Carl-Friedrich von Weizsäcker date back to 1979.

shows that mutual openness can lead to accepting and implementing parts originating from other religions, and that Buddhists are ready to share parts of their religion in a secularized, non-missionary way, when it can be helpful.

Buddhism challenged by the secular (Gender Issue)

Today, manifold forms of secularism across the world have either banned religion from the political platform (e.g. France, Mexico, Turkey) or do not strictly separate religion and state. Some other states take the responsibility to ensure the protection and equality of all religions (e.g. Germany) or at least guarantee their free exercise, i.e., to operate within a certain legal and political framework (e.g. India). Asia is in transition with regard to political systems. Democracies have been established, but democratic thinking is not yet fully implemented.

In the West, about two centuries ago, Buddhism became part of mainly Judeo-Christian dominated societies where nowadays gender equality is taken for granted – at least theoretically. Thus we must ask how gender equality is understood from a Buddhist perspective and how far it is taken into consideration within Buddhist institutional structures. Can Buddhist women participate equally in preserving, teaching and representing their religion? No. Do they have equal access to religious leadership positions? No. Can they independently observe all of the obligatory rules and rituals? No. And the Buddha? Did he treat them equally to men or differently? The Buddha treated them differently. But in view of the ancient India context, he created incredible possibilities to practise Buddhism almost equally. Studying Buddhist societies today, however, we cannot avoid the impression that compared to the Buddha's lifetime setbacks occurred. Against this background, the Four Immeasurables are very important, since they explicitly state that our love and compassion should be equally directed to *all* sentient beings. Studying Buddhist societies nowadays, however, we cannot avoid the impression that men are "more equal" than women.

The understanding of equanimity plays a key role in modern societies. It should not only be understood as a peaceful state of mind – it has the potential to be interpreted according to secular values such as gender equality in the context of Human Rights. It could also sharpen the awareness of Buddhists and encourage them to become socially engaged and to take active responsibility and care for others, fighting other forms of discrimination and inequality. In Buddhism there is no technical term for "justice" (King 2005, 203) or "injustice." When dealing with human coexistence, one can therefore rely on the term "equanimity" or on the Four Immeasurables in total with regard to equality, social justice and gender justice, because the Buddhist mental training in love, compassion, sympathetic joy and equanimity includes *all* sentient beings without exception and irrespective of their religious affiliation, nationality or gender.

One may object that such reasoning is the attempt of a white feminist to influence or patronize Asian Buddhists by Western ideas. My emphasis on equanimity, however, derives from my experience with living Buddhism in Asia. The first conclave of the "International Buddhist Confederation" in Delhi (India) in September 2013, for example, adopted "equanimity" as an argument for demanding equality of women in Buddhism (Roloff 2014, 250). And in December 2013, the renowned Thai reformer, Sulak Sivaraksa, referring to the Thai Saṅgha Council asked, somewhat polemically: "Is their opposition to *Bhikkhunī* ordination based on the *Dhamma* and the *Brahmavihāra*s, or are they acting out of jealousy and ignorance?" (*International Network of Engaged Buddhists* petition 13 December 2014).[22] This remark reveals that the *Brahmavihāra*s are also cited by Asian Buddhists in the context of gender equality.

If Buddhists do not manage to treat other Buddhists including women and LGBTIQs,[23] at eye-level, how can they respectfully treat religious others? Already in ancient Indian Buddhist commentaries we find an inconsistency in relation to women, whether to fully include or partly exclude them. Two examples from indigenous Buddhist commentaries show where, from a Buddhist female perspective, I see such inconsistencies.

Buddhaghosa says in *The Divine Abidings* (*Brahmavihāra-niddesa*), the ninth chapter of his Theravāda commentary *Visuddhimagga* (*The Path of Purification*), that one considers all beings as equal with oneself:

> The mind-deliverance of loving-kindness is [practised] with specified pervasion in these seven ways: 'May all women be free from enmity, affliction and anxiety and live happily. May all men [...] all Noble Ones [...] all not Noble Ones [...] all deities [...] all human beings [...] all in states of loss be free from enmity, affliction and anxiety, and live happily (Paṭis II 131).' (Buddhaghosa and Ñāṇamoli 2010, 304)[24]

22. *International Network of Engaged Buddhists (INEB)*, 13 December 2014, www.change.org/>Petitions (Petition 13); 28 January 2016, www.change.org/p/Saṅgha-supreme-council-of-thailand-to-support-establishing-the-bhikkhuni-Saṅgha-in-siam-thailand

23. Since the 1990s LGBT or LGBTIQ is the acronym for lesbian, gay, bisexual and transgender communities; sometimes Q is added for those who identify as queer or are questioning their sexual identity, and the I includes intersex people.

24. *Cf.* the Four immeasurables in the *Saṅgīti Sutta*, *Reciting in Concert* D 33 (D iii 207):

Nevertheless in the same chapter Buddhaghosa writes:

> for Loving-kindness should not be developed […] towards the opposite sex, or towards a dead person. [...] Then, if he develops it specifically towards the opposite sex, lust inspired by that person springs up in him. (Buddhaghosa and Ñyāṇamoli 2010, 291–292)

Another example stems from a much later commentary by Pabongka Dechen Nyingpo (1879–1941), a famous teacher in the Gelug tradition of Tibetan Buddhism. It shows that there are Buddhist masters who teach the Four Immeasurables and are nevertheless convinced that being born as a man is superior to being born as a woman (see also Anālayo 2014). In the context of explaining the eight qualities of higher rebirth, Pabongka states in *Liberation in our Hands*: "we could not have found a better rebirth than the present one, except those of us, who have not been reborn as a man."[25]

It can be assumed that reticence – the opposite of openness – towards women may go hand in hand with reticence towards religious others. Furthermore, the examples illustrate that different readings and ambivalence or ambiguity are not only found within different traditions of Buddhism but also within the very same tradition, and even within *one* exegetical work. The same author also states by the way that faith in religions other than Buddhism should be given up.[26]

These examples give an idea how, after the Buddha's passing away and depending on sociological and cultural context, the notion of the religious other and the minor importance of the female sex have been constructed. Masculinity and "one's own" religious tradition have become the norm and whoever deviates from this norm is defined as "other," i.e., inferior. That means when dealing with the question of openness towards the religious other, Buddhists are well-advised not to forget the openness – or the lack of it – towards the *Buddhist* other as far as the female sex or persons with different sexual orientations are concerned. In principle, though, it is true that in Buddhism no sentient being is exempt from liberation. All, even religious others and non-religious people, are soteriologically included.

Sutta Central, www.suttacentral.net (06 March 2019), >Sutta>Long>Dīghanikāya>DN 33>Bhikkhu Sujato English and Pali, 2018: http://suttacentral.net/dn33 (under "Fours").

25. Tibetan text by Pha bong kha pa Bde chen snying po, *rNam grol lag bcangs*, ACIP S0004M.ACT, 159a3–4: *rang cag rnams a pho rang gis ma byung ba kho na ma gtogs | rten 'di las lhag pa zhig rnyed du med.*

26. Pabongka 1994, 207–212, in a chapter titled "Taking refuge by disavowing faith in other religions."

A critical look on openness within Tibetan Buddhism

As previously mentioned there are different interpretations of Buddhist teachings. Now we take a brief look at Tibetan Buddhism itself to illustrate the difficulty of creating openness towards the religious other when one has not yet cultivated openness within one's own religious tradition. Similar examples could be easily found in other religions too.

The Two Truths, for example, are understood differently not only by the various schools within Indian Buddhism, but also within Tibetan Buddhism itself. Although all of the principal Tibetan Buddhist schools (Nyingma, Sakya, Kagyü and Gelug) follow the Madhymaka (Middle Way) view, we find different interpretations leading among them to irreconcilable differences about the "true" Madhyamaka view of ultimate and conventional truths.[27] Although they will in general respect the authenticity of each other's understanding of the teaching of the Buddha, very often the different views go along with a feeling of superiority about one's own religious tradition.

Nowadays, initiated by the Dalai Lama, philosophical debates between followers of the different schools have been introduced. Similarly Tibetan nuns have been integrated into the learning system. Visiting one of these study centres in 2008 the Dalai Lama suggested to make their teachers' curriculum nonsectarian and to study not only the treatises of each of the Tibetan Buddhist sects, but also the Pāli and the Chinese traditions. His vision is to establish an international Buddhist institute "where every existing Buddhist tradition in the world can be studied in a single place" (Dalai Lama XIV 2009, 34).

The goal of such an approach may be seen as a kind of dogmatic tolerance trying to integrate other Buddhist traditions' (and in future perhaps even other religions') beliefs into one's own framework of religious theory. Such an approach could be described as an inclusivistic or pluralistic approach, depending on the motivation: the goal to study other traditions to promote openness and to learn from each other would be pluralistic, the goal to promote one's own tradition and to convince others of its superiority would be inclusivistic. If one aims at genuine dialogue, I would not consider it a missionary attempt, but rather an attempt to learn from other traditions, not because one's own tradition is incomplete, but as an enrichment and a tool for better mutual understanding.

It is obvious that nowadays when Tibetan Buddhist teachers are invited to foreign countries a lack of knowledge of the various traditions they

27. For a detailed study of great richness and diversity found among Tibetan Mādhyamikas see Thakchoe 2007.

encounter is prejudicial to them as well as to their students. Considering the importance of interreligious dialogue, it could be very helpful to further extend the curriculum in Buddhist monastic institutions to other religions as well. Thus, Buddhist monks and nuns could increasingly become active members of the inter-monastic dialogue, which will help Buddhists to shape their self-understanding in the context of many religions.

The readiness to engage in dialogue may also depend on mutual fears of expansionistic tendencies like missionizing. For Buddhism the *natural* spread of the *Buddhadharma*, i.e., the spread of the Buddha's teaching without intervention from outside, is seen to be positive *karma*, a wholesome action (Skt. *kuśalakarma*). An *organized* effort to spread the *Dharma* would *not* be considered as *un*wholesome (Skt. *akuśala*), provided the motivation is pure. This would entail avoiding the claim to sole representation and any kind of violence. The Buddha himself said in the *Ādhipateyya Sutta*[28] that his teaching is "inviting one to come and see." It is just an invitation, everybody is free to become a Buddhist – or not. Teachers are taught not to teach the *Dharma* to anybody who has not asked for it. And everybody is free to give up being a Buddhist. Apostasy only exists in the sense that monastics who have broken their major precepts such as celibacy will be expelled from the order.

First attempts towards a future Buddhist contextual dialogical theology

For the Dalai Lama, each religious tradition has two aspects: philosophical view and religious practice. More recently, however, he has added a third category that seems to have the potential to develop into a Buddhist contextual theology. He identifies three core characteristics of religion: (1) ethical teachings (behaviour, attitudes, practice): (2) doctrines of faith or metaphysics (views or philosophical perspectives with regard to an ultimate truth and hereafter, theory): and (3) cultural specifics. This third trait comprises the way believers behave at a particular time and place (Dalai Lama XIV 2010a, 150–151).

For example, in 1995, in a message sent to the Fourth International Sakyadhita Conference of Buddhist Women, he says:

> mere tradition can never justify violations of human rights. Thus, discrimination against persons of a different race, against women, and against weaker sections of society may be traditional in some

28. *Ādhipateyya Sutta, In Charge / Authorities* A 3.40 (A i 147): Sutta Central, www.suttacentral.net (14 February 2016),> Sutta> Numbered> Aṅguttaranikāya> 3. Tikanipāta>Paṭhamapaṇṇāsaka> 31–40. Devadūta Vagga> AN 3.40> Bhikkhu Bodhi English, 2012: https://suttacentral.net/an3.40

> places, but because they are inconsistent with universally recognized human rights, these forms of behavior should change. The universal principal of the equality of all human beings must take precedence. (Cited in Allison Goodwin 2012, 206 n14)

The Dalai Lama looks for common ground among religions in their practice of love and compassion, forgiveness, tolerance, satisfaction and self-discipline. In his view, differences and demarcations are primarily caused by diverging philosophical views, which exist in great numbers even within the Buddhist tradition (2005, 18–19). Notwithstanding, he consistently emphasizes that one should not conceal differences, but engage in dialogue because "finding common ground among faiths can help us bridge needless divides at a time when unified action is more crucial than ever" (2010b).

If we are ready to enter into an interreligious dialogue, we will surely discover common ground, but differences will also become more and more apparent, not only with regard to doctrines, but also with regard to ethics.[29] That should be accepted, otherwise interreligious dialogue would be meaningless. As already mentioned above, for Buddhism, we need to distinguish between openness in theory/doctrine, i.e., views, and openness in practice, i.e., attitude and behaviour. When it comes to views, "Buddhist doxographers distinguish a number of schools of thought organized in a hierarchy of degrees of supposed sophistication" (Garfield 2015, 157). While Tibetan Buddhists accept all these schools, despite their differences, as Buddhist schools, a demarcation line is drawn when the question arises who is – or is not – a Buddhist. In the past non-Buddhists have been considered to be on the "wrong" path, not on one's own "right" one. As Garfield emphasizes:

> the sectarianism of Tibetan Buddhism was always a mixed blessing. Politically it was often disastrous [...] But the philosophical and doctrinal rivalries often generated sharp debate and a honing of arguments and positions. While sometimes we find closed-minded sectarians among Tibetan philosophers, we also find eminent scholars who proudly meld ideas from distinct lineages to generate new syntheses. (2015, 23)

Thus, the existing potential to accept religious diversity may serve as a springboard to develop openness for new, enriching Buddhist and non-Buddhist viewpoints, doctrines or profound insights. When it comes to religious philosophical view, however, the question will remain, whether

29. For a discussion of Buddhist ethics and what distinguishes them from dominant Western ethical theory see Garfield 2015, 278–317.

being committed to one's own path one is able to give up hierarchization and the claim of superiority; both considered typical characteristics of an inclusivist.

Simplified, although all Tibetan Buddhist traditions accept that theoretically different salvific paths and different goals are taught and that the respective schools are part of Buddhism, they disagree whether, in order to become a saint (Skt. m. *ārya*, f. *āryā*), firstly theory is necessary – or rather a hindrance – in order to achieve insight, and secondly whether in practice saints who have followed slightly different paths do achieve the same insight. Vélez de Cea, however, distinguishing between "pluralism as a view of OTMIX and the pluralistic attitude," argues that:

> the Buddha displays a pluralistic attitude because he proactively engages religious diversity through dialogue, but without subordinating dialogue to agreement or conversion. Dialogue, for the Buddha, is an open-ended process that seeks mutual understanding and harmonious relationships with others, not necessarily agreement or conversion. (Vélez de Cea 2013, 177)

The Dalai Lama (2010a, 158–161) advises not to cling to one's own object of investigation because this could prevent impartial research:

> this, I think, is an important insight that we in the religious world should also embrace. It means that I, as a Buddhist, must not feel ego-centric attachment to my own faith of Buddhism, for doing so obstructs me from seeing the value of others traditions. (2010a, 158–159)

Nevertheless, he is still convinced of his own religion: "For me Buddhism is the best, but this does not mean that Buddhism is the best for all" (2010a, 158).

Practising openness we have to ask ourselves too, if our tolerance is or should be limited. Therefore, I suggest to implement Paul Griffiths's approach of mutual enrichment and understanding within interreligious dialogue, a practice of positive apologetics on themes where we disagree taking the other's position seriously (Griffiths 1991, 107–108). Such an approach demands a way of dialogue that is not polemical but constitutes an honest debate (Tib. *rtsod pa*, Skt. *vāda*) (Cf. Roloff 2014, 247) that does not end in competition between religious traditions and/or in hierarchization. Griffiths claims that if we get into serious polemics or apologetics (understanding these terms in a neutral sense), we will learn from each other. Thus, I want the term *apologist* to be understood in its original sense, i.e., as somebody who is committed to defending a certain position. This method should become part of dialogical theology.

Results and perspectives

What about the openness of Buddhism for the religious other? Is Buddhism ready for dialogue? That is where we started. We see that Buddhism indeed has attributes that can serve as a springboard for openness towards the religious other, a basis partly shared with other religions. Thus, there is potential for fruitful exchange and common ground with others in the religious as well as in the secular sphere. Buddhism has long since made its entry into modern societies.

For the peaceful and respectful coexistence of religious communities it is crucial to address – and not to exclude or minimize – the different views of their respective religious truth and also how religious others are encountered in practice. Cultivating an inner attitude of benevolence and openness will prove advantageous for our interaction with others. Thus, for example, the Fourteenth Dalai Lama shows a strongly pluralistic attitude by explicitly asking members of other religions to pursue their own way to salvation but to show respect to others' views. Without renouncing his Buddhist faith position, he himself likewise extends his openness towards Buddhist and non-Buddhist religious traditions, regarding religious harmony and understanding between the world's major religions as more important than to share a common belief in the same ultimate truth. He considers most important that despite philosophical differences, all major world religions have the same potential to create good human beings.

To sum up, I have considered three devices to illustrate Buddhism's capability for openness towards the religious other. The Four Immeasurables that are shared by all three main Buddhist traditions - Theravāda, East Asian Buddhism (including Zen), and Tibetan Buddhism - embrace all beings no matter whether they follow a religion or not or which religion they follow. Skill (Skt. *upāya*), or the Skill in Liberative Technique (Skt. *upāyakauśalya*), also carries the idea that the "Words of the Buddha" and their commentaries need to be understood dependent on context: different people in different contexts have different needs for which there is no panacea/universal remedy. Thus it is another tool suitable for creating common ground.

The third one is the framework of the Two Truths, the conventional truth and the ultimate truth. The conventional truth is also referred to as *upāya,* i.e., as means or as a useful tool that leads to the goal of liberation, *upeya.* The Two Truths allow us to create common ground by using the conventional truth to find shared ethical values, which may become the starting point to deal with the more difficult question of ultimate truth. We can discuss at first the different religious traditions' respective ultimate truths before we attack the question whether there is or can be *one single* ultimate truth compulsory for all of them.

The Two Truths theory allows me to open up and to understand various Buddhist, but also non-Buddhist religious doctrines that communicate salvific truth as different *upāya*s, i.e., different attempts to move closer to truth, whatever this may be. Openness will allow us to better understand each other and may lead to the development of a canon of shared values. Such an approach would equally consider the others' theory and practice as well as one's own in mutual respect. Focusing on peaceful co-existence such an attitude can even have a laicistic aspect, because of its social relevance.

To answer the question we started with – yes, irrespective of the religious other's understanding of ultimate reality, the non-theist/a-theist Buddhism has the potential for openness towards the religious other, for peaceful and respectful co-existence and cooperation with non-Buddhist others.

Acknowledgements

A German version of this chapter was first published in 2016 as "Offenheit gegenüber dem religiös Anderen im Buddhismus." *Perspektiven dialogischer Theologie. Offenheit in den Religionen und Hermeneutik interreligiösen Dialogs,* edited by K. Amirpur, T. Knauth, C. Roloff, and W. Weiße, 49–81. Münster: Waxmann.

The findings presented here are the results of the research project "Religion and Dialogue in Modern Societies Interdisciplinary and Internationally Comparative Studies on the Possibilities and Limitations of Interreligious Dialogue (ReDi)." From 2013–2018 it was based at the Academy of World Religions, University of Hamburg, funded by the Federal Ministry of Education and Research, Germany (BMBF), whose help is gratefully acknowledged. I am deeply indebted to Jay L. Garfield, Doris Silbert, professor in the humanities and professor of philosophy at Smith College (USA), who not only challenged an earlier version of this paper, but also kindly took the time to go through the next version and comment on it in detail. His useful questions gave me a lot of further thought. Many thanks for their feedback and input at different times also go to all the scholars, heads, advisors and colleagues in the ReDi project. Although I cannot name all of them here, I specially thank Katajun Amirpur, Ephraim Meir, Sallie King, Volker Küster, Perry Schmidt-Leukel and Wolfram Weisse for commenting on earlier German versions of this paper and for their encouragement. Thus, this paper, although still "mine." became the product of honest dialogue. Last but not least, I am extremely grateful to Monika Deimann-Clemens for her support in editing and to Shaykha Halima Krausen for her help with the first translation into English.

References

Anālayo, B. 2014. "Karma and Female Birth." *Journal of Buddhist Ethics* 21: 109–153.

Anālayo, B. 2015. "Brahmavihāra and Awakening. A Study of the Dīrgha-āgama Parallel to the Tevijja-sutta." *Asian Literature and Translation* 3(4): 1–27. https://doi.org/10.18573/j.2015.10216

Anderssen-Reuster, U. and J. Meibert. 2013. "Grundbegriffe einer buddhistischen Psychologie." In *Psychotherapie und buddhistisches Geistestraining. Methoden einer achtsamen Bewusstseinskultur*, edited by U. Anderssen-Reuster, P. Meibert, and S. Meck, 59–74. Stuttgart: Schattauer.

Apple, J. B. 2009. *Stairway to Nirvāṇa. A Study of the Twenty Saṃghas Based on The Works of TSONG KHA PA*. Albany: State University of New York Press.

Berzin, A. 2008. "Buddhist-Muslim Doctrinal Relations: Past, Present and Future." In *Buddhist Attitudes to Other Religions*, edited by P. Schmidt-Leukel, 212–236. St. Ottilien: EOS.

Bodhi, B. 2013. "Arahants, Buddhas and Bodhisattvas." In *The Bodhisattva Ideal, Essays on the Emergence of Mahāyāna*, edited by B. Ñāṇatusita, 1–30. Kandy: Buddhist Publication Society.

Buddhaghosa and Ñyāṇamoli, B. 2010. *The Path of Purification: Visuddhimaga. The Classical Manual of Buddhist Doctrine and Meditation* (fourth edition). Kandy: Buddhist Publication Society.

Dalai Lama XIV (Tenzin Gyatso). 1989. *Yoga des Geistes*. Hamburg: dharma edition.

———. 2005. "Altes Wissen für die moderne Welt." In *Einheit in der Vielfalt. Moderne Wissenschaft und östliche Weisheit im Dialog*, edited by X. Tarab Tulku and L. Handberg, 15–23. Berlin: Theseus.

———. 2009. *Speech Delivered by His Holiness the 14th Dalai Lama During the Inauguration Ceremony of the Main Assembly Hall at Jangchup Choeling Nunnery, Mundgod, India. 6 January, 2008*. Hamburg: Foundation for Buddhist Studies.

———. 2010a. *Towards A True Kinship of Faiths. How the World's Religions Can Come Together*. Great Britain: Abacus.

———. 2010b. "Many Faiths, One Truth." *The New York Times*. 24 May. https://www.nytimes.com/2010/05/25/opinion/25gyatso.html

Dalai Lama XIV and T. Chödrön. 2014. *Buddhism: One Teacher, Many Traditions. Bhikṣu Tenzin Gyatso, The Fourteenth Dalai Lama, and Bhikṣuṇī Thubten Chodron*. Boston: Wisdom.

Frauwallner, E. 2010 [1956]. *The Philosophy of Buddhism. (Die Philosophie des Buddhismus).* Translated by Gelong Lodrö Sangpo, Jigme Sheldrön, and Ernst Steinkellner. Delhi: Motilal Banarsidass. https://doi.org/10.1524/9783050088099

Freiberger, O. 2013. "How the Buddha dealt with Non-Buddhists." In *Buddhism and Religious Diversity,* Volume 4, edited by P. Schmidt-Leukel, 46–56. Abingdon: Routledge.

Freiberger, O. and C. Kleine. 2011. *Buddhismus. Handbuch und kritische Einführung* (first edition). Göttingen: Vandenhoeck & Ruprecht.

Garfield, J. L. 2015. *Engaging Buddhism. Why it Matters to Philosophy.* Oxford: Oxford University Press. https://doi.org/10.1093/acprof:oso/9780190204334.001.0001

Gentz, J. 2008. "Buddhism and Chinese Religions." In *Buddhist Attitudes to Other Religions*, edited by P. Schmidt-Leukel, 172–211. St. Ottilien: EOS.

Goodwin, A. 2012. "Right Views, Red Rust, and White Bones. The Eight Garudhammas and Buddhist Teachings on Female Inferiority." *Journal of Buddhist Ethics* 19: 198–343.

Griffiths, P. J. 1991. *An Apology for Apologetics. A Study in the Logic of Interreligious Dialogue.* Eugene, OR: Wipf & Stock.

Gross, R. 2005a. "Excuse Me, but What's the Question?." In *The Myth of Religious Superiority: Multifaith Explorations of Religious Pluralism*, ed. P. F. Knitter, 75–87. Maryknoll, N.Y: Orbis.

———. 2005b. "Religious Identity and Openness in a Pluralistic World." *Buddhist-Christian Studies* 25(1): 15–20. https://doi.org/10.1353/bcs.2005.0048

Harris, E. J. 2013. "Buddhism and the Religious Other." In *Understanding interreligious Relations*, edited by D. Cheetham, D. Pratt and D. Thomas, 88–117. Oxford: Oxford University Press.

Harvey, P. 2008. "Between Controversy and Ecumenism: Intra-Buddhist Relationship." In *Buddhist Attitudes to Other Religions*, edited by P. Schmidt-Leukel, 114–142. St. Ottilien: EOS.

Hayes, R. P. 1991. "Gotama Buddha and Religious Pluralism." *Journal of Religious Pluralism* 1(1): 65–95. www.unm.edu/~rhayes/bahuvada.pdf

Hayes, R. P. and D. M. Hsin Tao. 2014. "Buddhism. Views on Overcoming Obstacles to Universal Friendship: Pali Theravada and Mahayana Perspectives." In *The Religious Other. Hostility, Hospitality, and the Hope of Human Flourishing*, edited by A. Goshen-Gottstein, 123–150. Lanham, MD: Lexington.

Hedges, P. and A. Race. 2008. *Christian approaches to other faiths*. London: SCM.

Hessel, S. and Dalai Lama XIV. 2012. *Wir erklären den Frieden! / Stéphane Hessel; Dalai Lama,* edited by Sylvie Crossman and Jean-Pierre Barou. Translated by Patricia Klobusiczky and P. Klobusiczky. Berlin: Ullstein.

Hick, J. 1983. "On Conflicting Religious Truth-Claims." *Religious Studies* 19: 485–491. https://doi.org/10.1017/S0034412500015511

Kiblinger, K. B. 2008. "Buddhist Stances Towards Others: Types, Examples, Considerations." In *Buddhist Attitudes to Other Religions*, edited by P. Schmidt-Leukel, 24–46. St. Ottilien: EOS.

King, S. B. 2005. *Being Benevolence. The Social Ethics of Engaged Buddhism.* Honolulu: University of Hawai'i Press.

Knauth, T., C. Roloff, K. Drechsler, F. Jäckel & A. Markowsky. 2016. "Auf dem Weg zu einer dialogisch-interreligiösen Hermeneutik." In *Perspektiven Dialogischer Theologie. Offenheit in den Religionen und eine Hermeneutik des interreligiösen Dialogs*, edited by K. Amirpur, T. Knauth, C. Roloff and W. Weiße, 207–324. Münster: Waxmann.

Knitter, P. F. 2002. *Introducing Theologies of Religions*. Maryknoll, NY: Orbis.

———. 2008. "Buddhist and Christian Attitudes to Other Religions: A Comparison." In *Buddhist Attitudes to Other Religions*, edited by P. Schmidt-Leukel, 85–112. St. Ottilien: EOS-Verlag.

Küster, V. 2011. *Einführung in die Interkulturelle Theologie*. Stuttgart: UTB – Verlag Barbara Budrich.

———. 2015. "Dialog und Kunst in Indonesien: Unterwegs zu einer Ästhetik interreligiöser Begegnung." In *Religionen – Dialog – Gesellschaft: Analysen zur gegenwärtigen Situation und Impulse für eine dialogische Theologie*, edited by K. Amirpur and W. Weiße, 99–128. Münster: Waxmann.

Maithrimurthi, M. 1999. *Wohlwollen, Mitleid, Freude und Gleichmut von den Anfängen bis hin zum frühen Yogācāra. Eine ideengeschichtliche Untersuchung der vier apramāṇas in der buddhistischen Ethik und Spiritualität.* Stuttgart: Franz Steiner.

Makransky, J. 2008. "The Emergence of Buddhist Critical-Constructive Reflection in the Academy as a Resource for Buddhist Communities and for the Contemporary World." *Journal of Buddhist Ethics* 9: 113–153.

McCagney, N. and Nāgārjuna. 1997. *Nāgārjuna and the Philosophy of Openness*. Lanham, MD: Rowman & Littlefield.

Ngawang, G. T. 1995. "Die Vier Grenzenlosen Geisteshaltungen: Eine Meditation für die Wesen und ihre Umwelt." In *Genügsamkeit und Nichtverletzen. Natur und spirituelle Entwicklung im tibetischen Buddhismus*. Mit Beiträgen von S.H. Dalai Lama, Tenzin P. Atisha und Peter von Stamm (Spektrum, vol 4356), edited by G. T. Ngawang and B. Stratmann, 77–91. Freiburg: Herder.

Nhất Hạnh, T. 1991. *Old Path, White Clouds: Walking in the Footsteps of the Buddha*. Berkeley, CA: Parallax.

———. 1998. *The Heart of the Buddha's Teaching: Transforming Suffering into Peace, Joy and Liberation*. London: Rider.

———. 2007. *Teachings on Love*. Berkeley, CA: Parallax.

Nyanatiloka, B. 2002. *The Buddha's Path to Deliverance. A systematic exposition in the words of the Sutta Piṭaka, compiled, translated, and explained by Nyanatiloka Thera*. Onalaska, Washington: BPS Pariyatti.

Oldenberg, H. 1881. *Buddha: sein Leben, seine Lehre, seine Gemeinde*. Berlin: Wilhelm Hertz.

Pabongka Rinpoche. 1994. *Liberation in our Hands. Part Two: The Fundamentals*. Transcribed and edited by Yongzin Trijang Rinpoche Lobsang Yeshe Tenzin Gyatso. Translated by Sera Mey Geshe Lobsang Tharchin and Artemus B. Engle. Howell, NJ: Sutra and Tantra.

Patañjali and Dvivedi, M. N. 1980 [1890]. *The Yoga-Sūtras of Patañjali. Sanskrit Text and English Translation together with an Introduction and an Appendix, and Notes on each Sūtra based upon several authentic commentaries – all in English*. Delhi: Sri Satguru. https://digi.ub.uni-heidelberg.de/diglit/dvivedi1890

Roloff, C. 2014. "Interreligious Dialogue in Buddhism from a Gender Perspective." In *Religions and Dialogue. International Approaches*, edited by W. Weiße, K. Amirpur, A. Körs and D. Vieregge, 245–281. The Academy of World Religions. Religions in Dialogue Series, Volume 7. Münster: Waxmann.

Roloff, C. and W. Weiße, eds. 2015. *Dialogue and Ethics in Buddhism and Hinduism*. Documentation Series Akademie der Weltreligionen, Volume 2. Münster: Waxmann.

Samdhong Rinpoche, V. 2015. "Impulses from a Buddhist Perspective on Religion and Dialogue in Modern Societies." In *Dialogue and Ethics in Buddhism and Hinduism*, edited by C. Roloff & W. Weiße, 53–64. Dokumentationsreihe Akademie der Weltreligionen, Volume 2. Münster: Waxmann.

Schmidt-Leukel, P. 2005. "Exclusivism, Inclusivism, Pluralism. The Tripolar Typology – Clarified and Reaffirmed." In *The Myth of Religious Superiority. Multifaith Explorations of Religious Pluralism*, edited by P. F. Knitter, 13–27. Maryknoll, NY: Orbis.

———. 2008b. "Buddhist-Hindu Relations." In *Buddhist Attitudes to Other Religions*, edited by P. Schmidt-Leukel, 143–171. St. Ottilien: EOS-Verlag.

———. 2009. *Transformation by Integration. How Inter-faith Encounter Changes Christianity*. London: SCM.

———. 2011. "Interkulturelle Theologie als interreligiöse Theologie." *Evangelische Theologie* 71(1): 4–16. https://doi.org/10.14315/evth-2011-71-1-4

Schmidt-Leukel, P., ed. 2008a. *Buddhist Attitudes to Other Religions*. St. Ottilien: EOS.

———, ed. 2013. *Buddhism and Religious Diversity. Religious Pluralism*. Abingdon: Routledge.

Schumann, H. W. 1994 [1982]. *Der historische Buddha. Leben und Lehren des Gotama*. München: Eugen Diederichs.

Sopa, G. L. & J. Hopkins. 1976. *Practice and Theory of Tibetan Buddhism*. London: Rider and Company.

Tatz, M. 1994. *The Skill iṇ Means (Upāyakauśalya)*. Delhi: Motilal Banarsidass.

Tauscher, H. 1995. *Die Lehre von den Zwei Wirklichkeiten in Tsoṅ kha pas Madhyamaka Werken.* Wiener Studien zur Tibetologie und Buddhismuskunde, Volume 36. Wien: Arbeitskreis für tibetische und buddhistische Studien Universität Wien.

Thakchoe, S. 2007. *The Two Truths Debate. Tsongkhapa and Gorampa on the Middle Way.* Boston: Wisdom.

Thurman, R. A. 1976. *The Holy Teaching of Vimalakīrti: A Mahāyāna Scripture.* University Park: Pennsylvania State University Press.

Vasubandhu. 1988–1990. *Abhidharmakośabhāṣyam.* Translated by Leo M. Pruden. Berkeley, CA: Asian Humanities Press.

Vélez de Cea, J. A. 2013. *The Buddha and Religious Diversity*. Abingdon: Routledge. https://doi.org/10.4324/9780203072639

5

Buddhism and the Religious Other: Twenty-First Century Dambulla and the Presence of Buddhist Exclusivism in Sri Lanka

Elizabeth J. Harris

University of Birmingham

Elizabeth J. Harris is an Honorary Senior Research Fellow within the Cadbury Centre for the Public Understanding of Religion, University of Birmingham, UK. Before this, she was an Associate Professor at Liverpool Hope University. She specializes in Buddhist Studies and Interreligious Studies, and has published widely in both disciplines. Her publications include: *What Buddhists Believe* (Oneworld, 1998); *Theravāda Buddhism and the British Encounter: Religious, missionary and colonial experience in nineteenth century Sri Lanka* (Routledge 2006); *Hope: A Form of Delusion? Buddhist and Christian Perspectives* ed. (EOS 2013); *Religion, Space and Conflict in Sri Lanka: colonial and postcolonial contexts* (Routledge 2018); *Meditation in Christian-Buddhist Encounter: A Critical Analysis,* edited with John O'Grady (EOS 2019). She was President of the European Network of Buddhist-Christian Studies from 2009 to 2019 and serves and as an international adviser to the Society for Buddhist-Christian Studies.

Introduction

On 28 October 2013, the Bhadrakālī Amman Kovil in Dambulla, Sri Lanka, was demolished by a group of Buddhists because it was situated on the soil of what had been designated, over thirty years beforehand, a Buddhist sacred area. On 21 October, the roof had been forcibly removed and, three weeks before that, an image of the deity, Bhadrakālī, had been smashed and thrown into a well (Colombo Telegraph 2013). Protests had been made by opposition Parliamentarians and the devotees themselves, but to no avail.[1] Even when devotees, bowing to the inevitable, had asked for more time to perform the necessary rituals for the abandoning of a Hindu

---

1. The devotees were Hindu but would have included some Buddhists, since the worship of Kālī has become more popular among Buddhists in the last fifty years, during war and economic hardship. See Gombrich and Obeyeskere, 1988.

temple, this was not granted (Hindu Existence 2013).[2] The year before, on 20 April 2012, Buddhists had attacked a small mosque in Dambulla, the Khairiya Juma Masjid, for the same reason: that it lay within a designated Buddhist sacred area. It was not, however, demolished, but the pressure on Muslims in Dambulla continues to the present, necessitating a police guard at the mosque.

The attacks were seemingly motivated by the conviction of the then chief incumbent of the Buddhist Golden Temple in Dambulla, Ven. Inamaluwe Sumangala Thero,[3] that, when Dambulla was made a Buddhist sacred area in the early 1980s, "there was no provision for any religion other than Buddhism to have their own place of worship" within its boundaries (Kannangara 2012). The language he used appealed to the need to defend and protect the Buddhist heritage of Dambulla and the country against external threat. And the way he sought to do this was through enforced spatial exclusion, seemingly predicated on the conviction that religious others defiled Buddhist sacred space. It was an attitude that can be called, exclusivist.

Buddhism in Sri Lanka, however, has traditionally been known for its inclusivist attitude towards religious others. Studies of the independent Kandyan Kingdom, before it was incorporated through conquest into British rule in 1815, demonstrate that a plurality of religious identities were respected within the Kingdom, albeit within a hierarchy of the sacred. Stanley Tambiah was absolutely right to argue that the Kingdom possessed a "galactic polity," within which the processes of the state could be inclusive of minorities and immigrants, but only if they were capable of being "incorporated within the larger [Buddhist] cosmological and economic framework" (Tambiah 1992, 175). In other words, if the Buddha and the King, as underwriter of Buddhism's dominance, were seen to be supreme in the landscape and ritual of the Kingdom, then other religious practices could be tolerated, and even welcomed, in a subordinate religious and socio-political position (See also Duncan 1990). This is the default position of the majority of Sri Lankan Buddhists to this day and the principle of subordination underpinning it can be traced back to Early Buddhism, as I demonstrate later.

This chapter examines why an exclusivist approach to "religious others"

2. This article on the Hindu Existence website quotes articles written in the Sri Lankan press on 29 October and 3 November 2013.

3. In June 2016 Ven Dr Godagama Mangala Thera was appointed by the Saṅgha Council of the Asgiriya Chapter to replace Ven Inamaluwe Sumangala Thero as Head of the Golden Temple in Dambulla.

emerged in Sri Lanka in the second decade of the twenty-first century, using the case study of Dambulla as illustration.[4] It is divided into four sections. The first examines recent theoretical approaches to Buddhism and inter-religious encounter, together with my own argument that a spectrum of approaches to religious others has been present in text and tradition from the beginnings of Buddhism. The second offers background information both about the Dambulla Golden Temple (*Vihāraya*) and Inamuluwe Sumangala Thero. The third explores three differing narratives of the mosque attack, those of Sumangala, the Hindus of Dambulla and secular analysts. It is the attack on the mosque rather than on the Bhadrakālī Amman Kovil that is the focus of this chapter. The fourth, drawing on the theoretical underpinning of the first section, suggests three conditioning factors for the dominance of Sumangala's representation and the emergence of what could be considered an uncharacteristically exclusivist Buddhist approach to religious others in Dambulla. I conclude, in line with Ananda Abeysekara, that the motivation of the religious actors within my case study was as contingent on local and global factors as on considerations connected with doctrinal beliefs (Abeysekara 2002).

Theoretical approaches to Buddhist encounters with religious others

Buddhism's response to religious others has attracted much scholarly attention in the last fifty years. In the West, two monographs stand out, both of which attempted to influence contemporary Buddhists, by constructing a Buddhist past that demonstrates openness to religious others. Both utilized and expanded the threefold typology that was first developed by the Anglican priest, Alan Race, to describe Christian attitudes to religious others: exclusivism, inclusivism and pluralism (Race 1993).[5] In the first, published in 2005, Kristin Kiblinger argued for a form of Buddhist inclusivism that was able to appropriate and value truths from religious others, whilst respecting that different religious traditions might have different goals. She labelled this an "alternative-ends-recognising

4. A shorter version of this chapter was given at the XVIIth Congress of the International Association of Buddhist Studies held in Vienna in August 2014 entitled, "Buddhism and the Religious Other: six responses in text and tradition." I also included a brief account of the Dambulla case study in Harris 2018, 200–201.

5. As first described by Race, exclusivism asserts that Christianity alone possesses salvific truth. Inclusivism recognises truth in religious others but asserts that this is not sufficient "apart from Christ" (Race 1993, 38). Pluralism contains "a range of other possible options" (Race 1993, 71), including that religions are on a pilgrimage towards a truth that is beyond all.

inclusivism" (Kiblinger 2005, 69–89). Citing texts from the Pāli tradition, she identified three inclusivistic strategies used in Early Buddhism in the context of Vedic religion: subordination, reinterpretation and new application (Kiblinger 2005, 40). For instance, she offered the *Kevaddha Sutta* in the *Dīgha Nikāya* (D 11) as a "clear example of subordination," the *Kūṭadanta Sutta* in the same *Nikāya* (D 5) as an example of the reinterpretation of a brahmanical practice, namely sacrifice, and the *Aggañña Sutta* (D 27) as a reinterpretation of what it is to be a Brahmin (Kiblinger 2005, 41–43).

In the second monograph, published in 2013, Abraham Vélez de Cea made an important distinction between views (openness to the Other in theory) and attitudes (openness to the Other in practice) (Vélez de Cea 2013, 15). In contrast to Kiblinger, he argued that the historical Buddha had a *view* of religious others that was pluralistic inclusivist[6] and an *attitude* that was pluralistic, namely a view that was open to seeing ultimate truths in other religious traditions but with some non-negotiable constraints and an attitude that was willing to recognize that enlightenment was possible outside Buddhism. Convinced that most contemporary Buddhists combined an exclusivist view of other religious traditions with an inclusivist attitude, Vélez de Cea sought to retrieve and to reconstruct a Buddhist past that moved beyond exclusivism or inclusivism, towards pluralistic inclusivism and pluralism, in the hope that this might influence the present.

In my own work on Buddhism and religious others, I have also delved into the texts of Early Buddhism in order to understand why particular responses to religious others have arisen in particular times and locations. I have argued that a spectrum of responses can be found in Buddhist text, tradition and history, some of the components of which were as dependent on political and social context as on what could be termed "religious" considerations. Within the Pāli Canon, I have suggested that the spectrum contained five broad categories: adherence to a code of conduct predicated on respect, co-existence and non-violent debate; the teaching of ideas that opposed or challenged those of other religious leaders; ridicule of the "religious other;" the demotion or subordination of other practices or beliefs; the appropriation or modification of practices and symbols of the "religious other" (Harris 201, 89). These overlap with Kiblinger's

6. Vélez de Cea argues that pluralistic inclusivism must be added to the typology for completeness: the capacity to recognize instances of ultimate value/ultimate truth in other religious traditions albeit constrained by "nonnegotiable doctrinal claims found in my religion" (2013, 16).

categories of subordination and new application, and with Gombrich's work on the development of Buddhism within its Indic context, within which he points, for example, to appropriations of brahmanical ritual that "look less like a debate than a takeover bid" (Gombrich 1996, 65–72).

To illustrate just two of these categories, the first can be seen in the *Mahāsīhanāda Sutta* of the *Dīgha Nikāya* (D 8), which shows Kassapa, an ascetic, coming to the Buddha to ask whether the Buddha condemned austerity and self-mortification. The Buddha is shown appealing to the tool of discernment: only if these practices lead to moral progress can they be endorsed. Before this, however, the Buddha comments on how similarity and difference between religious teachers should be negotiated. In awareness that some "ascetics and Brahmins" are "practised in disputation," the Buddha is reported as declaring:

> sometimes their views [of ascetics and brahmins] accord with mine, sometimes they do not. What they sometimes applaud, we sometimes applaud. What they sometimes do not applaud, we sometimes do not applaud; what they sometimes applaud, we sometimes do not applaud, and what they sometimes do not applaud, we sometimes applaud.

After reversing this pattern so that the "we" comes first, the Buddha says:

> on approaching them [ascetics and brahmins], I say: "In these things there is no agreement, let us leave them aside. In these things there is agreement: there let the wise take up, cross-question and criticise these matters with the teachers or with their followers, saying, 'Of those things that are unskilful and reckoned as such, censurable, to be refrained from, unbefitting a Noble One [...] who is there who has completely abandoned such things and is free of them; the ascetic Gotama, or some 'other venerable teachers?' (D I 162–163; Walshe 1995, 152)

This passage, therefore, recommends an interreligious ethic that avoids dispute about difference in favour of respectful discussion about what is considered by the partners in the conversation to be either good or censurable.

When discussing the subordination of the Other, the third of my categories, I have cited the same *sutta* as Kiblinger, the *Kevaddha Sutta*, which represents the gods as unable to answer a core question about truth present in the Buddha's teaching. In 2013, I wrote, "In such discourses, early Buddhism reduces the gods of the brahmanical tradition to the level of the mundane, the *laukika*," and referred to the work of David Seyfort Ruegg, who has argued that "the *laukika* becomes what Buddhism shares with other Indian religious groups and the *lokuttara*, the supramundane, becomes what is unique to Buddhism." (Harris 2013, 91–92; citing Ruegg 2008, 80).

If we turn to later centuries in Buddhist history, I have argued that these five responses continued but that others arose as Buddhism travelled beyond India. The trope of subordination, for instance, continued to utilize the *laukika/lokuttara* distinction, through a tendency to push the religious others it encountered outside India into the realm of the mundane. In Sri Lanka, in line with this, the gods of Hinduism, local spirits and exorcist ceremonies were subordinated to the Buddha as the only embodiment of the supramundane. When this subordinating tendency met a religious tradition that refused to be subordinated or that boasted a supramundane truth as all-encompassing as the *Dharma*, however, other responses developed, conditioned by local power relations and socio-economic factors. These included pragmatic co-existence in contexts where courtesy was shown to Buddhism and vigorous, often polemical, defence of Buddhism, if a threat to the *Dharma* from a religious Other was perceived (Harris 2013). In nineteenth-century Sri Lanka, for instance, the latter response became particularly strong when the discourtesy and contempt shown by evangelical Christian missionaries towards Buddhism was identified as a threat to Buddhism's existence (See Harris 2006 and 2012). My own research, therefore, has emphasized the importance of contextual analysis if the "attitudes" of Buddhists to religious others, used in Vélez de Cea's sense, are to be correctly understood.

The case study of Dambulla

The Jambukola Vihāra or the Rangiri Dambulu Vihāraya (the Golden Temple) in Dambulla is located on a rocky cave-filled outcrop at the northern edge of the central hills in Sri Lanka, which has probably seen monastic settlement since the third century BCE. Seventy three caves on the western and southern faces of the outcrop have been identified (Bandaranayake 2006, 140). A group of five caves, however, came to form the devotional centre of the complex. Over centuries, they were excavated further and richly painted and re-painted, in a process of palimpsest, to form shrines that were works of Buddhist art. In the eighteenth century, they were completely restored and one temple, Vihāra 5, was repainted again in 1915. In addition, Sumangala added modern constructions to the complex. At the time of the attack on the mosque, one new building housed the Rangiri Sri Lanka Media Network, which had its own radio, television and newspaper sections, and pilgrims entered the cave complex through another new building, topped with a magisterial golden Buddha image and a line of life-sized images of Buddhist monks.

The Viharāya is part of Sri Lanka's Cultural Triangle and, as such, is a UNESCO World Heritage Site. It is also extremely wealthy with considerable land-ownings in the Dambulla area, which generated accusations against Sumangala, because of his monetary dealings.[7] Sumangala's leadership in Dambulla began in the early 1980s and he was a controversial figure from the beginning. Ananda Abeysekara (1999; 2002, 174–200) has examined the discursive strategies underpinning the new higher ordination movement he started in 1985, which claimed to challenge the caste-based recruitment of the Asgiriya Chapter of the Siyam Nikāya to which the Rangiri Dambulu Vihāraya belonged and which resulted in Sumangala forming the Rangiri Dambulu Monastic Chapter. According to Abeysekara, in doing this, Sumangala placed his temple out on a limb as an "ancient, sacred, independent" Vihāraya (Abeysekara 1999, 272), although Sumangala continued to claim that the Head of the Asgiriya Chapter was "our Chief Priest," when he wanted to deflect criticism about the validity of his new ordination (e.g. Ariyawansha 2012).

In the 1990s, Sumangala was associated with campaigning movements and organizations that sought to end the ethnic war through peace talks and a negotiated solution rather than military might. For instance, he was present on the platforms of the Movement for Inter-Racial Justice and Equality (MIRJE) and the Anti-War Front.[8] In the early 1990s, he was also central to an interreligious movement that opposed the building of a luxury four star hotel, by a private corporation supported by the government, near a man-made reservoir or "tank" at Kandalama, a village close to Dambulla, on the grounds that it would both harm the tank's catchment area and endanger the livelihood of the villagers (National Christian Council 1992; Abeysekara 2002, 194–200). On 12 July 1992, a protest attended by Buddhists, Christians, Muslims and Hindus was held in the grounds of the Dambulla Vihāraya at the invitation of Sumangala. Several days later, a positive account of this appeared in *The Sunday Times* but it was accompanied by a picture of Roman Catholic nuns and priests sitting on the ground in the Vihāraya with a large wooden cross (Sirisena 1992). A paper controlled by the government, *The Daily News*, seized on this

7. The Sri Lanka Cricket Board, for instance, leased land from the Viharāya (i.e. from Sumangala) for the building of a new cricket ground in 2000. The Viharāya continued to have ownership rights to it and, according to local reports, has demanded high usage rent. See for instance, Roberts 2007.

8. Personal conversation in January 2016 with a Sri Lankan human rights activist, who had witnessed his presence.

about a week later, claiming that it had received numerous representations criticizing both the presence of a cross in a Buddhist Vihāraya and the actions of Sumangala. There can be no doubt that this was politically motivated, since a rival newspaper was quick to point out that it had not received a single protest (e.g. *The Island* 1992, 10). The building of the hotel was not stopped by the campaign and Sumangala eventually seemed to withdraw quietly from it, although in 2012, he could still assert that "I will continue that protest as long as I live" (Ariyawansha 2012).

To return to Sumangala's involvement with ordination issues, a caste-free higher ordination for males was not Sumangala's only vision. He also became involved with the controversial issue of higher ordination (*upasampadā*) for women.[9] At a time when Sri Lankan members of the international Buddhist women's organization, Sakyadhita (Daughters of the Buddha, formed in 1987), were working with *bhikkhuṇī*s (nuns with *upasampadā*) in countries such as Taiwan, to offer higher ordination to some of the ten-precept contemporary nuns in Sri Lanka,[10] Sumangala, in March 1997, founded the Sri Lanka Bhikkhuṇī Re-Awakening Organization and began to train selected ten-precept nuns for higher ordination, believing that the Buddha's initial vision of a four-fold community of monks, nuns, lay men and lay women should and could be re-activated. Eventually the two movements co-operated, with Sumangala becoming its media face. Some of Sumangala's trained contemporary nuns were, therefore, ordained at Bodh Gaya at the beginning of 1998, in a ceremony organized by members of Sakyadhita. They returned to Sri Lanka and, in turn, ordained 22 more nuns at Dambulla on 12 March of the same year.[11] There are now several hundred Sri Lankan *bhikkhuṇī*s but they have not yet gained official recognition from the state, in spite of the vocal support of Sumangala (e.g. Nathaniel 2013).

In the 1980s and 1990s, therefore, the Rangiri Dambulu Vihāraya, with its incumbent monk, Sumangala, was linked in the popular imagination with the Buddhist history of the island, innovation, power, wealth and

9. Sri Lanka once possessed an Order of Bhikkhuṇīs. It was lost in the eleventh century CE. At the beginning of the twentieth century, ordination for women into a Ten Precept discipline was brought from Myanmar to Sri Lanka by Catherine de Alwis, who became Sister Sudharmacarī. These nuns became known as *dasa sil mātā*s (ten precept mothers) or Sil Maniyos.

10. Sakyadhita members had already funded five *dasa sil mātā*s to be ordained at a ceremony in Los Angeles in 1988 and had helped to organize an ordination ceremony in Sarnath in 1996. For the early history, see Harris 1997.

11. This information has been gathered through my personal involvement with Sakyadhita since its foundation in 1987.

unconventionality but, significantly, not with religious exclusivism. However, as mentioned earlier, Dambulla was one of the locations established as a Buddhist sacred area under the premiership of J.R. Jayawardene in the early 1980s. Kemper rightly suggests that this move was not disinterested: Jayawardene sought to deflect the monastic *Saṅgha* away from his own resistance to some of their demands, including that Sri Lanka should become a Buddhist state (Kemper 1991, 79). This nevertheless became the hanger upon which exclusivist attitudes were hung.

Diverse perspectives on the mosque attack

There are at least three conflicting narratives surrounding the conflict over the mosque: that of Sumangala, that of the Muslims in the city and that of secular analysts. Sumangala's narrative went like this and I reconstruct it from the newspaper articles named in a footnote at the end of the paragraph. The Golden Temple at Dambulla traditionally owns 12,000 acres of land, although it has no legal documentation to prove this. When the Sacred City Development Project for Dambulla was drawn up in 1981and 1982, the temple provided 300 acres of its land to the government to further the project. The Survey Department examined the area and the resulting plan of the city did not identify the location of a mosque. The Gazette Notice concerning the Dambulla sacred city area was issued in 1992 and, again, it did not mention a mosque. There was, therefore, no place of religious worship for the Islamic faith or a mosque when the plan for a sacred city was drawn up. The land on which the makeshift mosque now stands belonged to a Muslim trader who came from the east of the country in 1972 for business. When he died, none of his family claimed the land and it was only recently made into a place where Muslims pray. There are about 30 scattered Muslim families in Dambulla but now about 300 come to worship and they have the backing of a powerful minister in the Government, who is anti-Buddhist. The growth in numbers is due to a Muslim fundamentalist group. This is a direct threat to the Buddhist history of Dambulla. To lead a protest that went to the mosque was justified to defend Buddhism and the Buddhist history of the island. The protest was peaceful. Video footage presenting the protest as violent was fake (Colombo Telegraph April 2012). The mosque must be taken down or, at least, relocated. If relocated, it must be relocated outside the 12,000 acres of land owned by the temple.[12]

12. To reconstruct this narrative, I have used: Kannangara 2012, Wickrematunga and Ariyawansha 2012, LankaNewspapers 2012.

When Niranjala Ariyawansha, after the attack on the mosque, reminded Sumangala that Sri Lanka was a "multi-religious, multi-cultural and multi-ethnic society," he replied, "What nonsense. You are speaking of a nonsensical society. This country has fourteen million Buddhists. How many Muslims are there?" He added later:

> are you trying to wrest away our Buddhist rights? We have respected all. What we have here is none of that. It is about protecting the Buddhist legacy against the wresting of it. There is no need for talking nonsense here. We are fighting to save the 2300 year old Buddhist heritage that is ours! They [Muslims] in turn are trying to wrest away our heritage. (Ariyawansha 2012)

The narrative of Muslims in the area was very different and went like this and again I construct the narrative from newspaper articles. The mosque is sixty-five years old. Deeds date back to 1967. The land had originally belonged to a Tamil and had been gifted to a Muslim, who donated it to the whole Muslim community. It was registered as a religious site for Muslims with the Muslim Religious Affairs Committee. Therefore, it is legally registered and existed long before the area was designated a sacred zone. It is possible that the Survey Department did not discover its existence, because, in 1982, it was very small. As for our relationships with Buddhists, Muslims and Buddhists have co-existed in Dambulla for centuries without a problem. However, on Friday, 20 April 2012, around noon, a mob of about 80 people, led by Buddhist monks, who displayed anger and disrespect, entered the mosque. Lights, fans, windows, the stage where the prayers are conducted, and copies of the Holy Qur'an were damaged. It was a pre-planned attack, since the radio station based at the Vihāraya (Rangiri FM) had announced the day before that there would be a protest. The police did not protect the mosque. Given this fact, it appears that there is a campaign underway to incite Sinhala Buddhist people against us.[13]

The Muslim narrative implicitly pleaded: "Why should there not be a place of worship of another religious community within a Buddhist sacred city? The Muslims who come to the mosque are patriotic and wish Buddhism no harm."

The secular narrative of the attack on the mosque concentrated on Sumangala's political links. In spite of Sumangala having been praised during the Kandalama protest for remaining independent of politics (See Abeysekara 2002, 197–198), this representation stressed that Sumangala

13. To reconstruct this narrative, I have used: Kannangara 2012, Wickrematunga & Ariyawansha 2012, BBC News Asia 2012, Farook 2012.

had always been a political monk, who could be swayed by money. The rumour, after the unsuccessful ending of the Kandalama campaign, was that "the management of the Kandalama Hotel had given the Thero several lakhs of rupees" (Lanka News Web 2012). The secular narrative took this rumour as fact and attributed the attack on the mosque to the close links between Sumangala and the then President, Mahinda Rajapakse. The probable explanation for this uncharacteristic attack on the mosque, according to this narrative, was, therefore, that the President of Sri Lanka or one of his brothers had directed Sumangala to do it, in order to create an environment of tension in Sri Lanka that would justify continued militarization, even after the ending of armed conflict (Lanka News Web 2012).

If the attack on the mosque is to be analyzed correctly, all three of these representations must be taken into account. When this is done, the attack on the mosque, although justified robustly by Sumangala, appears to have been unprovoked by the Muslim community, to be uncharacteristic of traditional, inclusivist Buddhist attitudes, and to have been politically motivated. Nevertheless, it was not without precedent as the next section demonstrates.

Three conditioning factors for the emergence of Buddhist exclusivism in Dambulla

The argument of this chapter is that the Buddhist exclusivism demonstrated in Dambulla in 2012 and 2013 can only be understood if conditioning factors from the local and national context are taken into account. I will briefly survey three sets of relevant factors: those that date back to colonialism and the precedent of Anurādhapura; those connected with the victory over the Liberation Tigers of Tamil Eelam (LTTE) in 2009; the political sympathies of Sumangala.

The Nineteenth Century and the Precedent of Anuradhāpura[14]

At the beginning of the twentieth century, a controversy arose over who should own the ancient Buddhist city of Anurādhapura, the British imperial administration or the Buddhists of Sri Lanka. The ruined city had long been a place of Buddhist pilgrimage. Under the British, an Assistant Agency was established there in 1833. In 1868, under Governor

14. A longer account of the spatial changes that occurred in Anurādhapura under the British and of the development of this controversy in the late nineteenth and early twentieth centuries can be found in Harris 2018, 116–141. It draws on Nissan 1985, 1988, 1989, Jeganathan 1995, Sivasundaram 2007, 2013 and Kemper 1991 as well as archival evidence.

Hercules Robinson, an Archaeological Commission to examine the ancient architectural works of Ceylon was established, which, in turn, led to surveys of the Buddhist ruins in Anurādhapura (Bell and Bell 1993, 30). In 1873, the city was made the capital of the North-West Province. This resulted in the development of the city and an influx of people, of all ethnicities and religions, so that the ruins of old monastic establishments vied, in the same space, with markets, dwellings, administrative offices and non-Buddhist places of religious worship.

One revivalist Buddhist voice became central to the controversy that developed: that of Välasinha Harischandra. In 1902, he was instrumental in forming the Anurādhapura Buddhist Defence Committee. In 1908, he published *The Sacred City of Anuradhapura* – a guide book that demanded a Commission of Inquiry to address the "desecration" of the city through archaeological excavations and its pollution through the entry of non-Buddhist elements.

His plea was for a clear demarcation of territory between the political and the monastic at Anurādhapura, essentially between Buddhist and non-Buddhist. The sacred city itself, he argued, should be the exclusive possession of Buddhists and should be "set apart" (Harischandra 1908, 15) for the Sinhala Buddhist "nation," as a centre of contemporary Sinhala Buddhist consciousness. All "foreign" elements should be removed, for example churches. Harischandra included in his "guide" a letter that one of the foremost Buddhist revivalists in Sri Lanka, Anagārika Dharmapāla (1864–1933), wrote in 1904 to the King of England, which included these words about the city:

> It is not wise neither is it just to satisfy a few hundred Muhamedan immigrants and Jesuitical Christians, that the imperishable associations of the holy City hallowed for 2,200 years should be violated and disturbed. The removal of the liquor saloons and butcher shops and foreign churches from the sacred precincts of this historic City is what the Buddhists demand. (Harischandra 1908, 9–80)

This attitude to space was not based on ancient Sri Lankan Buddhist precedent, which, as I have pointed out, was characterized by a spatially-embodied inclusivist hierarchy of the sacred. It was new, conditioned by the power relationships of imperialism. Its precedent, I would argue, was not Buddhist at all but Christian. In effect, Harischandra's view mimicked that of the British evangelical Christian missionaries who had arrived in Sri Lanka from 1805 onwards[15] with an exclusivist proselytizing

15. Five representatives of the London Missionary Society arrived in 1805, followed by Baptists in 1812, Wesleyan Methodists in 1814 and members of the Anglican, Church Missionary Society in 1818.

agenda that divided space into that which had been Christianized and that which remained "heathen" (Harris 2012, Harris 2018, 25–42). Converts to Christianity were expected to remain pure by moving away from "heathen" space completely. Buddhist books and symbols were banned from Christian schools, and churches that were situated away from busy markets and *vihāra*s were lauded (Harris 2018, 31–32). Harischandra's stance was, therefore, part of what Obeyesekere termed Protestant Buddhism, in that it protested against Christian missionaries by employing the very methods that the missionaries used (Obeyesekere 1970). In Sumangala, the same model re-emerges with the same rationale: defence of Buddhism. This conditioning factor, therefore, suggests that Buddhist exclusivism emerged as a result of the experience of British colonialism and evangelical Protestant missionaries.

The aftermath of the victory over the LTTE

In May 2009, the military forces of the Sri Lankan state defeated the LTTE, ending almost three decades of armed conflict between Tamil militants and the state.[16] Victory resulted in a new confidence among Sri Lankan Buddhists, and a determination to affirm the Buddhist heritage of the country by expressing Buddhism in space, even in areas where Buddhists were not in the majority. Some Buddhist shrines connected with army and navy camps in the north and east, the former war zones with a Hindu Tamil majority, were expanded. Ancient Buddhist sites, including ones in the north and east, were renovated. *Vihāra*s in the south of the country were graced with new, magisterial Buddha images. New Buddhist sites and centres, particularly in the north and east, were created, and other sites that had not been linked explicitly with Buddhism in the recent past, for example the hot wells (Sinhala: Kanniya; Tamil: Kanniyai) near Trincomalee, were re-imagined as Buddhist.[17] Sumangala's stance was consistent with this post-war movement to affirm the Buddhist identity of the island. During the war, Sumangala was silent about the mosque, although Dambulla had been designated a Buddhist sacred area in the early 1980s. Until 2009, the LTTE was the main threat to the *Dharma*, the principal Other to be tackled, although antagonism towards the Christian

16. There are many scholarly resources on the Sri Lankan ethnic conflict, including: Richardson 2005 and Hoole 2001.

17. I have given several papers on this, drawing from fieldwork in Sri Lanka in 2009, 2010 and 2012, including at the American Academy of Religion, the Spalding Symposium on Indian Religions and an annual conference of the UK Association for Buddhist Studies. The research also forms the last chapter of my 2018 monograph (Harris 2018, 192–237)

Other surfaced intermittently (See Harris 2006, 208–212). After the war ended, the opportunity arose both to affirm what many (but not all) Sinhala Buddhists believed - that Sri Lanka was once totally Buddhist and Sinhala - and to tackle what was perceived by some of these Buddhists as a new threat to the realization of this conviction, namely an increasingly visible and confident Muslim presence. Sumangala aligned himself with this mood. This conditioning factor, it could be argued, was also linked to Protestant Buddhism in the sense that the mosque attack responded to an exclusivism that was perceived in the Muslim community. However, as I argued in 2018, drawing particularly on the research of the Sri Lankan scholar, Roberts (e.g. Roberts 2003), it also drew from Sinhala Buddhist imaginaries or world views concerning the nature of the island that were present before the British colonial period and Protestant Buddhism, and which encouraged a form of inclusivist subordination (Harris 2018, 13–24)

The political affiliation of Sumangala

Buddhism in Sri Lanka has possessed a political face for centuries. Since independence from the British in 1948, political parties that have appealed to the Sinhala majority have visibly been supported by members of the monastic *Saṅgha* at their rallies and political meetings. Sumangala is known to have aligned himself with the party of Mahinda Rajapakse, who was President of the country between 2005 and January 2015. Under Rajapakse, between 2009 and 2014, there was a rise in interreligious tension in Sri Lanka, within which Buddhist monks played a part, particularly members of a new minority group, the Budu Bala Sena (BBS – Buddhist Strength Army or Force), which rose to prominence in 2012 with an agenda that was both anti-Christian and anti-Muslim. The government did little to curb this "Army/Force," prompting speculation that it had the support of key figures close to the President. Although Sumangala was not to my knowledge a member of the BBS, and although the attack on the mosque occurred before the BBS rose to prominence, his actions in Dambulla were consistent with the ethos of this group. The accusation that Sumangala had been encouraged to attack the mosque by the government itself cannot, therefore, be discounted, although it may never be proved.

Conclusion

In this chapter I have examined why a spacially-expressed Buddhist exclusivism arose in Dambulla between 2012 and 2014. I first surveyed scholarly research supportive of a non-exclusivist Buddhist attitude to interreligious relations. I then suggested, drawing on my own research, that a spectrum of Buddhist responses to religious others has existed from the beginnings of Buddhism and that what Buddhists have selected from and added to this spectrum has been conditioned by contextual factors. In the case of contemporary Dambulla, these contextual factors have included: the legacy of colonialism which continues to offer to Buddhists an exclusivist model of religion and space; the post-war Buddhist tendency to express Buddhist identity through spatial markers; the ethos of the Rajapakse regime after 2009, when little was done to curb attacks on Muslims and Christians. These factors, combined with a long-standing fear among Sinhala Buddhists in Sri Lanka that there will always be threats to their identity and their very existence, produced in Dambulla a Buddhist exclusivism that appears out of character with the previous commitments of the main agent within my case study, Inamaluwe Sumangala Thero, the traditional inclusivism of Buddhism within the island, and the attitudes to religious others that are traceable within the Pāli textual tradition.

References

Abeysekara, Ananda. 1999. "Politics of Higher Ordination, Buddhist Monastic Identity, and Leadership at the Dambulla Temple in Sri Lanka." *Journal of the International Association of Buddhist Studies* 22(2): 255–280.

———. 2002. *Colors of the Robe: Religion, Identity, and Difference*. Columbia: University of South Carolina Press.

Ariyawansha, Nirangala. 2012. "'We are fighting to save the 2,300 year old Buddhist heritage that is ours': Ven. Inamaluwe Sumangala Thero interviewed by Nirangala Ariywansha." *The Sunday Leader*, 5 May. http://dbsjeyaraj.com/dbs/archives/6092

Bandaranayake, Senaka. 2006 [1993]. "Dambulla: The Golden Mountain Temple." In *The Cultural Triangle of Sri Lanka*, 136–155. Paris: UNESCO. https://doi.org/10.30875/1d732d65-en

Bell, Bethia N. and Heather M. Bell. 1993. *H.C.P. Bell: Archaeologist of Ceylon and the Maldives*. Denbigh, Clwyd: Archetype.

BBC News Asia. 2012. "Sri Lanka Muslims decry radical Buddhist mosque attack." 23 April. http://bbc.co.uk/news/world-asia-17816285

Colombo Telegraph. 2012. "Dambulla Attack Videos Fake says Inamaluwe Sumangala." *Colombo Telegraph*. 24 April. https://www.colomhotelegraph.com/index.php/dambulla-attack-videos-fake-says-Inamaluwe-Sumangala-Thero/

———. 2013. "Dambulla Kovil Attacked; Hindu Politico Says Mosques And Kovils Must Not Be Shifted." 24 October. https://www.colombotelegraph.com

Duncan, James S. 1990. *The City as Text: The Politics of Landscape in the Kandyan Kingdom*. Cambridge: Cambridge University Press.

Farook, Latheef. 2012. "Attack on Dambulla Mosque: Latest Hooliganism Under

Organized "Hate Muslim" Campaign." *Colombo Telegraph*, 29 April. https://colombotelegraph.com/index.php/attack-on-dambulla-mosque-latest-hooliganism-under-organized-hate-muslim-campaign/

Gombrich, Richard and Gananath Obeyeskere. 1988. *Buddhism Transformed: Religious Change in Sri Lanka*. Princeton, NJ: Princeton University Press.

Gombrich, Richard. 1996. *How Buddhism Began: The Conditioned Genesis of the Early Teachings*. London: Athlone.

Harischandra, Brahmacari Walisinha. 1908. *The Sacred City of Anuradhapura*. Colombo: Colombo Apothacaries.

Harris, Elizabeth J. 1997. "Reclaiming the Sacred: Buddhist Women in Sri Lanka." *Feminist Theology* 15: 85–111. https://doi.org/10.1177/096673509700001507

———. 2006. *Theravāda Buddhism and the British Encounter: Religious, missionary and colonial experience in nineteenth century Sri Lanka*. Abingdon: Routledge.

———. 2012. "Memory, Experience and the Clash of Cosmologies: The Encounter between British Protestant Missionaries and Buddhism in Nineteenth Century Sri Lanka." *Social Sciences and Missions*. 25(3): 265–303. https://doi.org/10.1163/187489412X648927

———. 2013. "Buddhism and the Religious Other." In *Understanding Interreligious Relations*, edited by David Cheetham, Douglas Pratt, and David Thomas, 88-117. Oxford: Oxford University Press.

———. 2018. *Religion, Space and Conflict in Sri Lanka: Colonial and Postcolonial Contexts*. Abingdon: Routledge.

Hindu Existence. 2013. "Struggle for Hindu Existence." http://hinduexistence.org/2013/11/03/tamil-hindus-in-sri-lanka-are-still-in-danger-why-buddhists-of-sl-are-attacking-tamils-and-destroying-hindu-temples/

Hoole, Rajan. 2001. *Sri Lanka: The Arrogance of Power*. Colombo: University Teachers for Human Rights (Jaffna).

Jeganathan, Pradeep. 1995. "Authorizing History, Ordering Land: The Conquest of Anuradhapura." In *Unmaking the Nation: The Politics of Identity and History in Modern Sri Lanka,* edited by Catherine Brun and Qadri Ismail, 106–134. Colombo: Social Scientists Association.

Kannangara, Nirmala. 2012. "'No Provision for any other faith only Buddhism so move the mosque,' says Thero." *Lanka Standard.* 25 April. www.lankastandard.com/2012/04/no-provision-for-any-other-faith-only-Buddhism-so-move-the-mosque-says-thero/

Kemper, Steven. 1991. *The Presence of the Past: Chronicles, Politics, and Culture in Sinhala Life*. Ithaca and London: Cornell University Press.

Kiblinger, Kristin Beise. 2005. *Buddhist Inclusivism: Attitudes Towards Religious Others*. Aldershot: Ashgate.

Lanka Newspapers. 2012. "Won't Rest till justice is meted out, Dambulla priest insists." LankaNewspapers.com. 20 May. http://www.lankanewspapers.com/news/2012/5/76615_space.html

Lanka News Web. 2012. "President Instigates Inamaluwe Thero Against Muslims." 21 April. http://www.lankanewsweb.com/english/index.php?option=com_content&view=article&id=1724:president-instigates-inamaluwe-thero-against-muslims&catid=1&Itemid=29

Nathaniel, Camelia. 2013. "Sri Lanka Bhikkhuni Order in Deadlock." *Sunday Leader*. 3 March. www.thesundayleader.lk/2013/03/03/sri-lankas-bhikkhuni-order-in-deadlock/

National Christian Council of Sri Lanka, Commission of Justice and Peace. 1992. Pamphlet on Kandalama.

Nissan, Elizabeth. 1985. *The Sacred City of Anuradhapura: Aspects of Sinhalese Buddhism and Nationhood.* Unpublished PhD dissertation. London School of Economics and Political Science, University of London.

———. 1988. "Polity and Pilgrimage Centres in Sri Lanka." *Man* 23(2): 253–274. https://doi.org/10.2307/2802805

———. 1989. "History in the Making: Anuradhapura and the Sinhala Buddhist Nation." *Social Analysis* 25, September: 64–77.

Obeyesekere, Gananath. 1970. "Religious Symbolism and Political Change in Ceylon." *Modern Ceylon Studies* 1 no.1: 41–63.

Race, Alan. 1993 (1983). *Christians and Religious Pluralism: Patterns in the Christian Theology of Religions*. London: SCM.

Richardson, John. 2005. *Paradise Poisoned: Learning about Conflict, Terrorism and Development from Sri Lanka's Civil Wars*. Kandy: International Centre for Ethic Studies.

Roberts, Michael. 2003. *Sinhala Consciousness in the Kandyan Period 1590s to 1815.* Colombo: Vijitha Yapa.

———. 2007. "Inamaluwe Sumangala Thero, Rangiri Cricket Stadium and Thilanga Sumathipala." Cricinto.com, 10 July. http://dbsjeyaraj.com/dbs/archives/6004 on 09.01.2016

Ruegg, David Seyfort. 2008. *The Symbiosis of Buddhism and Brahmanism/Hinduism in South Asia and of Buddhism with "Local Cults" in Tibet and the Himalayan Region*. Vienna: Oisterreichische Akademie der Wisshenschaften.

Sirisena, S.M.D. 1992. "Spiritual Protest at Kandalama." *The Sunday Times*. 19 July.

Sivasundaram, Sujit. 2007. "Buddhist Kingship, British Archaeology and Historical Narratives in Sri Lanka c. 1750–1850." *Past and Present* 197(November): 111–142. https://doi.org/10.1093/pastj/gtm040

———. 2013. *Islanded: Britain, Sri Lanka and the Bounds of an Indian Ocean Territory.* Chicago: University of Chicago Press.

Tambiah, Stanley J. 1992. *Buddhism Betrayed? Religion, politics and violence in*

Sri Lanka. Chicago: University of Chicago Press.

The Island. 1992. "Foot in Your Mouth, Brother." 26 July: 10.

Vélez de Cea, J. Abraham. 2013. *The Buddha and Religious Diversity*. Abingdon: Routledge. https://doi.org/10.4324/9780203072639

Walsh, Maurice, transl. 1995. *The Long Discourses of the Buddha: A Translation of the Dīgha Nikāya*. Boston, MA: Wisdom.

Wickrematunga, Raisa and Niranjala Ariyawansha. 2012. "Dambulla Mosque controversy: Conflicting versions prevail." 29 April. http://dbsjeyaraj.com/dbsj/archives/5910

6

The Contemporary Tibetan Buddhist *Rimé* Response to Religious Diversity

Rachel Pang

Davidson College

Rachel H. Pang is Lester D. Coltrane III Assistant Professor of East Asian Religions in the Religious Studies Department at Davidson College. A graduate of the University of Virginia's doctoral programme in Religious Studies, her research focuses on the life and works of the Tibetan Buddhist poet-saint Shabkar Tsokdruk Rangdrol (1781–1851), the non-sectarian movement, auto/biography, and interfaith dialogue. Dr. Pang's work has been published in *a/b: Auto/Biography Studies*, *Journal of Buddhist Ethics*, *Journal of Inter-Religious Studies*, and *Révue d'Etudes Tibetaines.*

Introduction

The term "*rimé*" – the Tibetan word for "impartial" or "unbiased" – has become a "buzzword" in contemporary Tibetan Buddhist contexts, especially in Europe and America. In the context of inter-sectarian and interreligious relations, it is most often translated as "non-sectarian," "eclectic" or "ecumenical." And yet, upon closer examination, there remains a remarkable lack of sustained engagement with this topic by both Buddhists and Buddhist studies scholars alike. Moreover, the term is often tossed around without an awareness of its history, semantic range and theological underpinnings. In a world where communities across the globe are becoming increasingly interconnected, encounters with diverse cultures and faiths is inevitable. A pressing question is: how can diverse communities approach these encounters in a way that fosters dialogue rather than conflict, peace rather than war? Specifically, in the context of Buddhism, how should Buddhists relate to other faiths in a way that is simultaneously informed by their own spiritual traditions while being open-minded and respectful towards the beliefs and practices of other faiths?

Luckily, there already exists a vast body of largely unexamined historical literature available to Buddhists and Buddhist studies scholars for investigating and reflecting upon this subject. In addition, Buddhist leaders such as the Fourteenth Dalai Lama and Thich Nhat Hanh have made significant contributions towards interfaith understanding. In an effort to encourage both scholarship and conversations about Buddhist approaches to religious diversity, this essay will: (1) give a brief overview of the history of non-sectarianism in Tibetan Buddhist history; (2) examine how the non-sectarian response to religious diversity manifests in contemporary Tibetan Buddhist communities; and (3) discuss the significance of *rimé* in the modern world. I argue that it is essential for both Buddhists and Buddhist studies scholars to devote significant attention to the concept of *rimé*. For Buddhists, the very survival of their religion depends on it. For Buddhist studies scholars, it contributes to the development of an accurate understanding of one of the most significant intellectual moments in Tibetan and Buddhist history.

Historical *rimé*

According to Ringu Tulku, the concept of nonsectarianism in the Buddhist tradition is very old, dating back to the historical Buddha (Tulku 2006, 4). That is, this ideal of being unbiased towards religious difference is not unique to nineteenth-century Tibet, but rather, has its origins in the teachings of the historical Buddha (Tulku 2006, 4–5; Oldmeadow 2012, 23-28). Examining the earliest available Buddhist literature on the topic, the Pāli canon, Abraham Vélez de Cea argues that the historical Buddha's "view of religious diversity is best understood as a form of pluralistic-inclusivism and his attitude as pluralistic" (2013, 1). In other words, in contrast to the prevalent interpretation among Theravāda Buddhists and contemporary scholars who argue that the Buddha was exclusivist but nevertheless respectful towards other religions, Vélez de Cea demonstrates that "liberation and highest holiness are not sectarian or tradition-specific concepts, and therefore, they need not be interpreted as being the monopoly of Buddhist traditions" (2013, 2).

Buddhism was introduced from India into Tibet in two major transmissions: the early transmission period (seventh to ninth centuries CE) and the later transmission period (tenth to twelfth centuries CE). With the transmission of a great variety of Indian Buddhist lineages spread out over several centuries, it is perhaps no surprise that the celebrated Tibetologist, Gene Smith, once remarked, "The roots of eclecticism and tolerance are sunk as deep into the soil of Tibetan traditions as those of sectarianism and bigotry" (Smith 2001, 237).

While the most famous example of religious eclecticism and tolerance in Tibetan Buddhist history is without a doubt the non-sectarian movement of the nineteenth century, it is also important to note that there have been countless masters who have embraced this unbiased approach to their religious practice and pedagogical endeavours throughout Tibetan Buddhist history. Famous examples include Longchenpa (1308–1364), Tsongkhapa (1357–1419), Rangjung Dorjé (1284–1339), Tangtong Gyalpo (1361?–1485), and Shakya Chodken (1428–1507) (Smith 2001, 241; Stearns 2007; Komarovski 2012). These spiritual masters studied under teachers from different sects and adopted an unbiased approach towards religious difference.

The nineteenth century marks a critical turning point for the history of non-sectarianism in Tibet. During this period, a group of Tibetan Buddhist luminaries developed what later came to be known in contemporary Euro-American scholarship as the non-sectarian "movement." Revolving around Jamgön Kongtrul (1813–1899) and Jamyang Khyentsé Wangpo (1820-1892), the group consisted of an eclectic network of spiritual masters from the Dergé region of eastern Tibet, all committed to an unbiased approach to Buddhist and non-Buddhist teachings. The group included the philosopher Mipam (1846–1812), the celebrated itinerant meditation master Patrul (1808–1887), the treasure revealer Chokgyur Lingpa (1829–1870), the Bön master Shardza Tashi Gyaltsen (b.1859), and others (Smith 2001, 235, 250). While there is debate over whether or not the label "movement" is appropriate for this religio-cultural phenomenon (Gardner 2006, 112), the influence of this group of nineteenth-century masters on contemporary Tibetan Buddhism is undisputed. Indeed, Gene Smith notes that the activities of this group of masters "had enormous significance for the cultural history of Tibet" (2001, 235).

Contemporary Euro-American scholarship characterizes the nineteenth-century non-sectarian movement in the following ways: (1) an attitude of eclecticism and unity with regards to the various Buddhist (and non-Buddhist) teachings; (2) studying with teachers from many different lineages; (3) the collection and compilation of works from the various lineages of Tibetan Buddhism, many of them endangered; (4) the encyclopedic and systematic presentation of the various Buddhist tenet systems; and (5) a return to the Indian original texts to resolve sectarian disagreements (Smith 2001a, 246, 248, 263–264; 2001b, 232). In Ringu Tulku's reading of Jamgön Kongtrul's *Five Treasuries*, he emphasizes the latter's attitude, rather than his written legacy. He writes, "The Ri-me approach is an inclusive one, recognizing the distinctions of the various lineages and teachings, while seeing them all as valid instructions that lead to the same ultimate understanding" (2006, xiii). Indeed, in Jamgön Kongtrul's autobiography, non-sectarianism is first and foremost portrayed as an attitude of impartiality towards the various Buddhist traditions that fosters spiritual development:

> nowadays, as far as even the most famous lamas and scholars are concerned, other than those who hold their own specific traditions and several mainstream lineages of teaching, there are few who could equal Khyentsé Rinpoche's extremely fine regard and pure view for all the teachings of the Sage without bias, and accounts of their spiritual careers are meager. In particular, in these latter times there are many who, while they themselves do not act forthrightly and do not have a pure spiritual outlook, still speak of the relative superiority and inferiority of different Buddhist traditions, or the relative purity or impurity of different lineages, saying things such as, "Well, at least such-and-such tradition has empowerments." To say nothing of other traditions, they are full of meaningless suspicions and resistance concerning even their own traditions, like the proverbial skittish old yak that causes himself to shy.
>
> I, too, although I have been someone who has longed from his heart for the Buddhist teachings, have not turned out to have the mental strength to make up my own mind, and so have not accomplished my wishes successfully. From this point on, however, gradually the lotus of my faith in all the teachings of the Sage (without sectarian distinctions) and in the holders of those teachings unfolded in an unbiased manner. My spiritual career, too, has improved, and I have not committed the grievous fault of rejecting the teachings. All this is due to the grace of this precious lord guru. (Kongtrul 2003, 86)

Resonating with Jamgön Kongtrul's sentiments are the ideas of Shabkar Tsogdruk Rangdrol (1781–1851), a non-sectarian master whose activities predate those of Kongtrul and his contemporaries by approximately three decades. Like Kongtrul, Shabkar describes *rimé* as being an attitude of impartiality towards religious difference. In an aspiration prayer, he sings:

> may all male and female beings who hear this song pacify bias – aversion and attachment – to tenet systems and be in harmony with all – with faith, devotion, and pure perception – impartially benefitting the teachings and beings! (Zhabs dkar 2003b, 367.1)

Thus, according to Shabkar, to be "sectarian" is to engage in bias and partiality, and to be non-sectarian is to be impartial, non-judgmental and to have pure perception towards all, including those belonging to other religions (Zhabs dkar 2003a, 57.6, 66.5). An interesting element of Shabkar's conception of non-sectarianism that has yet to be found in the *Collected Works* of Jamgön Kongtrul and his contemporaries is its strong visionary, apocalyptic and theological dimensions (Pang 2015). This element of non-sectarianism as described by Shabkar reminds us of the way in which traditional Tibetan Buddhist non-sectarian approaches to religious diversity are rooted in a rich theological worldview.

Contemporary *rimé*

In contemporary contexts, the term *rimé* is used in several ways: (1) in reference to the non-sectarian movement in nineteenth century, eastern Tibet; (2) in the context of Buddhist masters advising their audiences not to exhibit bias towards other sects and religions; (3) to refer to a spiritual lineage that stems from one of the nineteenth-century non-sectarian masters; (4) to refer to a Buddhist community that does not directly stem from one of the nineteenth-century non-sectarian masters, but nevertheless adopts non-sectarian ideals; and (5) as a label for a religious event that espouses non-sectarian ideals. Because the first usage is discussed above, the next section will discuss usages (2) to (5).

Non-Sectarian advocacy by contemporary Tibetan Buddhist teachers

It has been suggested that the non-sectarian movement had a profound influence upon the way that Tibetan Buddhism is practised and taught in contemporary contexts (Samuel 1993, 537). While this has as yet to be demonstrated through textual evidence, there is no doubt that a non-sectarian approach was central to the life and works of the most prominent Tibetan Buddhist leaders of the past century, including the Fourteenth Dalai Lama (b. 1935), Dilgo Khyentsé Rinpoche (1910–1991) and Deshung Rinpoche (1906–1987). In a lecture to an audience in Los Angeles in 1983, Deshung Rinpoché observed:

> I have seen this narrow-minded spirit [of sectarianism] detract from Buddhism in my own land of Tibet and, during the past 20 years of my stay in America, I have also seen it grow among the many Dharma centers founded here by Tibetan teachers and their disciples. It is always with sorrow that I observe sectarianism take root among Dharma centers. It is my karma, as a representative of Buddhism and as a Tibetan, to have the opportunity and responsibility to speak out, when asked, against this 'inner foe' [...]

> Sectarianism turns the pure Dharma into poison, through it, one accumulates great sin. In this life one will be frustrated in one's own Dharma efforts. Upon death, one will fall into hell as swiftly as an arrow shot from a bow. These are the consequences of spending a lifetime in rejecting others' spiritual efforts on such narrow-minded grounds. (Deshung Rinpoche 1983)

Deshung Rinpoche's sentiments are echoed in the following speech by the Fourteenth Dalai Lama:

> fourth, I would like to insist upon the importance of non-sectarianism. It sometimes happens that people attribute an exaggerated importance to one or another of the different schools and different traditions within Buddhism, and this can lead to an accumulation of extremely negative acts with regard to the Dharma. The advantage of non-sectarianism is that after receiving the transmission of the instructions, initiations, and explanations pertinent to each different tradition, we will be able to have a better understanding of the different teachings. From my own experience, this is without doubt very beneficial. Consequently, if we keep a non-sectarian attitude, as we receive teachings from different traditions, think about them, and put them in practice, it is certain we will improve our understanding of the Dharma. This is why non-sectarianism is so important. (Dalai Lama 1993)

This short citation provides a succinct summary of the Fourteenth Dalai Lama's advocacy of non-sectarianism within the Buddhist tradition. He has also been a tireless advocate for interfaith understanding amongst religions of the world. In *Towards True Kinship of Faiths: How the World's Religions Can Come Together*, he singles out interreligious relations as the source of much historical and contemporary conflict and states: "this challenge of peaceful coexistence, I believe, will define the task of humanity in the twenty-first century" (2010, viii–ix, xiii).

Contemporary Rimé Lineages and Buddhist Centres

While the majority of Buddhist communities in Tibet, the Tibetan diaspora, Europe and North America belong to one of the main sects of Tibetan Buddhism, such as Geluk or Nyingma, there are a few that identify as "*rimé*," tracing their lineage directly to the masters of the non-sectarian movement in nineteenth-century Tibet.[1] For example, Rimay Gyalten Sogdzin Rinpoche originates from Tsar Tsar Monastery in Derge

1. There are also Buddhist lineages who trace their lineage directly to the non-sectarian masters of nineteenth-century Tibet but identify with a single lineage, such as Kagyu or Nyingma.

and traces his lineage to Jamgön Kongtrul. He heads Dharma centres in Taiwan, Hong Kong, Canada and the US (Welcome 2020). While Mahāmudrā and Dzogchen are the main practices of his disciples, this Dharma centre is explicitly described as being "*rimé*." Another example of a *rimé* community that traces its lineage to Jamgön Kongtrul is the Rimay Buddhist community in Arvillard, France, currently headed by Denys Rinpoche (Rimay 2019). Denys Rinpoche is a spiritual heir to Kalu Rinpoche (1905–1989) and traces his lineage back to Jamgön Kongtrul. Rimay is part of the Communauté Shangpa Rimay International (SRI), a network of *rimé* centres across Europe (Rimay 2019).

It is important to note that not all Buddhist communities who trace their lineages to nineteenth-century non-sectarian masters necessarily identify as *rimé* explicitly. For example, the fourth incarnation of Jamgön Kongtrul (b. 1995) is generally seen as being a reincarnate lama of the Karma Kagyu tradition (Jamgon Kongtrul Labrang 2012). Similarly, Shechen Monastery, the monastic seat of Dilgo Khyentse Rinpoche (who is an emanation of Jamyang Khyentse Wangpo), belongs to the Nyingma tradition. Yet, despite their stated sectarian traditions, neither of these monasteries are sectarian in outlook; one can have an unbiased approach to religious diversity but not state it explicitly. Therefore, explicitly describing one's community as "*rimé*" is a conscious choice by particular contemporary Buddhist communities.

Still, there are some *rimé* Buddhist centres who do not trace their lineage directly to Jamgön Kongtrul, but nevertheless, describe themselves as "*rimé.*" A prominent example is the Tibetan Buddhist Rimé Institute in Australia, headed by Khentrul Rinpoche, and belonging to the Jonang tradition. Their website notes that while Jamgön Kongtrul and Jamyang Khyentse Wangpo popularized *rimé* during the nineteenth century, they argue that the movement's roots were in fact laid by Jonang Tāranātha in the sixteenth century (Tibetan Buddhist Rimé Institute 2017). They also believe that Jamgön Kongtrul was a reincarnation of Tāranātha.

There are also *rimé* centres that are founded by Western teachers who have studied under Tibetan Buddhist masters, and that claim to be distinctly American. One example is the Nying Je Ling (Universal Compassion Buddhist Organization) in Texas. Its preceptor is Tashi Nyima, who was originally educated in the Dominican and Jesuit Orders, but also studied under Tibetan Buddhist masters. He describes himself as the "heart son" of Kyabje Tashi Norbu Rinpoche. The community's website notes that it is "a western branch of Great Middle Way Buddhism" that takes an eclectic approach to their Buddhist study (Great Middle Way n.d.). Another *rimé* centre with even looser links to Tibet is the Rime Buddhist Center in Kansas City, Missouri. Founded by Chuck Stanford (also known as Lama Changchup Kunchok Dorje) and Mary Stanford, its current spiritual director is Lama Matthew Rice (Rime Buddhist Centre n.d.). It offers meditation and *Dharma* classes, and is active in community outreach. Stanford's biography describes him as having received teachings from the Dalai Lama and a "root teacher" from Golok who remains unnamed. In this way, out of all the *rimé* centres described thus far, this one has the loosest links to Tibetan lineages although it does maintain several Tibetan spiritual teachers on its advisory committee.

Another example of a contemporary *rimé* Buddhist centre in the United States is RimeShedra.NYC. More textual and intellectual in its approach than any of the Buddhist organizations discussed so far, RimeShedra. NYC describes itself as "a group dedicated to studying advanced classical Buddhist texts to the extent they are available in English translation." It is led by a senior teacher, Derek Kolleeny, who has studied Buddhism both as a scholar and practitioner, and has translated Tibetan Buddhist texts as part of the Nalanda Translation Committee. The group describes itself as "*rimé*" because they examine root texts traditionally studied in Tibetan Buddhist monastic colleges from the perspective of all sectarian traditions. Traditionally, study of these root texts was often limited to one sectarian perspective. This is an example of a Buddhist group in the United States that calls itself "*rimé*" because its approach to Buddhist study is "in the spirit of the Rime or unbiased movement" (RimeShedra n.d.).

Finally, the term "*rimé*" is used to describe Buddhist events in Europe and America that adopt a non-sectarian ethos. A prominent example is the Rimay Monlam, a non-sectarian prayer festival held annually since 2006, first at the Blazing Wisdom Institute and the Garrison Institute in upstate New York, and now for the first time in Portugal. The Rimay Monlam Invitation Committee consists of Tibetan Buddhist spiritual teachers of both Tibetan and Euro-American origin from various sectarian denominations. These committee members are all prominent spiritual teachers in their own right. The mission statement of the prayer festival is true to its non-sectarian label: a "call for harmony and prosperity in all schools, lineage, traditions, monasteries, and sanghas, and in our society and the natural world" (Rimay Monlam 2017).

The significance of historical *rimé* literature in contemporary times

For contemporary Buddhist communities

While Jamgön Kongtrul's religious lineage is flourishing, there is not much attention paid to the *rimé* aspect of his legacy by contemporary Tibetan Buddhist communities. In the nineteenth century, Shabkar warned of the dangers of not embracing a non-sectarian approach. Around the year 1845, the Indian Buddhist saint Padmasambhava (eighth century) appeared to Shabkar in a vision with advice on composing the text that would become the *Emanated Scripture of Orgyen*. Padmasambhava made the following prophecy:

> in the future, during the degenerate age, according to the prophecy of King Kriķi's dream: "the precious teachings of the Buddha will not be destroyed by outsiders, etc. Rather, Buddhists, having mutually divided the Dharma into categories of good and bad, will quarrel due to attachment and aversion, destroying the teachings." In the future, during the degenerate age, when the *Emanated Scripture of Orgyen* is placed upon the heads of people – whether Dharma practitioners or worldly individuals, it will dispel all partiality concerning the Dharma, and cause pure perception to arise everywhere. Thus, it is good to compose these unprecedented elegant sayings that benefit the teachings and beings. (Zhabs dkar 2003b, 576.1-.4.)

In this passage, Padamsambhava identifies a causal link between inter-sectarian conflict and the demise of Buddhism. Reading this passage, one cannot help but think of the internal divides that currently plague Tibetan Buddhist communities, including the New Kadampa Tradition (NKT) and its campaigns against the Dalai Lama, and the factions within the Karma Kagyu that challenge the succession of the Karmapa. These conflicts may be seen to weaken the Tibetan Buddhist community as a whole, in effect, "destroying the teachings from the inside" as described in the above prophecy. If contemporary Tibetan Buddhists were to consider such texts within their tradition seriously, they would be more vigilant about abandoning narrow-minded sectarianism as the very survival of Buddhism depends on it.

It is important to note, however, that the version of non-sectarianism that Shabkar advocates is not uncritically tolerant of all doctrines and practices in Buddhism and other religions. His non-sectarian works contain many examples where he refutes the doctrinal positions of others. The non-sectarianism he advocates is more about the attitude with which one approaches religious difference. For Shabkar, it is important not to essentialize certain tenet systems as truly "good" or "bad." In *Dharma Discourse: Beneficial Jewel*, Shabkar advises:

> if you follow the intention of the Buddha's words, then don't categorize teachings into "good" and "bad" [...] Have pure perception towards all tenet systems unbiased like the sun. This is a critical instruction. If you don't understand this, but fall under the sway of attachment and aversion – categorizing the teachings and slandering other tenet systems – you will have lost the Buddha's instructions. (Zhabs dkar 2003a, 108.4)

In this mode, one can practice the tenet system towards which one feels the most affinity, while maintaining an attitude of unbiasedness towards all others (Zhabs dkar 2003a, 550.1). Shabkar's definition of non-sectarianism resonates with several contemporary interpretations of the concept, most notably those of Ringu Tulku and the Dungkar dictionary. For instance, Ringu Tulku states:

> Ri-me is not a way of uniting different schools and lineages by emphasizing their similarities. It is basically an appreciation of their differences and an acknowledgement of the importance of variety to benefit practitioners with different needs. (2006, 3)

Similarly, the Dungkar dictionary defines non-sectarianism as "upholding one's own school's theories and practices, yet not looking down on or insulting those of others" (Gayley and Schapiro 2017, 4).

In particular, Tibetan Buddhists would benefit from studying discussions of non-sectarianism from their own rich scriptural tradition. Studying the works of Jamgön Kongtrul, Shabkar and others would give contemporary Tibetan Buddhists the theological apparatus for articulating their approach to religious diversity to other faith communities. So far, Buddhists have not been as involved as Christians, for example, in interfaith dialogue initiatives. However, if we look at important advocates of non-sectarianism within the Buddhist tradition such as the Dalai Lama and Shabkar, we see that they encourage followers to embrace religious diversity not just within Buddhism, but within other religions as well (Zhabs dkar 2003a, 57.6, 66.5, 68.4). Thus, sustained encounters with both historical non-sectarian texts and other faiths will help contemporary Buddhists better understand the relationship between Buddhism and religious diversity, and enhance their own spiritual practice as well.

For Buddhist Studies scholars

While the importance of the nineteenth-century non-sectarian movement is widely acknowledged, there has been a significant lack of scholarship on this topic. Buddhist studies scholars would also benefit from more research into non-sectarianism. That is, while it is generally acknowledged that the non-sectarian movement had a profound influence on contemporary Tibetan Buddhism today, the exact nature and mechanisms of that influence is not concretely understood. Gene Smith, Ringu Tulku, Peter Oldmeadow and the translators of Jamgön Kongtrül's *Treasury of Knowledge* have made groundbreaking contributions to our knowledge of this topic. However, there is still much to be uncovered. Without an accurate characterization of the non-sectarian movement, our understanding of a key event in Tibetan and Buddhist history cannot be said to be complete.

For interfaith dialogue

With the exception of several Buddhist figures (such as the Dalai Lama, Thich Nhat Hanh, Masao Abe, Rita Gross), most discussions on religious diversity have been initiated and led by Christians. As many Christian theologians have pointed out, it has become increasingly impossible to ignore the issue of religious diversity in a rapidly globalizing world. Interestingly, it has been contemporary Christian – and not Buddhist – theologians who have made the most significant contributions to the topic of Buddhist responses to religious diversity. Important research on this topic include the work of Kristin Kiblinger, Paul Knitter, Perry Schmidt-Leukel, and Abraham Vélez de Cea. Amongst scholars working on the issue of Buddhist responses to religious diversity, Rita Gross has been the most distinctive, as she approaches the discussion using vocabulary and ideas from Buddhism and comparative religions rather than Christian theology. She argues that while many of the tools developed to discuss religious diversity by Christian theologians have been useful for Christians, they are not so much useful for non-Christians (Gross 2014, 3). She believes that the Buddhist constructive-critical perspective can make a unique and useful contribution to these dialogues.

Gross's criticisms come at a crucial moment in the history of Buddhism in Europe and America. Buddhism is a relatively new religion in these societies, and if it is to develop a significant presence in the religious mainstream, it is necessary for its adherents to participate in dialogue with its religious and non-religious neighbours. Throughout history, Buddhists have often had the tendency to be introverted. Yet, in a rapidly globalizing world, such reclusive behaviour may no longer be in its best interests. By engaging in dialogue with other faiths, Buddhists will not only contribute to mutual understanding and harmony between different religious groups, but will also secure a place for its own voice in discussions about religious diversity. This is important for preserving Buddhist traditions for future generations and for fostering peace amongst diverse religious communities. Buddhist leaders such as the Fourteenth Dalai Lama and Thich Nhat Hanh embody compelling examples of how one might approach interfaith dialogue.

Conclusion

In an age of increased religious intolerance, hatred and violence all over the world, the call for interfaith dialogue and understanding has never been more urgent. As Rita Gross has observed, "Making exclusive truth claims does not often result in people being kind and gentle: instead people become rigid and combative and defensive, brittle and very impoverished spiritually" (2014, 3). She argues that "in contemporary circumstances, it is the ethical responsibility of every person to acquire a basic working knowledge of the world's religions and suggests how to go about acquiring this knowledge in nonthreatening and effective ways" (Gross 2014, 16). Perhaps it might be too optimistic to hope for a "Copernican revolution in how religious people think about religious diversity," as advocated by John Hick and Rita Gross (Gross 2014, 5). Nevertheless, it is clear that the way in which we choose to address the inescapable reality of religious diversity will radically influence the course of our immediate history. Buddhists, like all others, must develop constructive ways of thinking about the detrimental effects of inter-sectarian and inter-religious conflict in religious history, their own rich tradition of non-sectarian literature and how to interact with other faith traditions in a constructive way.

References

Abe, Masao. 1995. *Buddhism and Interfaith Dialogue*. Edited by Steven Heine. London: Macmillan. https://doi.org/10.1007/978-1-349-13454-0

Dalai Lama XIV, His Holiness. 1993. "Advice to Buddhists in the West." http://hhdl.dharmakara.net/hhdlquotes111.html

———. 2010. *Toward a True Kinship of Faiths: How the World's Religions Can Come Together*. New York: Doubleday Religion.

Deshung Rinpoche. 1983. "Buddhism Without Sectarianism." Translated by Jared Rhoton. Los Angeles, CA: Quiet Mountain. http://www.quietmountain.org/links/teachings/nonsect.htm

Gardner, Alexander. 2006. "The Twenty-five Great Sites of Khams: Religious Geography, Revelation, and Nonsectarianism in Nineteeth-Century Eastern Tibet." PhD dissertation. Asian Languages and Cultures. University of Michigan.

Gayley, Holly and Joshua Schapiro. 2017. "Introduction." *A Gathering of Brilliant Moons: Practice Advice from the Rimé Masters of Tibet*, edited by Holly Gayley and Joshua Schapiro. Somerville: Wisdom Publications.

Great Middle Way. n.d. "Nying Je Ling." https://greatmiddleway.wordpress.com/about/

Gross, Rita. 2014. *Religious Diversity What's the Problem?: Buddhist Advice for Flourishing with Religious Diversity*. Eugene: Cascade.

Jamgon Kongtrul Labrang. 2012. "The 4th Jamgon Kongtrul Rinopche." Office of H.E. Jamgon Kongtrul Rinpoche. http://www.jamgonkongtrul.org/section.php?s1=2&s2=3

Kiblinger, Kristin. 2005. *Buddhist Inclusivism: Attitudes Toward Religious Others*. Farnham: Ashgate.

Knitter, Paul F. 1995. *One Earth Many Religions: Multifaith Dialogue and Global Responsibility*. Maryknoll, NY: Orbis.

———. 1996. *Jesus and the Other Names: Christian Mission and Global Responsibility.* Maryknoll, NY: Orbis.

———. 2002. *Theologies of Religions*. Maryknoll, NY: Orbis.

———. 2009. *Without Buddha I Could Not Be a Christian*. London: Oneworld.

Kongtrul, Jamgön. 2003. *The Autobiography of Jamgön Kongtrül Lodrö Thayé.* Trans. Richard Barron. Ithaca: Snow Lion.

Komarovski, Yaroslav. 2001. *Visions of Unity: The Golden Pandita Shakya Chokden's New Interpretation of Yogacara and Madhyamaka*. Albany: State University of New York Press.

Oldmeadow, Peter. 2012. *Rimé, Buddhism without Prejudice: the Nineteenth Century Non-Sectarian Movement and its Tibetan Context*. Carlton North: Shogam.

Pang, Rachel. H. 2014. "The *Rimé* Activities of Shabkar Tsokdruk Rangdrol (1781–1851)." *Revue d'Etudes Tibétaines* 30(October): 5–30.

Pang, Rachel H. 2015. "Rimé Revisited: Shabkar's Response to Religious Difference." *Journal of Buddhist Ethics* 22: 449–473.

Rimay: Communauté Shangpa Rimay International. 2019. "Denys Rinpoché." https://www.rimay.net/denys-rinpoche/

Rimay Monlam. 2017. http://www.rimaymonlam.org/en/about-rimay-monlam/

Rime Buddhist Center: Achieving Peace through Compassion. n.d. "Rime Center Founders." https://www.rimecenter.org/rime-center-founders/

RimeShedra.NYC. n.d. "Shedra Curriculum and History." https://www.rimeshedra.nyc/curriculum

Samuel, Geoffrey. 1993. *Civilized Shamans: Buddhism in Tibetan Societies.* Washington, D.C.: Smithsonian Institution Press.

Schmidt-Leukel, Perry, ed. 2008. *Buddhist Attitudes to Other Religions.* Germany: St. Ottilien.

Smith, E. Gene. 2001a. "Jam mgon Kong sprul and the Nonsectarian Movement." In *Among Tibetan Texts: History and Literature of the Himalayan Plateau,* ed. Kurtis R. Schaeffer, 235–272. Boston: Wisdom.

———. 2001b. "Mi pham and the Philosophical Controversies of the Nineteenth Century." In *Among Tibetan Texts: History and Literature of the Himalayan Plateau*, edited by Kurtis R. Schaeffer, 227–234. Boston: Wisdom.

Stearns, Cyrus. 2007. *King of the Empty Plain: The Tibetan Iron-Bridge Builder Tangtong Gyalpo.* Ithaca: Snow Lion.

Tibetan Buddhist Rimé Institute: Holder of Jonang Kalachakra. 2017. "Rimé Philosophy." rimebuddhism.com/about/rime-philosophy/3/

Tulku, Ringu. 2006. *The Ri-Me Philosophy of Jamgon Kongtrul the Great: A Study of Buddhist Lineages of Tibet.* Boston, MA: Shambhala.

Vélez de Cea, J. Abraham. 2013. *The Buddha and Religious Diversity.* Abingdon: Routledge. https://doi.org/10.4324/9780203072639

Welcome to the Official Website: His Holiness Rimay Gyalten Sogdzin Rinpoche and Rimay Dzam Ling Zhi Dei Chö Khor Ling. 2020. "Rimay." rinpoche.ca/index.php/en/about-us/rimay

Zhabs dkar [Shabkar]. 2003a. *chos bshad gzhan phan nor bu.* Vol. 11 in *Zhabs dkar tshogs drug rang grol kyi bka' 'bum.* New Delhi: Shechen.

———. 2003b. *o rgyan sprul pla'i glegs bam. Zhabs dkar tshogs drug rang grol kyi bka' 'bum.* Volume 9. New Delhi: Shechen.

7

How Nonsectarian is "Nonsectarian"?: Jorge Ferrer's Pluralist Alternative to Tibetan Buddhist Inclusivism

Douglas S. Duckworth

Temple University

Douglas Duckworth is Professor at Temple University and the Director of Graduate Studies in the Department of Religion. He is the author of *Mipam on Buddha-Nature: The Ground of the Nyingma Tradition* (State University of New York 2008) and *Jamgön Mipam: His Life and Teachings* (Shambhala 2011). He also introduced and translated Distinguishing the *Views and Philosophies: Illuminating Emptiness in a Twentieth-Century Tibetan Buddhist Classic by Bötrül* (State University of New York 2011). His latest works include *Tibetan Buddhist Philosophy of Mind and Nature* (Oxford University Press 2019) and a translation of an overview of the Wisdom Chapter of the *Way of the Bodhisattva* by Künzang Sönam, entitled *The Profound Reality of Interdependence* (Oxford University Press 2019).

Introduction

This paper queries the logic of the structure of hierarchical philosophical systems. Following the Indian tradition of *siddhānta,* Tibetan Buddhist traditions articulate a hierarchy of philosophical views. The "Middle Way" philosophy or Madhyamaka – the view that holds that the ultimate truth is emptiness – is in general held to be the highest view in the systematic depictions of philosophies in Tibet, and is contrasted with realist schools of thought, Buddhist and non-Buddhist. But why should an antirealist or nominalist position be said to be "better" than a realist position? What is the criterion for this claim and is it, *or can it*, be more than a criterion that is tradition-specific for only Tibetan Buddhists? In this paper, I will look at criteria to evaluate Buddhist philosophical traditions, particularly as articulated in what came to be referred as the "nonsectarian" (*ris med*) tradition. I draw from the recent work of Jorge Ferrer to query the assumptions of the hierarchical structures of "nonsectarian" traditions and attempt to articulate evaluative criteria for a nonsectarian stance that are not based solely on metaphysical or tradition-specific claims.

Tibetan Buddhist hierarchies of truth

In the nineteenth century a constellation of Buddhist traditions emerged in eastern Tibet that forged alliances amongst different philosophical traditions. Despite the shared aims among the traditions that came to be called the "nonsectarian movement," we clearly find hierarchies of philosophical views as well as strategies of marginalization laid out to show the superiority of one tradition over another. A common practice in Tibet is to set forth a hierarchy of philosophical systems and assert the superiority of one view (one's own) over another. The "nonsectarian" movement was no exception, with the Madhyamaka view of "other-emptiness" (*gzhan stong*) or the view of Great Perfection (*rdzogs chen*) commonly found at the top of these hierarchies, in contrast to what are positioned as inferior Buddhist views such as those of the "Lesser Vehicle" (*hīnayāna*) and non-Buddhist schools of thought at the bottom of the ladder.

In the nineteenth century many different traditions came to be allied in reaction to the overwhelming dominance of the Geluk (*dge lugs*) tradition. The Geluk school champions a unique view of Prāsaṅgika-Madhyamaka, which it holds to be not only the supreme philosophical view, but the only correct view through which *Nirvāṇa* is possible (e.g. Cabezón 1992, 217). The overt exclusivism of the Geluk school contrasts sharply with the inclusivism that characterizes the other schools that came to form what is commonly associated with the nonsectarian ideal in Tibet, particularly the Kagyü and Nyingma schools.

In the Kagyü tradition, Kongtrül (*kong sprul blo gros mtha' yas,* 1813–1899) was a particularly influential figure who assimilated the works of (non-Geluk) traditions in the nineteenth century. In his encyclopedic *Treasury of Knowledge,* he assembled the views of various schools, and formulated a hierarchy of philosophical systems that notably put the Madhyamaka interpretation of "other-emptiness" above Prāsaṅgika-Madhyamaka, which he categorized as the doctrine of "self-emptiness" (Kongtrül 2002, 41; translated in Callahan 2007, 74). In contrast to self-emptiness, which reflects the ultimate truth understood as a *negation* that is the emptiness of a phenomenon's own essence, other-emptiness is an *affirmation* of ultimate truth as an unconditioned ground that is empty of all relative phenomena.

Along with Prāsaṅgika-Madhyamaka and the "other-emptiness" interpretation of Madhyamaka, another tradition that is commonly found at the capstone of philosophical hierarchies in Tibet, in the works of Kongtrül and followers of the Nyingma tradition in particular, is the Great Perfection. Some scholars connect the Great Perfection with "other-emptiness" (e.g. Getsé Paṇchen 2001, 95), but other scholars, including Mipam (*'ju mi pham rgya mtsho,* 1842–1912), associate Prāsaṅgika-Madhyamaka with the way of approaching the empty aspect of reality in the Great Perfection.[1] For Mipam, the philosophy of Prāsaṅgika can be said to be primarily concerned with determining the indeterminacy of the ultimate.[2] That is, Prāsaṅgika denies any conceptual formulation of ultimate truth, and sharply contrasts with the traditions of "other-emptiness," which represent the experiential content of ultimate reality in affirming language.

We may wonder why "other-emptiness" is held to be superior to "self-emptiness" by some traditions in Tibet, or why Prāsaṅgika-Madhyamaka or self-emptiness is held above other-emptiness by others?[3] In the next section, I aim to probe the logic of these hierarchical schemes and show the demands that are placed by a more openly "nonsectarian," or pluralist, stance.

1. Mipam 1990, 76; English translation in Doctor 2004, 85. Mipam 1997, 19; English translation in Pettit 1999, 209; see Duckworth 2008, 39.
2. Prāsaṅgika-Madhyamaka is variously represented by different traditions in Tibet, and Mipam characterized Prāsaṅgika-Madhyamaka as "discourse that emphasizes the uncategorized ultimate free from assertions." The "uncategorized ultimate" is the nonconceptual ultimate, in contrast to the "categorized ultimate," which is a conceptual understanding of the ultimate, a concept or idea of emptiness. See Mipam 1990: 99; English trans. in Doctor 2004, 117; see also Duckworth 2008, 33.
3. For instance, one way this plays out is stated in the works of a Nyingma scholar, Lochen Dharmaśrī, who suggests that Prāsaṅgika-Madhyamaka can be said to be "better" than the Madhyamaka of other-emptiness if the criterion is set to be the one that is the best means for establishing the ultimate nature things as free from conceptual constructs in study. However, if the criterion is the one that is the best means of setting forth the way ultimate reality is understood as an experiential presence in meditation, other-emptiness is better. Lochen Dharmaśrī states: "If one thinks, "In the scriptures such as the *Treasury of Philosophies* and the root and [auto-]commentary of the *Wish-Fulfilling Treasury*, is it not a contradiction that: (1) in the context of identifying what is to be ascertained by means of study, Prāsaṅgika-Madhyamaka is established as the pinnacle of the Causal Vehicle of Mahāyāna, and (2) in the contexts of ascertainment by means of meditative experience, individual reflexive wisdom free from perceived-perceiver [duality] is asserted?" There is no contradiction because it is difficult for an ordinary being to deconstruct the reifications of the mind at the time of ascertaining the view by means of study and contemplation. Therefore, in negating these [reifications of the mind] through the supreme knowledge that arises through study and contemplation, Prāsaṅgika is a sharper awareness that cuts through superimpositions. Also, at the time of ascertaining by experience [the supreme knowledge] that arises in meditation, the view of the Middle Way taught in the last wheel itself is profound and much better because: (1) the naturally pure expanse, the ultimate truth that is the self-existing wisdom, is itself the primordial mode of reality of all phenomena, and (2) it is also in accord with the practice of the view that is accepted in the profound tantras of Secret Mantra" (Lochen Dharmaśrī n.d., 377–378).

Nonsectarian alternatives

One of the ways that a philosophical view could be said to be better than another is that it is a more accurate representation of reality. We might assume that views at the higher end of a spectrum of philosophical views are those that more accurately represent ultimate reality while those at the lower end are those that misrepresent it. Alternatively, it could be that traditions with the most effective emancipatory power are those that are said to be higher. Either of these criteria may not be problematic strictly within a Buddhist context (although arguably, a problem emerges when competing Buddhist views are considered on their own terms), yet when other traditions are brought into the conversation (e.g., Hindu, Christian) a problem comes into a more clear focus.

We encounter a problem when we cannot empirically reconcile conflicting claims about ultimate truth – whereas Buddhists assert no-self, Vedāntins claim a self, while some claim an impersonal ground of reality, others assert a personal or pantheistic deity at the ground of all, or the emptiness of all things... We can see this problem clearly when we consider the following thought experiment:[4] consider a Theravāda Buddhist monk who comes from his meditation retreat and reports an experience of having seen the eternal, independent Self, or, suppose he had another vision – an intimate experience with a personal and loving God upon penetrating the depths of the soul. After conveying either of these experiences to his teacher, he would most certainly be told to go back to his meditation cushion until he saw things "as they really are": impermanent, suffering and without a self. Yet we can expect that the result would be just the opposite if the teacher were a follower of Advaita Vedānta (in the former case) or Christian mysticism (in the latter).

If we take the claims of religious experience seriously—and not brush them aside as mere illusions or projections—the lessons to be drawn from this example are clear: given that the diversity of claims has yet to be resolved by such "experiential evidence" or by a clean philosophical or religious debate (and a dirty bomb has yet to settle these differences either), it may be time to look for another way around this problem, unless we remain content with tried alternatives: isolationism (in the ivory tower, a cave or on the iphone), relativism (which suffers from indifferent isolationism too, as well as being self-defeating), exclusivism (which claims the universal validity of one's own culturally-contingent view) or perennialism (which, while ignoring critical differences among traditions, is guilty of the problems of exclusivism, too). Jorge Ferrer,

4. I have taken this thought experiment from Jorge Ferrer 2002, 63.

however, points out that there may be another way to resolve the problem of religious diversity. Ferrer claims that many of the competing claims of religions present a problem only with an objectivist view, one that sees such conflicting truths as more or less accurate *representations* of ultimate reality. He states:

> the diversity of spiritual claims is a problem *only* when we have previously presupposed that they are referring to a single ready-made reality…if they intend to represent or convey the nature of a single referent with determined features. But if we see such a spiritual referent as malleable, undetermined, and creatively open to a multiplicity of disclosures largely contingent on human religious endeavors, then the reasons for conflict vanish like a mirage. (2008, 149)

Ferrer argues that this kind of religious diversity is only problematic when we assume that there is a determinate ultimate reality that can be exclusively depicted by a single representation. If ultimate reality is undetermined, there could be multiple ways it would manifest, and thus the "problem" of diversity would dissolve, echoing Wittgenstein's words in the *Tractatus* that "The solution of the problem of life is seen in the vanishing of the problem" (1922, 6.521). Thus, rather than seeing religious diversity as a problem, Ferrer celebrates pluralism's irreducibility.

Does this move to embracing pluralism and an undetermined ultimate reality leave us with relativism—equalizing all assertions and disclosures? Not necessarily. Empirical claims can still be distinguished on empirical grounds,[5] while claims about ultimate reality can be distinguished, too. Yet rather than one claim being *better* than another by more accurately referring to an objective, predetermined ultimate truth, it can be said to be better based on the potency of its emancipatory effects. With this, a representational or objectivist picture of language can be left behind, as there is no need for a conception of language that models a pregiven reality. Rather, language can be thought of here as a vehicle to elicit transformative experience, like the example of a finger that points to the moon. That is, when evaluating competing claims, a more effective or aesthetically pleasing, simpler or more elegant way *to evoke* an experience of ultimate reality could be said to be a better one, even if what is expressed is not something that could be represented. Thus, instead of seeing language about ultimate reality as *descriptive*, this is what Ferrer proposes in the *prescriptive* or performative language of mystical traditions:

5. Empirical validity, as Ferrer points out, is not reducible to objective (third person) verification or falsification, but encompasses intersubjective verification (and falsification) as well as disciplined introspection. See Ferrer 2002 chapter 2.

> the expression "things as they really are" is misguided only if understood in the context of objectivist and essentialist epistemologies [...] After all, what most mystical traditions offer are not so much descriptions of a pregiven ultimate reality to be confirmed or falsified by experiential evidence but prescriptions of ways of "being-and-the-world" to be intentionally cultivated and lived. In the end, mystical traditions aim at transformation, not representation [...] it may be more accurate to talk about them not so much in terms of "things as they really are," but of "things as they really can be" or, perhaps more normatively, "things as they really should be." (Ferrer 2008, 155)

In contrast to a criterion of representational adequacy, another way to evaluate the claims of traditions is through their transformational potency.

Thus, the presumption that ultimate reality is undetermined does not necessarily lead to relativism, but could support a hierarchical model of truth, too. The logic of such a hierarchy could be based on what has more emancipatory power, like we see in some Tibetan Buddhist philosophical hierarchies. In such a Buddhist context, claims that are more effective in eliciting *Nirvāṇa,* an end to suffering, are said to be better. This kind of inclusivism is hierarchical, too, as a tradition represents its own stance as the most accurate and complete, while those of others are seen as partial or incomplete. Yet Ferrer points out a problem with inclusivism as a picture that predetermines the way that opposing views fit into one's own framework and structures all divergent ideas into one's own, ready-made model. He states:

> once one believes oneself to be in possession of a picture of "things as they really are," dialogue with traditions maintaining different spiritual visions often becomes an uninteresting and sterile monologue. At its worst, the conflicting viewpoints are regarded as less evolved, incoherent, or simply false. At best, the challenges presented are assimilated within the all-encompassing perennialist scheme. In both cases the perennialist philosopher appears not to listen to what other people are saying, because all new or conflicting information is screened, processed, or assimilated in terms of the perennialist framework. Therefore, a genuine or symmetrical encounter with the other in which opposing spiritual visions are regarded as real options is rendered unlikely. (Ferrer 2002, 94)

Here Ferrer argues against a predetermined hierarchical scheme for spiritual truths, not only for the reason that he rejects exclusivism (because no tradition has exclusive priority to claims that are non-empirical) but because he rejects an objectivist model that presumes a structure that is pregiven, generalizable, and fixed for all individuals across space and time

(Ferrer 2011b, 8; see also Ferrer 2002, 164–165). This applies not only to ultimate truths, but to hierarchies of philosophical systems, as well as structures of paths understood to lay out "The Way" to liberation in a way that mirrors an intrinsic, objective reality that everyone must follow. He contends that not only does such a preconception preclude the possibility of genuine interreligious dialogue, but it delimits transformative possibilities to one's own preconceived notion of the result of a process of spiritual transformation. Thus, Ferrer challenges a hardwired, vertical hierarchy of religious Truth, and opts for a more fluid or multi-centred structure that embraces not only a plurality of *paths*, but a plurality of ultimate(s) *goals* as well, in what could be said to be, in a Deleuzian sense, a "rhizomatic" landscape.[6]

This kind of model still permits a (soft) hierarchy within traditions in terms of their efficacy in different contexts for varied individuals, and a fluid or soft hierarchy can also be laid out here with regards to claims about the ultimate as well. That is, there can be times when the monistic singularity of reality may serve as a "better" description (or prescription or performative "path") for someone and other times when the pluralistic diversity of reality may be better, and yet another time when a denial of both singularity and plurality may be preferable. Likewise, it may be better to emphasize the continuity of reality in some contexts while in others, rupture and disjunction may be better, depending on the desired outcome for the particular community or individual in the situation at hand. In other words, whether or not these expressions may be said to be "better" does not depend on how well they hook up to a universal structure or objective referent in the world, but to the efficacy for a desired outcome in a given context.

It is in this last criterion of efficacy, the pragmatic or transformative effectiveness of a tradition and its claims, where we find what pertains to the ethical rather than simply the metaphysical. It is in this domain where we find what does the work that determines the criteria for evaluating traditions according to Ferrer, as he states:

> although my work does not privilege any tradition or type of spirituality over others on objectivist or ontological grounds (i.e. saying that theism, monism, or nondualism corresponds to the nature of ultimate reality and/or is intrinsically superior), it does offer criteria for making qualitative distinctions among spiritual systems *on pragmatic and transformational grounds*. (2011b, 7)

6. For Deleuze (and Guattari) on the rhizome, see, for instance Deleuze and Guattari 1987, 21.

Rather than just a metaphysical criterion, Ferrer incorporates ethical standards for evaluating mystical traditions, too, and solicits two main criteria to evaluate them: the *egocentricism test* and the *dissociation test*. The egocentricism test evaluates "to what extent...a spiritual tradition, path, or practice free(s) its practitioners from gross and subtle forms of narcissism and self-centeredness?"(Ferrer 2008, 153). And the dissociation test evaluates "to what extent [...] a spiritual tradition, path, or practice foster(s) the integrated blossoming of all dimensions of the person?" (Ferrer 2008, 153). The "integrated dimensions of a person" refers to criteria that incorporate both cognitive and embodied aspects of an individual (Ferrer 2011a, 3). Ferrer further adds a third criterion (that could be considered a subset of the second) that he calls the *eco-social-political test,* which he says, "assesses the extent to which spiritual systems foster ecological balance, social and economic justice, religious and political freedom, class and gender equality, and other fundamental human rights." (Ferrer 2011a, 7)

The importance of these evaluative criteria is that they are nonsectarian, or rather are not tradition-specific, but attempt to provide a means to make qualitative distinctions across different religious traditions without taking on a privileged perspective from any one tradition's view. Arguably, this allows one to sidestep absolutist claims because no single tradition is held to presume an exclusive monopoly on truth, and furthermore, standards are not measured with reference to a predetermined, objective reality. Rather, the evaluative measures are based on pragmatic markers that are applicable across traditions. These criteria arguably avoid relativism too, because, despite a real diversity of empirically irreconcilable truth claims amongst different traditions, their varying qualities of truth can be differentiated qualitatively on the grounds of their enacted results—on (integrative and dissociative) psychological, sociological and ecological grounds—rather than based on which one most accurately depicts *the right* metaphysical picture of reality.

Since Ferrer's model is based on a pragmatic and "participatory" account of truth rather than a metaphysical one, his approach is different than the one proposed by John Hick, who relied on a Kantian metaphysic to formulate his "pluralistic hypothesis" of different religions experiencing "the Real" in different ways (See Hick 1989, 240–246). In contrast to Hick's metaphysical "Real," Ferrer does not subscribe to objectivist metaphysics. He stresses that reality is indeterminate (or undetermined) and that there is no real, pregiven structure to reality. Thus, he arguably avoids unwarranted metaphysical assumptions. While Ferrer's pluralist model of alternative religious ends resembles a position articulated by Mark Heim, he distinguishes his model from Heim's on precisely this point where he differs from Hick.

Ferrer argues that Heim is guilty of presuming an independent, pregiven reality (Ferrer 2002, 215n27) and perpetuating Kantian dualism (Ferrer 2008, 165–166n49), while Ferrer himself claims that "the model I am advancing here is that *no pregiven ultimate reality exists, and that different spiritual ultimates can be enacted through intentional or spontaneous creative participation in an indeterminate spiritual power or Mystery*" (Ferrer 2002, 151). Of course a lot hinges upon what is meant by this "indeterminate spiritual power or Mystery," but Ferrer maintains that his *denial* of any pregiven reality is not the same as his *affirming* a positive theory about it. Thus, he claims to avoid the ontological presuppositions of the metaphysical systems he critiques (Ferrer 2008, 168n63). The move Ferrer makes here to avoid self-contradiction is reminiscent of the one made by Nāgārjuna in support of his Middle Way doctrine of emptiness.[7] Indeed, there is a real affinity with Ferrer's position and the Buddhist Middle Way.

Yet the "one vehicle" of the Middle Way tradition in Tibet affirms that all Buddhist paths lead in the end to the same goal (of becoming Buddha). This is a classic view of inclusivism, not pluralism. This view is said to be better than the "Mind-Only" tradition's assertion of three vehicles (Auditor, Solitary Realizer and Bodhisattva) that lead to different final results (and only the last leads to becoming a Buddha). Probing this internal diversity of Buddhist tradition can be a good point of entry to query Buddhist attitudes toward other religions (See Kiblinger 2005). Here we have a place from which to ask critical questions about contemporary Buddhist inclusivism: why is it better to hold one final goal for all these Buddhist traditions (and for all other traditions, too, with the claim that all beings will eventually become Buddhas)? Is it because this accords with how reality is or is it better because subscribing to this is an effective means to overcome egocentrism and dissociation? The *Uttaratantra*, a classical text that supports the universality of Buddhist enlightenment, suggests the latter (see *Uttaratantra* I.157; see also Duckworth 2008, 136–137). Yet how is the single final destination reconciled with non-Buddhist paths that claim other ends (like heaven (or hell), union with God, Brahman, etc.)?

7. Nāgārjuna, *Vigrahavyāvartanī* v. 29: "if I had a thesis, I would have fault; since I have no thesis, I am only faultless," and *Mūlamadhyāmakakārikā* XIII.8: "the Victorious Ones have proclaimed emptiness as that which relinquishes all views; but those who hold emptiness as a view are incurable."

Is asserting one end for everyone better because it does not exclude people in other religions from the final fruit of one's own—for Buddhists at least? for everyone? This last question is particularly relevant for traditions in the contemporary world to address, Buddhist and non-Buddhist alike. A nonsectarian stance of *pluralism* rather than inclusivism—one that concedes multiple ends, like Ferrer—is one possible alternative. This kind of pluralism offers a nonsectarian stance in a global context. As a stance that stakes a certain claim, it indeed is not neutral, relativistic or apathetic, and certainly (and by definition) is not the only one.[8]

Conclusion

While Ferrer's notion of ultimate reality being undetermined resonates with Buddhist emptiness (as does his *egocentrism test*), his idea of an *undetermined* ultimate precludes emptiness from being the final word on reality because, being undetermined, ultimate reality can also be disclosed as theistic in a personal God. And importantly, this God is not a "lower" reality than emptiness because, of course, being lower depends on the criteria of a given context, not an objective truth. That is, its value is based on the pragmatic results or emancipatory functions it serves for an individual or community at a specific time, in the way it functions to overcome egocentrism and dissociation. It is with this logic that Ferrer challenges the structure of predetermined paths and sectarian hierarchies within a scripted Buddhist universe, and with this he offers a challenge to the assumptions of so-called "nonsectarian" traditions of Buddhist Tibet. However, the logic that drives his argument is precisely the logic of interdependence (or context-dependence), and this again can be seen as a Buddhist position.

Moreover, Ferrer's notions of the *dissociation-test* and *eco-social-political test* are also not foreign to a Buddhist worldview, but grow out of the notion of the *Bodhisattva.* Indeed, he articulates his own updated version of the *Bodhisattva* vow to engage the world that he calls "the integrated bodhisattva vow." With this he describes a commitment to cultivate fully the integrated dimensions of heart and mind, and not neglect the horizontal "breadth" of one's living body (e.g., the emotional, energetic and somatic dimensions) and world (e.g., the social, political and ecological dimensions) while vertically ascending the "heights" (and depths) of cognitive development (Ferrer 2011b, 16–19). In this light,

8. See Makransky 2008 for a defence of Buddhist inclusivism that sustains multiple ends for different religious traditions, but asserts a distinctive Buddhist end (for its distinct path).

Ferrer can be seen as a "Buddhist modernist," or rather, as offering a critical and constructive version of Buddhism for Northwestern European cultural traditions of the twenty-first century.[9]

The strengths of Ferrer's contribution are that he brings traditional religious systems, and Buddhism in particular, into conversation with the concerns of the contemporary world, a world that is not bound to the singular narrative of one premodern ethos, but which resonates with a multiplicity of voices – feminist and historical, empirical and theoretical, hermeneutic and scientific, mystical and secular, Hindu and Muslim. Yet Ferrer can be seen to clearly be drawing from Buddhist principles: emptiness (with his notion of an undetermined ultimate), interdependence (with his emphasis on context-dependence for evaluating normative values), no-self (which he formulates in the *egocentricism test*) and the *Bodhisattva* ideal (which he reformulates in the *dissociation* and *eco-social-political tests*). In this light, Ferrer is doing nothing more (and nothing less) than offering an updated version of Buddhism, a global Buddhism. Nonetheless, his most significant contribution may be in illustrating what a "nonsectarian" stance might look like in a contemporary, religiously diverse world. While doing so, he shows us what is lost, and what is gained, if we adopt such a truly "nonsectarian" or pluralist stance: what we stand to lose is our particular version of a determinate ultimate truth and a fixed referent of what the end religious goal looks like; what we stand to gain is the real possibility of a transformative dialogue with different traditions, and a new, open relation to the world, ourselves and each other.

Acknowledgements

Previously published in 2014 as "How Nonsectarian is 'Nonsectarian'?: Jorge Ferrer's Pluralist Alternative to Tibetan Buddhist Inclusivism." *Sophia* 53(3): 339–348.

References

Cabezón José. 1992. *A Dose of Emptiness: An Annotated Translation of the sTong thun chen mo of mKhas grub dGe legs dpal bzang.* Albany, NY: State University of New York Press.

Callahan, Elizabeth. 2007. *The Treasury of Philosophy: Frameworks of Buddhist Philosophy.* Ithaca: Snow Lion.

Deleuze, Gilles and Felix Guattari. 1987. *A Thousand Plateaus: Capitalism and Schizophrenia.* trans. Brain Massumi. Minneapolis, MN: University of Minnesota Press.

9. A similar project to reconstruct a modern Buddhist stance toward religious others is taken up in Vélez de Cea 2013.

Doctor, Thomas. 2004. *Speech of Delight: Mipham's Commentary on Śāntarakṣita's Ornament of the Middle Way.* Ithaca, N.Y.: Snow Lion.

Duckworth, Douglas. 2008. *Mipam on Buddha-Nature.* Albany, NY: State University of New York Press.

Ferrer, Jorge. 2011. "Participatory Spirituality and Transpersonal Theory: A Ten-Year Retrospective." *Journal of Transpersonal Psychology* 43(1): 1–34.

_____. 2011. "Participation, Metaphysics, and Enlightenment: Reflections on Ken Wilber's Recent Work." *Transpersonal Psychology Review* 14(2): 3–24.

_____. 2008. "Spiritual Knowing as Participatory Enaction." In *The Participatory Turn: Spirituality, Mysticism, Religious studies*, edited by Jorge Ferrer and Jacob Sherman, 135–169. Albany, NY: State University of New York Press.

_____. 2002. *Revisioning Transpersonal Theory: A Participatory Vision of Human Spirituality.* Albany, NY: State University of New York Press.

Getsé Paṇchen (*dge rtse paṇ chen, 'gyur med tshe dbang mchog grub*, 1761-1829). 2001. *Ornament of Buddha-Nature: A Discourse Ascertaining the Manner of the Definitive Meaning Middle Way* (*nges don dbu ma chen po'i tshul rnam par nges pa'i gtam bde gshegs snying po'i rgyan*). Collected Works, vol. 1, 75–104. Chengdu, China: People's Press.

Heim, S. Mark. 1995. *Salvations: Truth and Difference in Religion.* Mary Knoll, NY: Orbis.

Hick, John. 1989. *An Interpretation of Religion.* New Haven, CT: Yale University Press. https://doi.org/10.1057/9780230371286

Kiblinger, Kristen. 2005. *Buddhist Inclusivism: Attitudes Toward Religious Others.* Farnham: Ashgate.

Kongtrül (*kong sprul blo gros mtha' yas,* 1813–1899). 2002. *Encyclopedia of Knowledge* (*shes bya kun khyab*). Beijing, China: Nationalities Press.

Lochen Dharmaśrī (*lo chen dharmaśrī,* 1654-1717). n.d. *Cluster of Supreme Intentions: Commentary on "Ascertaining the Three Vows"* (*sdom pa gsum rnam par nges pa'i 'grel pa legs bshad ngo mtshar dpag bsam gyi snye ma*). Bylakuppe, India: Ngagyur Nyingma Institute.

Makransky, John. 2008. "Buddhist Inclusivism: Reflections Toward a Contemporary Theology of Religions." In *Buddhist Attitudes To Other Religions,* edited by Perry Schmidt-Leukel, 47–68. Germany: EOS.

Mipam (*'ju mi pham rgya mtsho,* 1846-1912). 1990. *Words That Delight Guru Mañjughoṣa: Commentary on the 'Ornament of the Middle Way'* (*dbu ma rgyan gyi rnam bshad 'jam byangs bla ma dgyes pa'i zhal lung*). Published in *dbu ma rgyan rtsa 'grel.* Sichuan, China: Nationalities Press.

Mipam. 1997. *Beacon of Certainty* (*nges shes sgron me*). *nges shes sgron me rtsa 'grel,* 1–54. Sichuan, China: Nationalities Press.

Pettit, John. 1999. *Mipham's Beacon of Certainty.* Boston: Wisdom.

Vélez de Cea, J. Abraham. 2013. *The Buddha and Religious Diversity.* Abingdon: Routledge. https://doi.org/10.4324/9780203072639

Wittgenstein, Ludwig. 1922 [1921]. *Tractatus Logico-Philosophicus.* Translated by Frank P. Ramsey and Charles Kay Ogden. London: Kegan Paul.

8

Buddhism and Beyond: The Question of Pluralism

Douglas S. Duckworth

Temple University

Douglas Duckworth is Professor at Temple University and the Director of Graduate Studies in the Department of Religion. He is the author of *Mipam on Buddha-Nature: The Ground of the Nyingma Tradition* (State University of New York 2008) and *Jamgön Mipam: His Life and Teachings* (Shambhala 2011). He also introduced and translated Distinguishing the *Views and Philosophies: Illuminating Emptiness in a Twentieth-Century Tibetan Buddhist Classic by Bötrül* (State University of New York 2011). His latest works include *Tibetan Buddhist Philosophy of Mind and Nature* (Oxford University Press 2019) and a translation of an overview of the Wisdom Chapter of the *Way of the Bodhisattva* by Künzang Sönam, entitled *The Profound Reality of Interdependence* (Oxford University Press 2019).

Introduction

This paper discusses Buddhist responses to religious diversity. I use the logical form of the tetralemma made famous by Nāgārjuna to clarify the ways that Buddhists can be seen to relate to other religions. With four alternatives, I discuss Buddhist claims to truth in terms of their being singularly absolute, one among many, both and neither. As is evident in the presence of the third and fourth alternatives of the tetralemma, rigid dichotomies (like one and many, exclusivism and pluralism) are often false, for both (and neither) are live options. Yet typologies like these can be useful to clarify distinctions, particularly when situating Buddhist claims in light of those of other religions.

A key difference I draw out rests on the interpretation of ultimate truth, and in particular, whether the ultimate truth of emptiness is interpreted as a claim to the *indeterminate* nature of reality or its *undetermined* nature. In drawing this distinction between the *indeterminate* and the *undetermined*, I take a cue from Jorge Ferrer, who prefers the latter term "to invoke the sense of not-knowing and intellectual humility."[1] In contrast to a certain claim of indeterminacy, the undetermined is not enframed by a determinate judgment. Rather, the undetermined involves a participatory attitude of openness, and a healthy suspicion of preconceptions that determine and delimit the ultimate truth. Thus, the *undetermined* refers not so much to a descriptive truth claim but rather to a comportment to the world – one of humility and openness.

In parallel with this distinction between openness and certainty, I also spell out differences between claims and attitudes in an example from Tibetan traditions, with reference to the so-called "nonsectarian" (*ris med*) movement in particular. Following Abraham Vélez de Cea, I argue that there is an important distinction to be made between a *claim* and an *attitude*;[2] whereas a claim is necessarily exclusive (for in affirming one thing, the counter claim is denied), for an attitude, this need not be the case. I wish to argue that the difference between claims and attitudes can help clarify what it means to be "nonsectarian," and thereby articulate the difference between maintaining an exclusively Buddhist claim and having an attitude that reaches beyond Buddhism.

Four alternatives

According to Nāgārjuna, emptiness is the nature of things and the highest truth (*paramārtha*). The closer we look to find the nature of things like a self, the further they pass beyond our reach. Nothing can be pinned down, and this emptiness is the way things are, for all things in time and space – including self and other – have fuzzy boundaries that defy identification within discrete kinds.

Stemming from an interpretation of Nāgārjuna that affirms ultimate truth as the determinate nature of things being empty, the Geluk (*dge lugs*) tradition of Tibet makes an explicit claim to Buddhist exclusivism. In this tradition, until one has identified the object of negation – that is, determined emptiness to be simply the lack of intrinsic nature of things and thereby "found" in the absence of intrinsic nature – there is no liberation. Following Tsongkhapa, the Geluk school champions a unique view of Prāsaṅgika-Madhyamaka that it holds to be not only the supreme

1. Ferrer makes the following claim that draws this distinction clearly: "Rather than affirming negatively (as the term indeterminate does), "undetermined" leaves open the possibility of both determinacy and indeterminacy within the mystery (as well as the paradoxical confluence or even identity of these two apparent accounts), simply suggesting that the genuinely creative qualities of the mystery cannot be determined a priori" (Ferrer 2008, 168n63).

2. For a summary of these differences, see Vélez de Cea 2013, 222–225.

philosophical view, but the only correct view through which *Nirvāna* is possible (see for example, Cabezón 1992, 217). This exclusivist position is one widely held in Tibet's most popular tradition.

As with other exclusivist traditions, the Geluk school claims an ultimate truth that is singularly framed within its own tradition.[3] That is, reality is predetermined in a way circumscribed by Buddhist doctrine *necessarily and exclusively*. As long as one sees the world otherwise, one is confused. This is a claim of Buddhist absolutism, or closure, regarding the nature of an incontrovertible, ultimate truth. That is, to say things are empty is to make a clear claim about what ultimate reality is (empty) and what it is not (an independent truth). This kind of claim represents an exclusivist paradigm of truth, the first lemma of our tetralemma.

In contrast to the singularity of truth claims in exclusivism, I will now outline a pluralist position that affirms the truth of "many" as opposed to the exclusivist "one" in the second alternative of the tetralemma. But the pluralism I sketch here is not the masked singularity of neo-Kantians like John Hick, who affirm that all religions represent merely phenomenal differences of the noumenal "One." Rather than the veiled exclusivism of this kind of inclusivism,[4] this version of pluralism takes seriously the *distinctiveness* of each religion's claims, including the distinctiveness of the Buddhist claim of emptiness (or indeterminacy) of things, and the distinctive results (e.g., *Nirvāṇa*) that arise exclusively from a Buddhist path of understanding this truth.[5]

In outlining a pluralist position, I want to draw upon the important distinction between the meaning of the ultimate truth of emptiness as *indeterminate* in contrast to this truth as *undetermined*. The (in-) determined versus undetermined ultimate marks the difference between a closed model of truth and one that is open-ended. Unlike the indeterminate ultimate (e.g., the emptiness of emptiness, which is a certain truth), the undetermined is not determined in any way; an undetermined ultimate is thus different from the certain truth of emptiness. That is to say, it is

3. An important character of Buddhist claims is that they articulate "beliefs" or "views" (*dṛṣṭi*) that are episodic; that is, beliefs do not endure but take place in a momentary mental event (*caitta*) of a mental continuum.

4. This kind of interpretation exemplifies a strategy of marginalization typical of inclusivism, fitting other views neatly within one's own hierarchical schemes of truth. That is, this kind of model lays out a picture that predetermines the way that opposing views fit into one's own framework and structures all divergent ideas into one's own, ready-made model.

5. Here I agree with John Makransky's argument for the distinctiveness of Buddhist paths and goals. See Makransky 2008, 47–49.

unbound. An undetermined ultimate is beyond determinate categories; not even emptiness can be the final word on reality because any determinate conception of anything is false. By assenting to the world as *undetermined* the ultimate remains unfinished, incomplete. Without (pre)determined claims about the ultimate, one remains *open to mystery*, to the possibilities of being. This kind of orientation to truth leaves open possibilities of transformation that a determinate claim closes off.

A Buddhist exclusivist can argue that an *un*determined ultimate is simply *under*determined, for as long as reality remains undetermined, one has not completed an analysis of reality, which will result in seeing it to be indeterminate (empty). Indeed, this is what Tsongkhapa has stated (Tsongkhapa 2005; English trans. in Hopkins 2008, 57). Emptiness (or indeterminacy) is the only ultimate truth in the exclusivist model of the Geluk tradition I sketched above, for there is no other ultimate truth to be known. The nature of things is held to be indeterminate because everything is necessarily empty – not identifiable under ontological analysis. As we see in the Geluk school, no other claim to ultimate truth is possible because any other notion will necessarily be relative, conventional and/or merely a false appearance. Yet in light of the undetermined, such determined affirmations of indeterminacy can be seen to constrain the creative potential of the ultimate.

As for the third lemma – that of both – we may wonder how it is possible for there to be common ground between exclusivist and pluralist positions. Firstly, affirming both need not entail a performative contradiction for there can be an analytic "certainty" of an undetermined ultimate akin to that of "finding" indeterminacy. As Anne Klein and Tenzin Wangyel remark, "Ontological undecidability does not preclude epistemological certainty. Indeed, one provokes the other, since the clearer one is about the open, unfettered, and indefinable nature of reality, the more confidence one has in it" (Klein and Wangyel 2006, 72). In other words, the more you understand the lack of any determinate essence in things, the more certainty you have in this indeterminate nature. Thus, the indeterminate and the undetermined need not be diametrically opposed, as the ultimate truth can be both determinate (in terms of what it is not) and undetermined (in terms of what it is), without conflict.

A common ground of the determined and the undetermined can also be laid out through contextual distinctions. We see this put forward in the work of Mipam (1846–1912), who outlined two contexts for making claims based on meditative equipoise and post-meditation. In the context of the former, no claims are made in accord with the orientation of meditative equipoise, unstructured by thought. In the latter context, actions are clearly delimited as ethical and unethical in accord with the orientation of discursive post-meditative states, where emptiness is also held to be a determinate absence (see Mipam 1982a, 487; Longchenpa 1996, 1164–1167; see also Duckworth 2008, 28–39).

In this way, the bivocality of the determined and undetermined can be split between distinctive analytic and meditative contexts. Indeed, there are clear differences between a Buddhist claim and the claims of others in contexts enframed by discursive analysis, where "all things conditioned are impermanent" for a Buddhist, and "all things contaminated are suffering." Yet in meditative equipoise and discourse in accord with it, such distinctive Buddhist claims can be left behind, along with differences (and similarities) with other traditions.[6] What remains can be simply undetermined, no more (and no less) than an open attitude or receptive orientation.

This brings us to the last of the four lemmas – that of neither. Since the ultimate is not tethered to categories of thought, it is open-ended and unbound; there is no room for a pluralist claim, needless to mention an exclusivist one, because without any assertions or identities to which one stakes claim, there are no "others" to define oneself against. Since the identities of "self" and "other" rise and fall together, there are not only no real differences, but no real similarities between Buddhist and non-Buddhist identities, either.[7] This can be understood as pointing to the all-embracing silence of the Buddha, enacted as the view in accord with meditative equipoise.

Buddhist alternatives

In contrast to the either-or logic of theological categories like exclusivism and pluralism, the tetralemma makes room for hybrids and abstentions. It thus can be helpful to extend the Christian-inspired model of exclusivism versus pluralism, particularly since these categories derive from only a claim about a result – whether someone is "saved" or not. Along with the

6. In contrast, in the Geluk tradition, the view of emptiness, determined as a lack of intrinsic existence, is to be cultivated in meditation as well. In this tradition, emptiness that is known conceptually is the same as that which is known directly in meditative equipoise, so there is only ultimate indeterminacy here (nothing undetermined) across the contexts of meditation and post-meditation - thus their singular voice of exclusivism. See Tsongkhapa 2005, 358; English trans. in Hopkins 2008, 142–143. See also, Thupten Jinpa 2002, 202–203n71.

7. Since all identities and differences are contingent constructions, real identity for a Buddhist is not even a lack of identity (so despite lacking any real religious identity, Buddhists should not be confused with the religiously unaffiliated – "the nones").

categories of both and neither from the tetralemma, we can supplement this dichotomous, teleological model with other markers of identity and difference drawn from Buddhists traditions.

In addition to distinctions among traditions in terms of claims to distinct results, the fourteenth-century Nyingma scholar, Longchenpa (1308–1364) also described differences in terms of: (1) refuge; (2) view; (3) meditation; and (4) action (Longchenpa 1996, 922–926). Thus, rather than a Christian-based model built around the result of salvation, a Buddhist framework of view, meditation and action is another way to frame religious diversity. This schema is a way that Buddhists like Longchenpa have drawn distinctions not only between Buddhist and non-Buddhist traditions, but among Buddhist traditions as well.

Along with differences in results, *actions* can also offer clear pragmatic markers of identity: manifestly violent and destructive, caring and benevolent, and so forth. Moreover, actions are inextricably tied to results and intentions in a Buddhist theory of *karma*, so results cannot be separated from the actions that are their causes. Additionally, actions are an extension of a *view*; that is, actions not only express a way of being (e.g., a view of the world can lead to an act of generosity), but can elicit a way of seeing the world (e.g., an act of generosity can lead to being less ego-centered). Thus, a view is intertwined with expressions in action, as an ethic stems from an ethos.

Meditation, yet another category of demarcation, refers to the process of internalizing a view, assimilating a way of seeing and being in the world through cultivating it in practice. Meditation is thus symbiotically related to view (ethos) and action (ethics), too; it can both elicit a view on one hand and express it on the other. As with the difference in the claims of a determinate and undetermined view, we can also see a difference in meditations structured by determinate objects on the one hand, and on the other, those that are oriented to be undetermined and objectless, without any explicit goal-directed effort.[8] Undirected (but not necessarily aimless) meditations represent an attitude of openness, as opposed to directed meditations with determinate (and predetermined) aims.

Refuge, another marker of Buddhist identity, is also tied to a view (e.g., views of suffering and the possibility of freedom). Yet as with any identity marker, when torn away from the networks in which it is embedded - those that involve the interconnected scaffolding of view, meditation, action and

8. In the Nyingma tradition, for instance, Mipam argued that the Great Perfection (*rdzogs chen*) is more profound than the completion stage of the *Kālacakra* because it is enacted without as much effort. See Mipam 1987b.

result – in isolation it is likely to be tied as much to acts of violence as it is to group cohesion.[9] This is because – as Amartya Sen has shown in his book, *Identity and Violence* – absolute, singular religious identities manifest as stark reminders of how these kinds of one-dimensional markers not only serve to shape communities, but also to exclude others and perpetuate violence (See Sen 2006). This fact is particularly pertinent today as we continue to see people kill each other under the banner of a narrowly conceived religious identity.

We cannot expect to extract from any tradition a single element, like refuge (a starting point among Buddhists) or salvation (the result among Christians), and presume that this marker will alone be sufficient to represent any other tradition that does not share the assumptions of the tradition in which this element is embedded. Rather, we are in a better position to appreciate other traditions - to learn about them and from them - when we can consider their complexity and see how a constellation of elements (such as view, meditation, action and results) are interconnected. With an exclusive focus on one ingredient – as in the case with the litmus tests of refuge (in Buddhism) or salvation (motivating the Christian-inspired categories of pluralism, inclusivism and exclusivism) – we court violence, and confine ourselves to view the world through a monochromatic lens.

Nonsectarian attitude

A nonsectarian attitude within Tibetan Buddhist traditions can be generally characterized as an impulse to engage with a variety of traditions in contrast to an insular model that only deals with texts and interpretations within the confines of one's own tradition. This impulse was stimulated in the nineteenth and twentieth centuries in eastern Tibet, when several lineages were marginalized due to the overwhelming hegemony of the Geluk tradition. But this is not something new to the nineteenth and twentieth centuries; it is exemplified in Buddhist scholarship and practice from early times, and goes beyond Tibet to Buddhism in India, as Buddhists like Śāntarakṣita, Śāntideva, Dharmakīrti, Nāgārjuna and Śākyamuni himself were engaged in a conversation outside of the narrow confines of their own bounded "Buddhist" tradition. Nonsectarianism has also become a dominant force beyond the nineteenth century among Tibetan Buddhists living in and outside of Tibet, in the twentieth and into the twenty-first

9. Exemplifying the simplistic tendency of singular identification, Donald Lopez, on the first page of his introduction to Buddhism in the *Norton Anthology of World Religions* (Lopez 2015), laconically remarks that "Someone who says three times, "I go for refuge to the Buddha, I go for refuge to the dharma. I go for refuge to the sangha," is a Buddhist."

centuries.

To adopt the label "nonsectarian" casually invites the danger of absolute tolerance, with the result that an idealized *rimé* (nonsectarian) becomes realized as a spineless *rumé* (boneless).[10] Hans Küng has described "the problem of an easy, cheap tolerance in Buddhism." And Hakamaya Noriaki, within the Critical Buddhism movement in Japan, has argued that "Buddhists should not give in to a compromising and mushy "tolerance" that uncritically accepts all things." Sir Charles Eliot also said that Buddhism is "dangerously tolerant" and that "their courteous acquiescence in other creeds enfeebles [...] their own" (cited in Kiblinger 2006, 3). What does "nonsectarian" mean for a Buddhist? Do only Buddhist traditions fall under the label of "nonsectarian"? Only Tibetan Buddhists? If Buddhism is a sect, is it not a contradiction in terms to say "nonsectarian Buddhist"? And if Buddhism is not a sect, then what is it? What is at stake in defining "nonsectarian" in this context is not only the nature of defining nonsectarianism, but in defining the nature of Buddhism, as well.

While the so-called "nonsectarian movement," stemming from eastern Tibet in the nineteenth and twentieth centuries, was sparked in a large part as a response to the dominance of the Geluk tradition on the Tibetan plateau since the seventeenth century, there are a range of responses to the hegemony of the Geluk tradition. While at times, the diversity of these responses has been all uncritically heaped into a single "nonsectarian" movement, it can be helpful to distinguish the differences among these responses to Geluk dominance: (1) one response is to hostilely reject the Geluk tradition, as we see modelled in the critiques of Tsongkhapa by Gorampa in the Sakya tradition; (2) another is to ignore the Geluk tradition, which can be done in a number of ways, too. One way to do this is to go back to the Indian classics, as we see in the renaissance movement in Tibet that looked to Indian Buddhist texts while ignoring the Tibetan sectarian disputes around them (like we see in Khenpo Shenga's interlinear commentaries on the "13 Great Treatises," that is taken up in the curriculum in prominent monastic colleges in the Kagyü and Sakya traditions) (See Duckworth 2008).

A third way is (3) to frame what is of highest value in another's tradition as merely a provisional teaching, a stepping stone to arrive at the real truth that is found in one's own tradition. This inclusivist move, common to many Mahāyāna Buddhist traditions, is adopted by Jamgön Kongtrül, and shapes his response to the Geluk tradition that inspired much of the "nonsectarian" movement. Another way is (4) to appropriate elements from

10. This is a play on the Tibetan words for "nonsectarian" and "boneless" (i.e., spineless relativism), respectively.

the Geluk tradition into one's own. That is, to assimilate the successes of the Geluk school in terms of *sūtra* scholarship and institutional structure by creating large monastic colleges and making a move toward a formalized curriculum. This distinctive approach is exemplified in the rise of monastic colleges initiated at Dzokchen monastery in the nineteenth century (Duckworth 2008). Importantly, this way permits a new expression of the Buddhist tradition to take shape out of a dialogue with another tradition. It is this model – as a model that embraces a transformative dialogue across traditions – that embodies what is best about a pluralistic, or cross-cultural, conversation.

A question we can ask about the nature of a "nonsectarian" identity among contemporary Tibetan Buddhists is: "how nonsectarian is nonsectarian?" That is, is there a sectarian boundary around the nonsectarian tradition so that it is only Tibetan Buddhists? Or Buddhists? In the last sixty years, to an unprecedented extent Tibetans have come face-to-face with Buddhists of other places, practices and traditions. As the twentieth century has brought Tibetan Buddhism into conversation with a diversity of religions of the world, Tibetan Buddhists around the world have been confronted with Christians, Jews, Muslims and Hindus. How does a nonsectarian respond to these religious "others"? This is an important question for Buddhists in the present and future and for those interested in the meaning of nonsectarianism.

The question of nonsectarianism no longer just pertains to the relations among Buddhist sects in Tibet, but to relations among a diversity of religious views. Being "nonsectarian" thus means something different now than it did in nineteenth-century Tibet. Now, we are confronted with questions like: is Buddhism exclusivist – such that there is no liberation other than through Buddhism? After all, even the Dalai Lama, who draws upon a variety of world religions, has said that *Nirvāna* can only be achieved through realizing the Prāsaṅgika-Madhyamaka view. Putting a Buddhist twist on the Gospel of John, a Buddhist exclusivist can imagine Candrakīrti saying: "No one gets to *Nirvāna* except through me!"

Also, we may now consider the question of whether there is anything like "anonymous Buddhists" corresponding to the "anonymous Christians" Karl Rahner has popularized for Christianity. An "anonymous Christian" is a term a Christian can use to include the noble "pagans," who live in places like Tibet and can be saved even though they have never heard about Jesus. It may be that there are anonymous Buddhists after all in Mahāyāna (most of it anyway), because everyone has buddha-nature whether they realize it or not. So, it seems that a Buddhist might be understood as an inclusivist rather than exclusivist, for although there are many religious paths, they all lead to the same goal. This is widely claimed in Mahāyāna: we are all aboard the *ekayāna* or "one vehicle" to Buddhahood. This still leaves the question open as to whether the practices of religious Jews are part of the one vehicle, too, and what about the practices of Muslims?

Can Buddhism also be a form of religious pluralism, such that there are many goals just as there are many paths? A Buddhist pluralist stance has the advantage of acknowledging the role of causality—*karma*—in that you reap what you sow and don't get something for nothing. It also gives an opportunity to discover new insights from other traditions and not just find truths from others that are already found in one's home tradition. But how is pluralism to be distinguished from relativism, where "anything goes"? Where is one to draw the line between right and wrong view?

One way is to appeal to ethics: despite whether someone practices the Great Perfection, Mahāmudrā, Vipassanā, Zen, Christianity, or Śaivism, and whatever is claimed about the ultimate truth in the end, if the practice leads someone to be less egotistical (lessens the afflictions) and to be engaged with the world in a positive way – socially, politically and ecologically – then it is a viable path; if not, then it is excluded (Ferrer 2008, Duckworth 2014). This is one way to demarcate what is acceptable and what is not, but whatever the criteria, I feel it is important for "the *rimépa*-s" (nonsectarian ones) to distinguish their Buddhist tradition from the relativists "the *rumépa*-s" (spineless ones), while at the same time, not be arbitrary about the criteria for inclusion and exclusion, us and them (as insiders and outsiders, Buddhists and non-Buddhists)—by acknowledging other traditions and engaging them.

I propose that a way this distinction can be responsibly maintained is by demarcating between *claims* and *attitudes*. Before concluding, I will show how this can be done with reference in particular to the so-called "nonsectarian" (*ris med*) movement in Buddhist Tibet. As I mentioned above, the "nonsectarian movement" is porous and internally diverse; the cohesion of this category can even be cynically (and paradoxically) defined by a shared rejection of the Geluk tradition. Yet what it means to be "nonsectarian" can be positively characterized by the impulse to engage with a variety of traditions – an attitude of openness – in contrast to an insular stance that only deals with texts and interpretations within the confines of one's own tradition. The exclusivism that came to characterize the Geluk school, in terms of not just claims but in attitude toward non-Geluk traditions, contrasts sharply with the attitude of openness that is the normative ideal of this movement.

The attitude of openness that characterizes a nonsectarian ethos rallies around the Great Perfection, a tradition with a view that can be characterized as undetermined and a meditation that is not explicitly goal-oriented. The Geluk tradition, in contrast, represents the opposite end of the spectrum, with claims to the ultimate that are closed and determined, and meditations that are explicitly directed toward the apprehension of this determinate ultimate truth.

Despite this difference, and the fact that the Great Perfection stems from another tradition (the Nyingma), the Fourteenth Dalai Lama (the *de facto* head of the Geluk school) has embraced the Great Perfection in contrast to other influential Geluk scholars, such as Pabongka (1878–1941), who have sharply criticized and distanced their own tradition from it. Pabongka, and the sectarian political movement that he has inspired that continues to stage protests at the Dalai Lama's public appearances,[11] exemplifies an exclusivist attitude toward other traditions (in addition to exclusivist claims). In contrast, the Dalai Lama (while maintaining exclusivist claims) represents an attitude of openness to others that is the ideal of what can be called a "nonsectarian attitude,"[12] a sincere receptivity toward others and the world, including those who hold conflicting claims from one's own. This kind of attitude or orientation to the world is rarely actualized within any tradition, "non-sectarian" or not.[13]

A nonsectarian attitude (not to be confused with a pluralist claim) embraces the transformative possibilities of dialogue across traditions. This kind of attitude instantiates what Francis Clooney called "deep learning";[14] that is, learning that is not simply framed within a single tradition's preconception of truth. A nonsectarian attitude need not assent to the validity of a plurality of conflicting claims – such as a claim to a non-empty, determinate essence of self or things. Rather, through a comportment to the world characterized by intellectual humility and openness, it enables possibilities that are precluded by predetermined claims. A nonsectarian *attitude* is thus open and undetermined.

11. See chapter on "Pabongka Rinpoche and Fundamentalism" in The Dolgyal Shugden Research Society 2014.

12. I prefer the terms *nonsectarian* to *pluralist* to describe this attitude because pluralism is still hinged to the dichotomy of many versus one, whereas "nonsectarian" (as a simple negation) is more radically open.

13. The Dalai Lama's appropriations of science can be seen to instantiate this openness to transformation, particularly in his remarks questioning the traditional Buddhist cosmology of Mount Meru. He has even said that if science can prove that a Buddhist claim is not true, Buddhists should reject that claim. See Dalai Lama 2005, 3.

14. I borrow this term from Clooney 2010.

Conclusion

As we can learn from a Christian-inspired lens of relating to religious others, we can take a lesson from Buddhist traditions in negotiating diverse religious identities as well. On the one hand, Buddhists like Nāgārjuna have shown us that identities are only ever contingent, so there is no real identity or difference. By acknowledging the fluid, contextual nature of identity, we can let go of the grip of rigid identities and absolute differences between traditions. Moreover, we can come to understand traditions as complex networks of ideas and practices that are not reducible to any single element in isolation, and thereby see more clearly the hybrid constructions and internal diversity within traditions, sects and even individuals.

Furthermore, as we see in the case of the Dalai Lama, a nonsectarian attitude need not be a pluralist claim, for an attitude reflects the way a tradition responds to others, how we encounter others rather than what we say or believe. A nonsectarian attitude need not compromise an exclusivist claim, including the claim to the universality of emptiness (understood as either a certain, determinate absence or as an undetermined reality). This kind of attitude enables us to learn from others regardless of whether their claims are compatible with our own. In contrast to the insular attitude of exclusion, a nonsectarian attitude acknowledges the value of others as others, and thus enables not only learning about other traditions, but learning from them. This attitude, modelled on dialogue rather than monologue, sustains an open-ended and unfinished orientation to the world—one that allows the world and its mysteries to continue to unfold in unexpected and transformative ways.

References

Cabezón, José. 1992. *A Dose of Emptiness.* Albany, NY: State University of New York Press.

Clooney, Francis. 2010. *Comparative Theology: Deep Learning Across Theological Borders.* West Sussex, UK: Wiley-Blackwell. https://doi.org/10.1002/9781444318951

Dalai Lama. 2005. *The Universe in a Single Atom: The Convergence of Science and Spirituality.* New York: Morgan Road.

The Dolgyal Shugden Research Society. 2014. *Dolgyal Shugden: A History.* New York: Tibet House.

Duckworth, Douglas. 2014. "How Nonsectarian is 'Nonsectarian'?: Jorge Ferrer's Pluralist Alternative to Tibetan Buddhist Inclusivism." *Sophia* 53(3): 339–348. https://doi.org/10.1007/s11841-013-0398-5

Duckworth, Douglas. 2008. *Mipam on Buddha-Nature.* Albany, NY: State University of New York Press.

Ferrer, Jorge N. 2008. "Spiritual Knowing as Participatory Enaction." In *The Participatory Turn: Spirituality, Mysticism, Religious studies*, edited by Jorge N. Ferrer and Jacob Sherman, 135–169. Albany, NY: State University of New York Press.

Hopkins, Jeffrey. 2008. *Tsong-kha-pa's Final Exposition of Wisdom.* Ithaca, NY: Snow Lion.

Kiblinger, Kristin Beise. 2005. *Buddhist Inclusivism: Attitudes Towards Religious Others.* Farnham: Ashgate.

Klein, Anne and Tenzin Wangyal. 2006. *Unbounded Wholeness: Dzogchen, Bon, and the Logic of the Nonconceptual.* Oxford: Oxford University Press. https://doi.org/10.1093/0195178491.001.0001

Longchenpa. 1996. *White Lotus: Autocommentary of the* Precious Wish-Fulfilling Treasury (*theg pa chen po'i man ngag gi bstan bcos yid bzhin rin po che'i mdzod kyi 'grel pa padma dkar po*). In *Seven Treasuries* (*mdzod bdun*), Volume 7, 139–1544. Sichuan: Tarthang Tulku.

Lopez, Donald, ed. 2015. *Norton's Anthology of Buddhism.* New York: W. W. Norton.

Makransky, John. 2008. "Buddhist Inclusivism: Reflections Toward a Contemporary Theology of Religions." In *Buddhist Attitudes Toward Other Religions,* edited by Perry Schmidt-Leukel, 47–68. Germany: EOS.

Mipam. 1987a. *Concise Summary of the Philosophical Systems in the Precious Wish-Fulfilling Treasury* (*yid bzhin mdzod kyi grub mtha' bsdus pa*). In *Collected Works* (Dilgo Khyentsé's expanded redaction of *sde dge edition*), Volume 21, 439–500.

———. 1987b. *Intelligent Presence* (*gnyug sems 'od gsal ba'i don la dpyad pa rdzogs pa chen po gzhi lam 'gras bu'i shan 'byed blo gros snang ba*). Mipam's *Collected Works* (Dilgo Khyentsé's expanded redaction of *sde dge edition*), Volume 24, 411–566.

Sen, Amartya. 2006. *Identity and Violence: The Illusion of Destiny.* New York: W. W. Norton.

Thupten Jinpa. 2002. *Self, Reality, and Reason in Tibetan Philosophy.* London: RoutledgeCurzon.

Tsongkhapa. 2005. *Middling Stages of the Path* (*lam rim 'bring*). Bylakuppe, India: Sera Je Library.

Vélez de Cea, Abraham. 2013. *The Buddha and Religious Diversity.* Abingdon: Routledge. https://doi.org/10.4324/9780203072639

9

The Dalai Lama and Religious Diversity

Abraham Vélez de Cea
Eastern Kentucky University

Born in Saragossa, Spain, Dr. **J. Abraham Vélez de Cea** is professor of Buddhism and World Religions at Eastern Kentucky University. He came to the US in 2002. Before joining Eastern Kentucky University in 2006, he taught Buddhism, Buddhist Ethics, and Buddhist-Christian Mysticism in the department of theology at Georgetown University. He is the author of *The Buddha and Religious Diversity* (Routledge, 2013), which discusses the Buddha's attitude towards religious diversity in conversation with Christian theology of religions. He is currently working on a book about multiple religious belonging and the possibility of being both a disciple of Buddha and Jesus.

The Dalai Lama's model of religious diversity

In his book *Towards True Kinship of Faiths: How the World's Religions Can Come Together*, His Holiness the XIVth Dalai Lama explains some of the main teachings of Hinduism, Christianity, Islam and Judaism. He also compares the basic teachings of these religions to Buddhism. He suggests that the ethics of all religions is compassion-centred, and that this is a "tremendous shared resource." For the Dalai Lama, universal compassion is the ultimate ideal of all religions. Religions can be a source of good for this planet, and they "can help overcome prejudices, deal with conflicts, and give succor for the poor and the week" (Dalai Lama 2010, 128). The ideal of interreligious harmony is, for the Dalai Lama, possible, but it must be based on mutual understanding and the explicit recognition of real differences. Religious diversity is a good thing given the variety of human predispositions. From a theistic perspective, the Dalai Lama says that differences among the religions represent the beauty of God's infinite wisdom, and, from a non-theistic perspective, the richness of the human spirit.

In order to achieve the ideal of interreligious harmony and promote mutual understanding and recognition of real differences, the Dalai Lama proposes four types of interreligious dialogue: (1) dialogue among scholars of religions at the academic level, which focusses on doctrinal similarities and differences with emphasis on the purpose of religions; (2) dialogue among genuine spiritual practitioners about deep religious experiences; (3) dialogue among leaders of religions to speak and pray from one common platform; (4) joint participation in pilgrimages to holy sites and rites of other religions.

Besides advocating interreligious dialogue based on mutual understanding and the explicit recognition of real differences, the Dalai Lama calls for "the emergence of a genuine spirit of religious pluralism" (Dalai Lama 2010, 146). The Dalai Lama tries to reconcile the tension that many people perceive between deep commitment to one's own tradition and acceptance of other religions as legitimate. The Dalai Lama explains that for many people accepting the legitimacy of other faiths somewhat compromises the integrity of their own tradition. In his words:

> a devout Buddhist may feel that acceptance of other spiritual paths as valid suggests the existence of ways other than of the Buddha toward the attainment of enlightenment. A Muslim might feel that acceptance of other traditions as legitimate would require relinquishing the belief that God's revelation to the Prophet, as recorded in the Qur'an, represents the final revelation of the highest truth. In the same vein, a Christian might feel that accepting the legitimacy of other religions would entail compromising the key belief that it is only through Jesus Christ that the way to God is found. (2010 145)

Thus, for the Dalai Lama we need to balance the acceptance of religious diversity with commitment to one's own tradition, otherwise there will not be interreligious harmony. Before advancing his proposal to achieve the aforementioned balance, the Dalai Lama discusses three basic responses to other religions, which he calls exclusivism, inclusivism and pluralism.

The Dalai Lama defines exclusivism as "a position that one's own religion is the only true religion and that rejects, as if it were by default, the legitimacy of other faith traditions." Inclusivism, on the other hand, considers other faith traditions as partially valid, "but maintains that their teachings are somehow contained within one's own traditions." The Dalai Lama acknowledges that inclusivism is more tolerant than exclusivism but equally problematic because it entails that other traditions are ultimately redundant. The Dalai Lama defines pluralism as the acceptance of other religions as valid. For the Dalai Lama, the pluralist accords validity to all faith traditions (2010, 147). This conception of pluralism does not imply relativism. Other traditions are valid as long as they are able to provide a foundation for ethical and spiritual practices, and as long as they can generate in their followers spiritual qualities such as love, compassion, simplicity, patience and forgiveness.

The Dalai Lama suggests that in order to achieve the ideal interreligious harmony we need to adopt some form of pluralism. However, not all conceptions of pluralism are acceptable. For instance, the Dalai Lama rejects the "multiple rivers" view of religious diversity because it presupposes the ultimate oneness of all religions, and this "demands a precondition that remains impossible for the majority of adherents of the world's great religions" (2010, 148). Instead, the Dalai Lama proposes a form of pluralism that recognizes and respects fundamental differences among the traditions. This recognition of diversity at a fundamental level "is not only essential but also the first step toward creating deeper understanding of each other" (Dalai Lama 2010, 148).

Another conception of pluralism that the Dalai Lama finds problematic is the one that seeks a universal religion. Whether this universal religion is a totally new religion or one of the old ones is irrelevant. For the Dalai Lama, the idea of a universal religion is "simply unfeasible" (2010, 148). First, because of the diversity of mental dispositions and spiritual inclinations, a single set of spiritual teachings will not serve everyone. Second, because of the history of religions, they are already adapted to specific cultures and environments, thus making the spread of one religion to all cultures and environments virtually impossible. Thus, a plurality of religions seems unavoidable, and accepting religious diversity is indispensable to advance the cause of peace and human happiness. Religious diversity, for the Dalai Lama, is consistent with the way things are. In contrast, the denial of religious diversity "represents a perspective that is not in accord with reality" (2010, 149).

In sum, for the Dalai Lama, in order to achieve interreligious harmony we need to practise interreligious dialogue and be pluralists in the sense of truly accepting the reality and the legitimacy of other faith traditions (2010, 149). The main reason for accepting and respecting other religions is that they serve and benefit human beings of different dispositions. More specifically, other religions "engender the beautiful qualities of the human heart and foster compassion and loving kindness – exactly the qualities one is striving to attain through one's own faith"(Dalai Lama 2010, 150).

The Dalai Lama distinguishes between three aspects of religions: (1) ethical teachings, (2) doctrines or metaphysics, and (3) cultural specifics. Among these three, ethical teachings are, for the Dalai Lama, the essence of religions. For the Dalai Lama, there is a profound convergence of the world's great religions on the level of ethical teachings. All religions share the same ethical purpose, which the Dalai Lama describes as the betterment of humanity and the creation of more compassionate and responsible human beings. The Dalai Lama claims that the ethical teachings of religions as well as the fruits of such teachings are essentially the same, namely love and compassion (2010, 151). On the level of culture and metaphysics, however, there are many differences, some of them fundamental and unbridgeable. There are differences about the concept of afterlife, the concept of well-being that takes place in the afterlife, the origin of the universe, the methods to achieve well-being in the future life, and about what exactly constitutes the ultimate truth. Any attempt to find convergence on this doctrinal and metaphysical level is, for the Dalai Lama, bound to fail (2010, 152).

For the Dalai Lama, however, the fundamental differences that exist on the doctrinal and metaphysical level have a practical purpose. In order to explain this purpose, the Dalai Lama uses "a Buddhist hermeneutical principle," namely, the concept of *upāya* or skilful means. For the Dalai Lama, the Buddha taught divergent, even contradictory teachings, depending on the context, the needs and the spiritual level of his listeners. The Dalai Lama extrapolates this understanding of the Buddha's teachings to the teachings of all religions. In the same way that the Buddha teaches many divergent and contradictory teachings depending on the needs and the capacity of his disciples, many religions teach different and even contradictory things because there are many people with diverse mental dispositions, and diverse spiritual and philosophical inclinations.

According to the Dalai Lama, the teachings of religions are like medicines. In the same way that it does not make much sense to prescribe one medicine for all kinds of illness, the idea that there should be only one religion or only one teaching for all beings is untenable. We can say "this is the best teaching" or "this is the best medicine," but always from a particular context. We cannot evaluate a teaching or a religion as "the best" independently of specific contexts: "therefore, a Buddhist cannot say, when relating to the Buddha's teaching, 'this is the best teaching,' as if one can make such evaluations independent of the specific contexts" (Dalai Lama 2010, 155). Similarly, when we talk about religions in general we have to qualify our claims of superiority and say that a religion is the best for us, but not necessarily the best for everybody. The Dalai Lama definitely believes that Buddhism is the best for him, but he does not consider Buddhism the best for all (2010, 158). Likewise, we can say that this specific medicine is the best for this particular ailment and for such and such patients, but we should never claim that it is the best medicine in absolute and universal terms independently of the context.

Rather than seeing religious diversity as a threat to one's own tradition, religious diversity should be seen as something to be embraced, appreciated and even celebrated. The Dalai Lama acknowledges that this understanding of religions as medicines and skilful means undermines the urge to convert others and leads to the acceptance of other religions as legitimate. In the Dalai Lama's words:

> understood thus, the urge to convert others to one's own faith loses its force. In its place arises a genuine acceptance of the reality of other faith traditions. Then, instead of seeing others as an aberration, or at worst as a threat, one can relate to others out of a sense of deep appreciation for their profound contribution to the world. (2010, 156)

According to the Dalai Lama, pluralists need to take seriously the concerns of exclusivists. The concern of exclusivists is that accepting other religions as legitimate may involve the relativization of the truths found in one's own religion. In order to avoid such relativization, the Dalai Lama proposes to uphold two distinct perspectives in two different contexts.

Whereas the first perspective is to be adopted in the context of individual religious practice, the second perspective is to be embraced in the context of society and religious diversity. The first perspective is called "one truth, one religion," and the second "many truths, many religions." The first perspective corresponds to the view of religious diversity held by one's own tradition, which, for the Dalai Lama, involves some form of exclusivism. In his words:

> as many religious believers feel, I would agree that some version of exclusivism—the principle of 'one truth, one religion'—lies at the heart of most of the world's great religions. Furthermore, a single-pointed commitment to one's own faith tradition demands the recognition that one's chosen faith represents the highest religious teaching. For example, for me Buddhism is the best, but this does not mean that Buddhism is the best for all. Certainly not. For millions of my fellow human beings, theistic forms of teaching represent the best path. Therefore, in the context of an individual religious practitioner, the concept of 'one truth, one religion' remains most relevant. It is this that gives the power and single-pointed focus of one's religious path. At the same time, it is critical that the religious practitioner harbors no ego-centric attachment to his faith. (2010, 158)

If I understand the Dalai Lama correctly, he seems to be suggesting that a version of exclusivism in the context of individual religious practice is not only unavoidable but also indispensable to have single-pointed commitment to one's own tradition. Whereas the first perspective in the context of individual practice is exclusivist, i.e. "one truth, one religion," the second perspective in the context of society is pluralist, i.e., "many truths, many religions." If the exclusivist perspective allows us to be committed to one's own tradition, the pluralistic perspective allows us to accept, respect and even celebrate religious diversity.

For the Dalai Lama, there is no conflict between these two seemingly contradictory perspectives:

> in the context of society, however, the concept of 'many truths, many religions' not only becomes relevant but also necessary. In fact, where there is more than one person, already the pluralistic perspective of 'many truths, many religions' becomes critical. Thus, if we relate these two seemingly contradictory perspectives to their differing contexts of society and the individual we can see no real conflict between the two. (2010, 159)

The two perspectives can be combined without contradiction because they relate to two distinct contexts, namely individual and social. Thus, by distinguishing between the exclusivist perspective of individual practice and the pluralist perspective of social relationships with other religions, the Dalai Lama is able to achieve two goals: (1) facilitating the acceptance of other religions as legitimate, and (2) avoiding the relativization of doctrinal claims that traditions consider definitive truth. In other words, the adoption of the aforementioned two perspectives fosters interreligious harmony because it balances the tension that many people feel between commitment to one's own tradition and acceptance of religious diversity.

The Dalai Lama's distinction between two perspectives also contributes to interreligious harmony because it avoids disputes on the level of doctrines and metaphysics, while promoting respect and appreciation for religions on the level of ethics and spirituality. It should be noted that the doctrines and metaphysical beliefs of one's own tradition are never relativized. Rather, such beliefs are set aside for pragmatic reasons at the social level and confined to the context of individual practice.

In order to achieve interreligious harmony, the Dalai Lama advocates three things: (1) the practice of diverse forms of interreligious dialogue; (2) keeping doctrinal and metaphysical claims outside the social context of religious diversity or the perspective of many truths, many religions; (3) acknowledging the overall common ground and positive contribution of religions on the level of ethics and spirituality. Although the Dalai Lama does not equate the individual, exclusivist perspective with the private sphere nor the social, pluralist perspective with the public sphere, in practice the doctrinal and metaphysical claims of religions are relegated to the "private" sphere of one's own community or, as the Dalai Lama puts it, to the context of individual practice (2010, 158).

The Dalai Lama concludes his discussion of the individual and social perspectives by offering two reasons for respecting religious diversity: (1) religions provide solace, spiritual development and a system of ethics for millions of people, (2) despite the doctrinal differences between religions, their teachings ground the ethical conduct of their followers in strikingly parallel and praiseworthy ways.

The Dalai Lama acknowledges that in order to uphold the two perspectives with integrity we need a creative approach. As an instance of this creative approach, the Dalai Lama speaks about two complementary attitudes: faith and respect. Faith relates to cognitive states such as "belief" as well as to affective states such as "trust" and "confidence." Respect, on the other hand, relates to mental states such as "appreciation" and "reverence." The Dalai Lama explains that in the Sanskrit Buddhist tradition faith and respect are interrelated (2010, 161). The term faith (*śraddhā*) can be understood as having three senses: admiration, conviction and emulation. Faith in the sense of admiration is similar to respect or reverence, whereas faith in the sense of conviction relates to belief, trust and confidence.

Faith in the sense of belief, trust and confidence is applied to one's own tradition because faith in this sense of belief pertains to truth, especially doctrinal truths. Faith in the sense of belief in the truth of one's own tradition, however, does not prevent us from cultivating faith in the sense of admiration, that is, respect and reverence for other traditions. For the Dalai Lama, faith in the sense of admiration and respect "can be fully extended to other religions" (2010, 161).

A critical assessment of the Dalai Lama's approach to religious diversity

The Dalai Lama's proposal is simple yet profound and practical. Given that religions are not going to agree with each other on the level of doctrines and metaphysical claims, it makes sense to set aside such claims and keep them outside the social context of religious diversity. By keeping doctrinal and metaphysical claims outside the social context of religious diversity, we can be pluralists in the sense of accepting and respecting many truths and many religions at the sociological level. This pluralism at the social level does not need to compromise the exclusivist claims of one's own tradition. In other words, for the Dalai Lama, being a pluralist in the social context is compatible with being an exclusivist in the context of individual practice. The doctrinal and metaphysical claims of other religions may be challenged and rejected in the context of individual practice. The exclusivist rejection of the doctrines and metaphysics of other religions is compatible with the pluralist acceptance of religious diversity, which includes sincere respect for the contribution of religions in ethical and spiritual matters.

Properly understood, the Dalai Lama is not suggesting that we accept other religions in the social context while we reject them in the context of individual practice. Religious diversity is to be accepted and respected both in the individual and the social contexts. First, religions are to be accepted and respected because they provide a foundation for ethical conduct and promote the cultivation of spiritual qualities such as love and compassion. Second, religions are to be accepted and respected because there are many different kinds of people with diverse predispositions and that requires the existence of a multiplicity of religions.

For the Dalai Lama, it is unrealistic to believe that only one religion can be the best medicine for everybody because we may have different needs and predispositions. Thus, what allows the Dalai Lama to accept and respect religious diversity is his understanding of religions as therapies with positive effects at the ethical and spiritual level. For the Dalai Lama, being a pluralist consists in accepting other religions as legitimate, not on doctrinal grounds, but rather on ethical and spiritual grounds. The pluralist accords ethical and therapeutic value to religions despite their incommensurable doctrinal differences. Yet pluralists in the Dalai Lama's sense can remain faithful to their respective religious traditions by holding some form of exclusivist view in the context of their individual practice.

The Dalai Lama genuinely accepts and respects other traditions without necessarily agreeing with all their teachings. Unlike other forms of exclusivism, the Dalai Lama's exclusivism is limited to the level of individual practice. This limited exclusivism does not reject religious diversity and it does not deprive other religions of value or legitimacy.

The Dalai Lama's pluralism does not reduce other traditions to different paths to the same goal or to mere stepping stones towards the practice of one's own religious tradition. It should be noted that the Dalai Lama's pluralism goes beyond the inclusivism characteristic of his Geluk school of Tibetan Buddhism, which views other traditions as mere stepping stones towards the highest goal, i.e., Geluk presentation and realization of emptiness. Yet the Dalai Lama's pluralism does not make him a relativist for whom all doctrines and practices are equally valid to attain the final goal of his Geluk School.

For the Dalai Lama, the existence of religious diversity does not pose any problem. The main foundation for the existence of religious diversity is human diversity. We need a plurality of religions because not all human beings have the same needs and predispositions. There is nothing wrong with religious diversity and the world would not be a better place with just one religion. Yet we need interreligious harmony and that requires different types of interreligious dialogue. Interreligious dialogue does not seek agreement or conversion. Rather, interreligious dialogue seeks harmony based on mutual understanding and the acknowledgment of fundamental differences among the religions.

The Dalai Lama's positive approach to religious diversity ultimately derives from the belief in *karma* and rebirth. People are born with different *karma* (inclinations, capacities, contexts) and they have many lives ahead of them in order to travel the spiritual path. Thus, it is only natural to accept the existence of many religions, each one suitable for different kinds of individuals in different contexts and at different stages of spiritual development.

The Dalai Lama's genuine acceptance and respect for religions does not entail uncritical acceptance of all doctrines and spiritual practices. For the Dalai Lama, not all paths lead to the final goal, and certain doctrines and practices are less effective than others for attaining liberation and highest holiness.

The Dalai Lama approaches other religions with unshakeable commitment to what he considers true, namely the teachings on emptiness of the Geluk tradition. For the Dalai Lama, the teachings about the ultimate truth found in the Geluk tradition are definitive. It is from the perspective of his Geluk individual practice that the Dalai Lama speaks about other Buddhist traditions in exclusivist terms. But the Geluk school does not seem to speak just from the perspective of individual practice. Thus, there seems to be a tension between the Geluk perspective and the Dalai Lama's dual perspective as formulated in *Towards True Kinship of Faiths: How the World's Religions Can Come Together* (2010). Maybe the ideas of the Dalai Lama about other religions have evolved; maybe he speaks differently depending on his audience, in a more pluralistic way when he talks to Westerners about religions, or in more exclusivist terms when he talks to fellow Geluks about other Buddhist schools. Be it as it may, the Dalai Lama combines a genuine pluralistic attitude with an exclusivist view of liberation. For the Dalai Lama, the final goal is exclusive to Buddhist traditions. More specifically, only emptiness as taught by the Prāsaṅgika-Madhyamaka philosophical school leads to the ultimate end. In the Dalai Lama's words:

> liberation in which 'a mind that understands the sphere of reality annihilates all defilements in the sphere of reality' is a state that only Buddhists can accomplish. This kind of mokṣa or nirvāṇa is only explained in the Buddhist scriptures, and is achieved only through Buddhist practice...The mokṣa which is described in the Buddhist religion is achieved only though the practice of emptiness. And this kind of nirvāṇa or liberation, as I have defined above, cannot be achieved even by Svātantrika Mādhyamikas, by Cittamātras, Sautrāntikas or Vaibhāṣikas. The followers of these schools, though Buddhists, do not understand the actual doctrine of emptiness. Because they cannot realize emptiness, or reality, they cannot accomplish the kind of liberation I defined previously. (1983, 169)

In sum, the Dalai Lama's view of religious diversity combines two distinct perspectives: the exclusivist view of liberation in the context of individual religious practice, and the pluralistic attitude that accepts other traditions as legitimate, respects them sincerely and accords them value due to their ethical and spiritual contribution. Within the context of individual practice, the Geluk perspective of one truth, one religion prevails. The Dalai Lama holds an exclusivist view of the ultimate end, which is attainable only through the Geluk presentation of emptiness. Yet, within the social context of religious diversity and interreligious interactions, the perspective of many truths, many religions prevails, and the Dalai Lama displays a most exemplary form of pluralism.

The Dalai Lama can uphold the individual and the social perspectives with integrity because he legitimizes the validity of religions only on the level of ethics and spirituality, not on the level of doctrines and metaphysics. Other religions are legitimate and worthy of respect because they provide a foundation for ethical conduct and help to generate qualities such as love, compassion. The Dalai Lama acknowledges that traditions make divergent and contradictory claims about doctrinal and metaphysical matters, but, in the social context, he makes no attempt to either legitimize or delegitimize such claims as true, false or indifferent. He legitimizes religions as useful methods or skilful means to morally improve human beings and society.

From the individual perspective, however, which is the perspective of his own Geluk tradition, the Dalai Lama can judge other traditions on doctrinal grounds and make exclusivist claims about them. As an orthodox follower of the Geluk school, the Dalai Lama cannot legitimize the contradictory teachings of other traditions on the level of ultimate truth. This legitimation would put such teachings on par with the Geluk teachings on emptiness, and that would relativize the Geluk teachings as being true only for those who share the Geluk perspective.

In order to uphold with integrity the individual perspective of his Geluk school, the Dalai Lama cannot claim at the social level that Geluk teachings about the ultimate truth are only true for him or just for members of the Geluk tradition. This is why, when the Dalai Lama says that Buddhism is the best for him he must be referring to matters of practice or method, not to matters of ultimate truth or wisdom. Yet for the Geluk tradition and its interpretation of emptiness, the integration of metaphysics and ethics or between wisdom and method is central. If the Dalai Lama went as far as to claim that the teachings of the Geluk tradition about the ultimate truth are true only for him, then he would not be faithful to the individual perspective of the Geluk tradition and he would no longer be an orthodox Geluk. In order to remain committed to his own faith tradition, the Dalai Lama must limit his pluralist acceptance of other traditions to the ethical level or the level of method, never to the doctrinal level of ultimate truth or the level of wisdom.

This limited acceptance of religious diversity merely on the level of method or ethical teachings renders the Dalai Lama's model problematic. The problem is that religious traditions that make universal claims of truth including the Geluk school cannot in good conscience keep such claims within the context of individual practice, as if such a context had nothing to do with the social context of religious diversity. The individual context of traditions and practitioners is also part of the social context of religious diversity. We can choose not to judge the doctrinal claims of other traditions on the social level, and this is an excellent way of being politically correct and avoiding interreligious conflicts, but we cannot pretend that the universal truth claims of our traditions are only true for our individual practice without at the same time undermining the truth of such claims.

The Dalai Lama's concept of two distinct perspectives is nonetheless a brilliant solution to the tension many people perceive between commitment to their own faith tradition and acceptance of religious diversity. The Dalai Lama legitimizes the existence of many religions without downplaying their doctrinal differences and without relativizing their doctrinal claims about the ultimate end and the ultimate nature of reality. However, many traditions may object to the Dalai Lama's attempt to keep exclusivist claims out of the social context of religious diversity. For these traditions, the context or the perspective of individual religious practice is inseparable from the social context or perspective of religious diversity.

References

Dalai Lama. 1983. "Religious Harmony" and "Extracts from the Bodhgaya Interviews." In *Christianity Through Non-Christian Eyes*, edited by Paul Griffiths. Maryknoll, NY: Orbis.

———. 2002. *The Buddhism of Tibet*. Third edition. Ithaca, NY: Snow Lion.

———. 2010. *Towards True Kinship of Faiths: How the World's Religions Can Come Together*. New York: Three Rivers.

10

Thoughts on Why, How and What Buddhists Can Learn from Christian Theologians

John Makransky

Boston College

John Makransky is Associate Professor of Buddhism and Comparative Theology at Boston College, senior academic advisor for Kathmandu University's Centre for Buddhist Studies in Nepal, and a former President of the Society of Buddhist-Christian studies. John is the developer of the Sustainable Compassion Training (SCT) model, and co-founder and guiding teacher of the Courage of Care Coalition and Foundation for Active Compassion, organizations that provide contemplative trainings in sustainable care and compassion for people in caring professions and social and environmental activism. John's academic writings have focused on doctrines and practices of Indian Mahāyāna and Tibetan Buddhism, on Buddhist meditation theory and practice with applications to current needs, and on theoretical issues in interfaith learning. Information on his work can be found at these websites: http://www.bc.edu/schools/cas/theology/faculty/jmakransky.html; http://courageofcare.org; http://foundationforactivecompassion.org

---

Introduction

For this paper, I was asked to respond to the question: "can and should Buddhists and Christians do theology (or buddhology) together, and if so why and how?" I will respond as a Tibetan Buddhist of Nyingma tradition. My answer is yes, we can and should, where "doing theology together" for me means learning things from Christian theologians that illumine significant aspects of my Buddhist understanding. How is one to learn things for Buddhist understanding from Christian theology – what method should be used? I find the method of comparative theology, as developed recently by scholars such as Francis Clooney and James Fredericks, to be a productive approach for interreligious theological learning, including Christian-Buddhist learning. But first the question of *why* must be addressed: a Buddhist comparative theology must be motivated and informed by a *theology of religions* that convincingly articulates for Buddhists why they can learn things from religious others that can make a positive difference for their own understanding and practice of awakening.

If the why and how to learn from religious others is well enough addressed, then one would have the motivation and orientation to explore specific Buddhist learnings from non-Buddhist theologies. In what follows, then, I will make a start at addressing the how, why and what of Buddhist inter-religious learning by briefly summarizing the method of comparative theology, considerations toward developing a Buddhist theology of religions that can support such learning by Buddhists, and some examples of Christian themes that have been resources for my Buddhist learning.

Comparative theology

The purpose of comparative theology is to learn from a different religious tradition in enough depth and specificity to shine significant new light on your own. By paying careful attention to elements of another religious tradition in its own context of doctrine and practice, your perspective on corresponding elements of your own faith may be shifted in ways that permit new insights to emerge. This does not merely involve learning at a distance *about* other religious beliefs and cultures that leaves your own religious self-understanding unaffected. Rather, comparative theological analysis provides a method to learn *from* religious others in specific ways that newly inform your understanding of your *own* faith and may also energize and deepen your practice of it.[1] For this kind of learning to occur, certain supportive dispositions are necessary, such as those identified in Catherine Cornille's book, *The Im-possibilty of Interreligious Dialogue*. These include: (1) doctrinal humility, the acknowledgement that the doctrinal formulations of your own tradition, including its formulations of other religions, are conditioned viewpoints that have never perfectly captured the whole truth; (2) knowledgeable commitment to your own religious tradition, so that whatever you learn from religious others may inform your religious community and tradition through you; and (3) in the context of potential Buddhist learning from Christians, a belief that there is enough common ground between Buddhism and Christianity that it is possible to hear things from Christians that make a positive difference for Buddhists in their own understanding and practice of awakening (Cornille, 2008).

1. For excellent introductions to methods and approaches of comparative theology, see Clooney 2010a; Clooney 2010b; and Fredericks 2004.

Theologies of religions

For such dispositions to support comparative theological learning, in turn, they must be motivated and informed by an adequate theology of religions. A theology of religions is an understanding of other religious systems that explores their potential truth from within the theological framework of your own religious tradition. You can, as an individual, learn many things from other religions. But for your learning to inform not only yourself but also your religious community and tradition, it must make sense to your tradition in its own framework of understanding. And as Mark Heim, John Thatamanil, and Kristen Kiblinger have argued, behind *any* interest (or disinterest) in learning from other religions lies a theology of religions that is either conscious or unconscious.[2] How do I see the potential to learn significant truths from religious others? If my theology of religions is uncritically exclusivist, I may see only errors in religious others unaware that my perspective on them is limited by my own vision. Or if my theology of religions is uncritically pluralist, I may only hear from religious others the presumed commonality of religions that I think I already know. In either of these cases, new learning is not permitted.[3] For example, if I were to see an unconditioned truth as the revelatory source of my own religious tradition while viewing other religions merely as conditioned human artifacts, how paltry other religions' teachings would appear to me compared to my own. To support learning for my religious tradition from a religious other that permits something significant and fresh to be heard, my theology of religions, while rooted in my own tradition, would have to see religious others as potential sources of profound truth, without reducing them just to what I thought I knew before engaging them.

Diverse theologies of religions are possible for any religious tradition, and a number of alternative theologies of religions have been operative throughout the history of Buddhism in Asia.[4] Below I will offer considerations toward constructing a contemporary Buddhist theology of religions that would support interreligious learning. Such a theology of religions, if it is to be taken seriously by Buddhists, must be based

2. Heim and Thatamanil have argued this point in oral presentations to Luce American Academy of Religion (AAR) seminar gatherings in Theologies of Religious Pluralism and Comparative Theology, 2010. Kiblinger makes this point convincingly in her article, "Relating Theology of Religions and Comparative Theology," in Clooney 2010b, 24–42.

3. The considerations in this paragraph on the need for a theology of religions to support comparative theology are developed more fully in Kiblinger 2010, 24–32.

4. For examples of diverse Buddhist theologies of religion operative through the history of Buddhism in Asia, see Makransky 2003.

in fundamental Buddhist understandings of core teachings. Some of the implications of those teachings could turn the attention of Buddhists toward religious others as potential sources of truth. But such teachings have been employed traditionally in ways that orient Buddhists away from the possibility of religiously important learning from non-Buddhists. So to explore how core Buddhist teachings could newly inform interreligious learning for Buddhists today, I must not only summarize them in their traditional forms, but also relate them to experiences of interreligious learning today and to current work in theologies of religions.

Buddhist principles not to be ignored in developing a contemporary Buddhist theology of religions

Why did the Buddha teach? A principal reason, Buddhists believe, is that different spiritual paths taught in the world lead to different spiritual results, many of which fall short of complete liberation from the inmost causes of confusion and suffering. This, Buddhists believe, compelled the Buddha to "turn the wheel of the dharma," to re-introduce the way of the Buddhas to the world, the way that leads to inmost liberation, the realization of *Nirvāṇa*. In the *Sallekha Sutta* (ascribed to Shakyamuni Buddha), the Buddha describes dozens of ways that religious practitioners, mostly of non-Buddhist traditions known in his time, believed they had accomplished complete liberation (*mokṣa*), the highest religious end, while falling far short of it unawares. The Buddha then explains in detail how proper practice of his liberating path provides a way to be released from every layer of clinging to conditioned experience, to realize the full freedom of the unconditioned state, *Nirvāṇa*. This is formulated in Indo-Tibetan Buddhist traditions like my own as follows: the fullest realization of reality is a stable, non-dual insight into the empty, unconditioned nature of all experience – the emptiness of all conceptualized appearances – accompanied by an impartial, powerful compassion for all beings who have not realized the inmost freedom of such insight. Any religious beliefs or practices that encourage reifying and clinging to any conceptualization of truth, God, scripture, religious identity, ritual, religious experience or ethical prescription as an ultimate would obstruct realization of the emptiness of all such constructed forms, and thus, even in the name of religion, prevent the attainment of the fullest religious end, the unconstructed, unconditioned, *Nirvāṇa*. Careful guidance is required to learn to pay such penetrating, stable attention to experience that even the subtlest clinging to reified concepts collapses.

The Buddhist understanding that different modes of practice lead to different soteriological results and the fullest result can only be attained by methods appropriate to it (methods that the Buddha imparted), has established the main purpose for communicating the Buddha's teaching in the world (see Makransky 2008).

In sharp contrast to this foundational Buddhist understanding, a popular contemporary option in theology of religions, developed by John Hick and others, called "theological pluralism," asserts the following: since all great world religions engage the same ultimate reality which they call by different names, then in spite of their differences in belief and practice, all such religions should lead to the same essential realization of that ultimate reality, the same basic salvific result.[5] But as the previous paragraph implies, to accept that assertion is to put aside a primary concern of the Buddha and his followers – to investigate the efficacy of specific beliefs and practices promulgated by religions because the results of religious practice, which could be inmost liberation or unconscious bondage to suffering in the name of religion, depend on the specific functions of those beliefs and practices – not on a grand narrative about the equality of religions.

Nevertheless, for Buddhist philosophers to assert that different kinds of spiritual path lead to different results does not mean that just one narrowly specified way of belief and practice is authentically liberating. Buddhist traditions have also commonly taught that there are many possible modes of learning and practice that lead to liberation, not just one way, as exemplified in Shakyamuni Buddha's diverse ways of guiding different kinds of people in the practices of his liberating path. This teaching is the doctrine of skilful means (*upāya-kauśalya*), according to which the teachings of the Buddhas are ever adapted to the diverse mentalities and needs of beings so as to meet them effectively in their own horizons of understanding.

In a number of Mahāyāna Buddhist scriptures that emerged in the early centuries CE, such as those of the *Avataṃsaka Sūtra* collection, the teaching of skilful means was expanded in connection with the cosmic dimension of buddhahood, *dharmakāya*, the infinite, non-dual awareness of the Buddhas that pervades all reality. The infinite mind of the Buddhas, these scriptures assert, communicates the *Dharma* in limitlessly diverse ways to meet the varied mentalities of beings in all realms of existence, compassionately entering persons of varied walks of life and religious culture into *Dharma* practices conducive to their mundane and

5. Some leading formulations of theological pluralism appear in Hick and Knitter 1987 and in Knitter 2005. For a Buddhist critique of theological pluralism, see Makransky 2008, 49–53.

supramundane well-being.[6] Indeed, the skilful means of Buddhahood, in communicating the Buddha's core teaching of the Four Noble Truths, goes beyond all established religious expectations and teaching norms, including familiar Buddhist ways of expressing those very truths. As the Mahāyāna *Avataṃsaka Sūtra* puts it:

> in this world there are four quadrillion names to express the four holy truths in accord with the mentalities of beings, to cause them all to be harmonized and pacified. [...] [And] just as in this world there are four quadrillion names to express the four holy truths, so in all the worlds to the east – immeasurably many worlds, in each there are an equal number of names to express the four holy truths, to cause all the sentient beings there to be harmonized and pacified in accordance with their mentalities. And just as this is so of the worlds to the east, so it is with all the infinite worlds in the ten directions. (Cleary 1993, 276, 281)

Such a scriptural passage implies that it is the infinite mind of the Buddhas that is the ultimate ground and source of liberating truth for all peoples, cultures and religions, analogous to the Abrahamic belief in the one God as the transcendental source of revelation for all humankind.[7]

But, from a Buddhist perspective, even if there is one underlying source for diverse expressions of truth in the world, it does not necessarily speak with equal clarity, depth and fullness in all the world's traditions. Even if the infinite mind of the Buddhas is the ultimate source of liberating truth for all, it is Shakyamuni Buddha, many scriptures proclaim, that is the preeminent manifestation of that buddha-knowledge for this eon. He is the one who has spoken the liberating truth of *Dharma* with the greatest specificity, depth and completeness, with a unique focus on core liberating principles that are not as central to other traditions—foundational Buddhist doctrines that proclaim no substantial self in persons and the emptiness of independent existence of all phenomena as keys to the deepest liberation of persons. And it is the Buddha's *Dharma* heirs, contained in the *Saṅgha* community that he established, who uphold this unique teaching for the world (Makransky 2008, 56–57).

For a theology of religions to make sense to Buddhists (including those in my Tibetan tradition), the principles summarized in preceding

6. For fuller discussion of skilful means as ways of relating to religious others in early and later Buddhist traditions, see Makransky 2003, 342–354.

7. See Makransky 2003, 346–354 on alternative ways the Four Noble Truths have been expressed in Asian cultures, including non-cognitive ways. See Makransky 2008, 53–60 for more on Buddhahood's infinite means and Buddhahood as ultimate source of all religions.

paragraphs cannot be ignored. The teaching that Buddhahood employs infinite means of communication that transcend the established expectations of all traditions, including Buddhist ones, could direct the attention of Buddhists to the possibility of profound truth in other religions. So can the Buddhist concern to critically analyze beliefs and practices of religious traditions (both Buddhist and non-Buddhist) for soteriological efficacy. But the tendency narrowly to identify the primary source of revelation with Shakyamuni Buddha and his community makes it difficult for many Buddhists to view non-Buddhist religions as possessing a ground of truth comparable to their own. And the concern to critically analyze all beliefs is usually marshalled for Buddhist critiques of beliefs of religious others (including beliefs of Buddhist others), not as an analytical tool to avoid missteps while learning from religious others. The traditional Buddhist allergy to the notion of learning important religious things from religious others, including Christians, has been exacerbated in the modern period by the Asian experience of Western colonialism, which many experienced, in part, as an aggressive assault by Christian missionaries on indigenous Asian beliefs in support of the Western domination of their societies.

The Buddhist principles summarized in this section, as traditionally employed, have tended to constrain the possibility of new learning from religious others by subsuming others within a Buddhist system of belief that is functionally closed to new input by them. Such principles, then, cannot be drawn on uncritically if they are to inform a Buddhist theology of religions today that would adequately support interreligious learning. Yet they must contribute to any theology of religions that would make sense to Buddhist traditions, including my tradition of Tibetan Buddhism. I believe those principles can be drawn on in fresh ways that avoid closing off new learning from religious others, if they are informed by fresh experience of interreligious learning and by some current work in theologies of religions.

Examples of Buddhist interreligious learning

This section will focus on elements of my learning as a Buddhist from Christians. Such learning has reinforced for me the Buddhist understanding that Buddhahood, as a source of limitless skilful means, can communicate through non-Buddhist modes of teaching in ways that transcend accustomed frames of reference, including my conditioned Buddhist expectations. In dialogue and study, I have encountered Christians whose spiritual insights and qualities profoundly illumined my own Buddhist understanding about which they knew nothing, for example by embodying absolute trust in the ground of being, by recognizing the holy, sacramental nature of everyday things, or by vividly expressing the intrinsically communal nature of spiritual awakening. What follows are examples of a few areas of Christian theology that are rich sources of reflection for me. This is not the place to provide extensive analysis of each, but to give a fuller sense of my learning process, I will discuss the first of these areas at some more length below.

Atonement

Christian models of atonement include the understanding that human beings are not in a position to redeem themselves from sin, rather God is the effective agent of atonement and redemption for humanity. This expresses what theologians call an objective aspect of atonement. Christian concern with salvific power from beyond the human ego deepens my engagement with analogous issues of agency and objectivity implicit, it seems to me, in elements of Buddhist practice, as in the method of exchanging self for others (*tong-len*) central to Tibetan Buddhism.

Faith and sacramental vision

The Judeo-Christian teaching of absolute surrender in faith to God as source and ground of all creation has helped anchor Christian reflections on poverty and sacramental vision. Because all beings, as creations *of* God, are grounded *in* God, to know them in their depth is to know them as visible manifestations of grace, as holy beings of immeasurable worth.[8] Such teachings have further informed and energized my Buddhist understanding of refuge (in Nyingma tradition) as absolute surrender to the expanse of openness and awareness that is the empty ground of all beings. To be surrendered to that ground (*gzhi)* is to be surrendered to the inmost being of persons, a purer vision of them that elicits reverence, love and compassion for them. Articulations of Christian sacramental vision have further inspired me, as a Nyingma Buddhist, to see persons not as ungrounded, isolated entities of no innate worth but as *expressions* of a primordial ground, embodiments of original wakefulness and positive potential (*tathāgata-garbha*, buddha nature), however obscured that may be in them by inner tendencies of delusion and grasping. Christian sacramental teaching somehow further informs and energizes this Buddhist way of knowing for me.[9]

---

8. See references to Augustine, Francis of Assisi, Jonathan Edwards, and Gerard Manley Hopkins on poverty and sacramental vision in Himes and Himes1993, 110–113. Also Metz, 1968.

9. One sign of deepening refuge in the Buddha is a deepening reverence for persons in their innate buddhaness, their profound dignity and potential. On pure perception,

The Two Great Commandments

The themes above inform (and are informed by) the two great commandments of Matthew 22.36–40. A Pharisee asks Jesus: "'Teacher, which commandment in the law is the greatest?' Jesus replies: 'You shall love the Lord your God with all your heart, and with all your soul, and with all your mind.' This is the greatest and the first commandment. And a second is like it: 'You shall love your neighbour as yourself.' On these two commandments hang all the law and the prophets." The New Interpreter's Bible comments: "One cannot first love God and then, as a second task, love one's neighbor. To love God is to love one's neighbor, and vice versa."[10]

The striking equation of the second commandment with the first has made me reflect (from my Nyingma perspective) on the relation between devotion to Buddhahood (*dharmakāya,* buddha nature) as the empty *unconditioned* ground (*gzhi*) *of* beings and *unconditional* love *for* all those beings. Because of this connection, to cultivate *unconditional* love, compassion and joy in persons empowers and is empowered by increasing surrender to Buddhahood as the *unconditioned*, empty, cognizant ground of persons. This becomes the unity of wisdom and love within the Bodhisattva path of my tradition. And the ancient Jewish term *commandment* in the quote from Matthew points me with further depth into the Tibetan concept of *dam tsig (samaya*), the exigence of deepest commitment to the ground and practice of wisdom-love for the sake of all.

Ecclesiology

As Dominican theologian, J. M. R. Tillard has written: "To be 'in Christ' is to find oneself under the power of the Spirit of God that [...] knits into the unity of one body those who receive the gospel of God. [...] Whoever is 'in Christ' and 'in the Spirit' is never in a relation of one to one with God" (Tillard, 2001, 6).

Human participation in God, in this view, is *intrinsically* communal, ecclesiological. The individual is *incorporated* into the *body* of Christ that reaches out to all in the building of God's kingdom. One's relationship to God can never be isolated from one's relation to others in God. Although communal participation has been a central part of Buddhist practice from the start, Buddhist communities were understood as collections of individuals, following in the Buddha's footsteps individually, while

see Chökyi Nyima Rinpoche and Shlim 2006, 5153, 62, 66, 108, 114 and Makransky 2007, 131–155.

10. New Interpreter's Bible 1995, Volume VIII, 423–426.

guided by common disciplines and rules of living (*Dhamma* and *Vinaya*). The rhetoric of path as ontologically individual was retained even as communal dimensions of path gained increasing emphasis and centrality in a number of Buddhist traditions, prominently in Mahāyāna movements. And the Buddhist doctrinal thread of individualism was given renewed emphasis in the meeting of Buddhism with the modern West, as it seemed to match the intense individualism of Western interest in spirituality.

Nevertheless, "ecclesiological" aspects of Buddhism took highly developed doctrinal expression in Mahāyāna traditions (including my own), in ways that indicated the path and fruition of awakening must be understood as *intrinsically*, ontologically communal. Seemingly separate individuals awaken to a communal dimension of reality that they were not previously conscious of, remaking them into a collective extension of the Buddhas' liberating activity on behalf of the world. The ultimate fruition of the Bodhisattva path, Buddhahood, embodies itself not just as an individual attainment (*rang don, dharmakāya)* but as a power to coalesce *communities* of awakening (*zhan don, rūpakāya)* and to *incorporate* Bodhisattvas into *bodies of Buddhahood*—enlightened dimensions known as *sambhogakāya* and *nirmanakāya*—as agents of enlightened activity for beings.[11] But unlike Tillard's Christian understanding, Bodhisattva path and fruition are intrinsically communal not because Bodhisattvas are "knit into one body" by a supernatural Spirit, but because their practices awaken them in wisdom and love to the inter-dependent, ultimately undivided nature of all beings (undivided suchness, *tathatā*).

11. The perfected form of Buddhahood, referred to as "*sambhoga-kāya*" in the three Buddha-body scheme of Mahāyāna treatises, is understood not just as an isolated embodiment of enlightenment but as a "body of communion in the joy of the dharma," a supramundane form that communes with advanced Bodhisattvas in the *Dharma* qualities and energies of immeasurable love, wisdom and joy which radiate to all beings. This is pictured in numerous Buddha-realm scenes of Mahāyāna scriptures and in Asian Buddhist art, contributing to the development of the tantric mandala. On this see Makransky1997, 39–108, 319–368; Makransky 2004, 76–79; and McMahan 2002, 111–178. Implicit Bodhisattva "ecclesiologies" in Mahāyāna scriptures include scenes in which Bodhisattvas function not just as isolate individuals on individual paths to enlightenment but as communal expressions of Buddha activity—many Bodhisattvas performing enlightened activities throughout numerous realms as one community (Bodhisattva *Saṅgha*), thereby functioning as part of the body of the Buddhas (*nirmanakāya*) through the power of their prior vows and merit, the blessings of the Buddhas (*adhiṣṭhāna*, radiance) and emergent qualities of buddha nature (*tathāgata-garbha*). For examples of Bodhisattvas depicted in Mahāyāna sūtras as a communal, "ecclesiological" *Nirvāṇa.*

Social justice

I am struck by the Christian concern with a God of justice, vividly embodied in Jesus as the one who challenges oppressive attitudes and structures with special attention to the poor and marginalized. It has pushed me to seek increased clarity on the meaning of the unconditional compassion associated with the Bodhisattva path of awakening. The Christian theme points me back into Buddhist sources further to observe how Bodhisattva compassion, as an unconditional expression of wisdom, *upholds* something in persons by simultaneously *confronting* something in them. To uphold persons in their deepest potential of freedom and goodness *is* to confront us in all the ways we hide from that potential—the individual and social inhibitions and structures that prevent us from responding fully to others with reverence and care. And to be pointed by Christian ecclesiological thought to "ecclesiological" aspects of Buddhism noted above, shifts my understanding of what it means as a Buddhist to respond to needs of the contemporary world. Instead of focusing on individual attempts to address social problems in the context of each individual's own practice of *Dharma*, we might freshly explore how communal dimensions of awakening in Buddhist praxis "knit" Buddhist individuals and communities into interconnected, integrated responses of service and action that respond to concrete needs and problems of societies and the natural world.

Each Christian theme above shifts my lens on a corresponding aspect of Buddhist thought and practice, shining light on further implications of corresponding Buddhist themes in their similarity and difference, infusing them with greater depth and energy in my understanding and practice. It is as if Buddhahood is speaking *in and through* the Christian mode of expression to empower a deeper engagement with Buddhist principles, in ways I had not expected, do not control and do not fully comprehend.

An objective aspect of Christian atonement that sheds light on Buddhist praxis

I will discuss a bit more the first theme mentioned above, atonement. The Christian doctrine of atonement concerns Christ's redemption of humanity from sin through his life, death and resurrection. Two aspects of this doctrine have caught my attention: 1) the *agent of atonement* for humankind is God in Christ, not sinful humans. Since humanity does not even know the full depth of its own sinful condition, including its distorted tendencies of will and judgement, human beings are powerless to rectify that condition; and 2) there is an *objective aspect* of God's atonement for our sins through Christ. The redemptive power of God's action comes not just through the *subjective* personal responses of human beings to such a loving God, but by Christ's self-offering on our behalf.[12] God came to us in Christ and Spirit to do the work of reconciliation we cannot do for ourselves. This expresses an objective structure to reality – both with regard to the fallen condition of humankind and to the *objective* power of God's grace to reintegrate his creatures back into his loving purpose. John Macquarrie, discussing Christ's salvific work as it reached completion on the cross, says:

> the classic view [of atonement] includes an objective side. The self-giving of Christ is continuous with the self-giving of God, and the whole work of atonement is God's [...] something needs to be done for man, something that he is powerless to do for himself [...]. Here that absolute self-giving, which is the essence of God, has appeared in history in the work of Jesus Christ, and this is a work *on behalf of* man, a work of grace. (Macquarrie 1977, 320)

In Tibet, one of the principal practices for progressing on the Bodhisattva path of awakening is the contemplative exchange of oneself for others, given vivid expression in the practice of *tong-len*, literally the practice of "offering and receiving." After experiencing the power of love and compassion through prior contemplative cultivations, the practitioner takes that power into the *tong-len* contemplative pattern of offering and receiving. From compassion, one imaginatively *takes* the sufferings of beings upon oneself, into the empty nature of one's mind. From there, out of love, one imaginatively *offers* them all of one's well-being, resources and positive capacities.[13]

There is a tendency in some Buddhist discussions of *tong-len* to articulate it as a technique to become more compassionate through the effortful use of imagination. In this articulation, the agent of *tong-len* is the ego-centered human being who is learning to reverse her ego-orientation by re-conditioning subjective patterns of her mind toward greater love and compassion for beings. This is true as far as it goes. But from the perspective of my own tradition, it doesn't capture the fuller Buddhist ontology behind *tong-len*, which Christian reflections on the agency and the objective dimension of atonement help point out.

In the contemplative understanding of my tradition, Tibetan Nyingma,

12. See e.g. Macquarrie 1977, 316–325; Tillich 1968, 165–172, 240–241; Kung, 1968, 419–436; Fiorenza and Galvin 1991, 275–297; Ward 2000, 56–62.

13. For a more detailed explanation of the theory and practice of *tong-len*, see for example: Kongtrul 1987; Chödrön 1994; Dilgo Khyentse Rinpoche 1993; Traleg Kyabgon 2007; and Makransky 2007, 157–199.

the ultimate *agent* of *tong-len* is the awakening mind of enlightenment (*bodhicitta)* that has been hidden within the human being; the innate Buddha awareness that is the infinite cognizant ground and backdrop of all our experiences. Buddha awareness (*dharmakāya, rigpa*) is our deepest nature, but has been obscured by the conditioned patterning of our ego-centred thought and reaction. The pattern of *tong-len* helps re-conform the person to her deeper nature, bringing out her innate capacity of enlightened response, of compassion and love for beings as her greater self. When engaged in depth, *tong-len* flows progressively more spontaneously from the empty-cognizant ground of one's being, taking the world's delusions and sufferings back into that ground, and from that place of oneness with the Buddhas, blessing beings. The liberating power that *tong-len* unleashes gradually *incorporates* the practitioner into the body of the Buddhas by drawing her into the stream of their enlightened activity. From this perspective, it would not be correct to say that the transformative power of the practice comes just from re-conditioning the subjectivity of the practitioner, as if the ego-centred personality were the primary agent of the practice. The ultimate *agent* of *tong-len*, gradually discovered from within its practice, is innate Buddhahood (*dharmakāya*), which works in and through the practitioner from beyond her ego-centered mind, to do what is not possible for that mind.

This is *not* to say that *tong-len,* though broadly analogous in its pattern of exchanging self for others, soteriologically equates with the cross of Christ. Each such concept is embedded in its own framework of doctrinal understanding that differs foundationally from that of the other tradition. But because the similarities are embedded in such radically different worldviews, elements of Christian reflection on subjective and objective aspects of salvation both reveal analogous tensions in Buddhist tradition and shine new light upon them for me – deepening my Buddhist understanding and practice.[14]

Where does the light of interreligious understanding come from?

It seems to me that the ideas and words that Christians employ in their theological reflections, *of themselves*, are not what shed so much light for me on Buddhist understanding, since no Christian with whom I am in dialogue (contemporary or ancient) has the expertise to know how so

14. My reflections on atonement and Buddhism have been informed by conversations with Mark Heim, in the context of his own comparative theological inquiries into atonement in light of Buddhism.

profoundly to inform my Buddhist worldview. Rather, it feels as though the deepest reality that my own tradition engages, Buddhahood, *dharmakāya*, communicates aspects of truth to me in my own religious location *through* the religious other, illumining elements of my tradition in surprising ways beyond anyone's planning. Buddhahood can do this, it is taught in my tradition, because the infinite mind of the Buddhas is undivided from the empty, cognizant ground of persons.[15] Meanwhile, Christian dialogue partners I have known have said analogous things about their dialogical learning from Buddhism. It is as if, they say, the Spirit of God is teaching them *through* the inter-religious encounter with Buddhist thought or practice.

In light of all that has been said thus far, a further question arises for me toward developing a Buddhist theology of religions that would support interreligious learning: how to give due weight to these two poles: (1) to my inherited Buddhist understanding that different kinds of path lead to different ends, with the fullest soteriological end involving a stable, non-dual awareness of the *empty nature* of all things, without which the deepest roots of inner bondage are not cut; and (2) my experience that Christian theologians who are unacquainted with, even uninterested in, such teachings of emptiness can function as revelatory sources for my Buddhist understanding and path. How can both those poles be adequately held? Some elements of theologian Mark Heim's theology of religions have begun to help me to navigate those poles.

Learning with and from a Christian colleague

In developing his own distinctive theology of religions, Christian theologian Mark Heim[16] has argued that people of different religions engage the same ultimate reality, which is endowed with many aspects, qualities and potencies – the Trinitarian God for Heim, Buddhahood for me. Through differing frameworks of thought and practice, different religious traditions direct the attention of their practitioners more intensively to certain qualities of that one ultimate ground than to others. Since people of different religious frameworks engage different qualities of the same ultimate reality with greater intensity, they would be expected to achieve different fulfilments from their practice – different soteriological results. And because they pay primary attention to differing aspects of ultimate

15. On this see Nyoshul Khenpo 1995; Sogyal Rinpoche 2002, 154–176; Chagdud Tulku 2001, 169–192, 247–255; Makransky 2007, 33–68.

16. In this section I draw selectively on just a few of Mark Heim's points. I am not adopting his full theology of religions here.

reality, they integrate its qualities differently in their realization of it.[17]

These points by Heim accord with the two Buddhist principles summarized in section IV and also nuance them. On the one hand, from the perspective of my Buddhist tradition, the deepest ground of liberating truth, which I call Buddhahood and Christians call God, in its power to communicate transcends established expectations of all religious traditions, including Buddhism. On the other hand, also essential to Buddhists is the principle that different kinds of path lead to different results, and it behooves the Buddha's followers critically to investigate any proposed framework of belief and practice for liberating efficacy, without assuming all such frameworks support the same soteriological result.

Implied in Heim's approach, I believe, is the understanding that conceptual frameworks distinctive of each religious tradition are both necessary and inherently limiting. They are necessary to establish systematic religious understandings that inform all practices and to provide a conceptual container that receives the findings of practice experience to make them accessible to future generations. A conceptual map of soteriological ground, path and result is essential to inform each stage of practice in any religious tradition. It is the framework based upon which practitioners are prepared to engage even non-conceptual ways of practice, such as the non-dual meditations of Tibet or apophatic Christian modes of contemplation. But any conceptual framework (whether Buddhist or non-Buddhist) is also limited, because *in* the very act of pointing our attention to particular areas of understanding and experience it *lessens* our attention to other areas. In addition, all such conceptual frameworks are limited by historical and cultural conditioning of which none of us are ever fully aware.[18]

When we relate the Buddhist principles of section IV, and examples of Buddhist-Christian learning in sections V and VI, to Heim's suggestions above, further light is shed on my experience of inter-religious learning. A Buddhist conceptual framework of belief and practice, by focusing my attention on certain aspects of reality in a certain way, both increases my receptivity to those aspects and implicitly prevents my fuller attention to other aspects, with which Christian theologians with a different religious orientation and practice may engage more fully. The same is true for practitioners of other religions. For this reason, people of each tradition

17. For Mark Heim's Christian Trinitarian perspective on these points, see Heim 2001, 167–168, 174–197, 210–222, 289–295. For a Mahāyāna Buddhist perspective on them, see Makransky 2005, 189–199 and Makransky 2008, 60–65.

18. On the unconscious limitations of historical conditioning, see Makransky 2008, 58–64.

have much to learn from religious others, precisely *because* of their otherness. Religious others may be empowered through their framework of practice to know certain aspects of ultimate reality in *greater* depth than one may yet know through one's own tradition. An implication of this is that we are driven by the ultimate reality that grounds our own religious understanding *to the religious other* for further teaching, further revelation.

A sign of becoming more intimate with Buddhahood or God in this view, would be a growing tendency for you to view others who are deeply formed by their traditions as potential *religious teachers.* Not because you have abandoned your tradition but precisely the opposite. To become more receptive to ultimate reality *through your tradition* is to be made increasingly attentive to the voice of that reality as it makes itself heard *through other religious frameworks.* Thus, as a Tibetan Buddhist, elements of Christian teaching can function for me like an encounter with a profound Tibetan lama—they interrupt my established preconceptions to allow reality to speak afresh, to make more of itself known to me in my own religious location.

At the same time, from this perspective, there is no reason to assume that different frameworks of belief and practice lead to the same soteriological result. For example, Mark Heim, operating within a Christian framework, understands the fullest spiritual fulfilment to be deepest communion with God in Christ, a *dualistic*, Trinitarian communion that retains relational conceptual frameworks as ultimate. I, operating within a Buddhist framework, understand fullest spiritual fulfilment to be realization of the *non-dual* wisdom and compassion of Buddhahood, in which no conceptual frameworks are ultimate. These different understandings are based in different systems of doctrine and practice, and the religious experiences they inform and express need not be equated. Nor can I step out of my own finite religious perspective to fully understand and rank the possible fulfilments of other world religions (or even of other Buddhist traditions). There may be individuals in other traditions whose beliefs and practices function in ways that deeply free them from inner causes of suffering beyond what I know, beyond how my own historically conditioned tradition has conceptualized what's possible.

As a follower of the Buddha I am required to maintain an exploratory perspective on practice and result that asks critical questions both of non-Buddhists and Buddhists – how might these beliefs and practices inhibit or support liberation? At the same time, based on all that has been said above, *as a follower of the Buddha*, it behooves me to learn *from* religious others–because their lens on reality may give them greater intimacy with some aspects of it, and because elements of their understanding may interrupt reified elements of my own understanding in importantly informing ways.

Even when Mark Heim and I disagree about fullest spiritual results, we are motivated to listen deeply to each other for further learning *in and through* our differences, since the ultimate ground of our traditions can teach each of us more *by means* of the other's perspective. Indeed, it is *because* we inhabit such different worldviews that such fresh revelation may come through the other. This implies that religious others in their difference exist not just to be overcome through the apologetics of one's own tradition, but are *needed* if one is to learn more fully from the ultimate reality that grounds one's tradition. To lose the religious other (by dismissing him or reducing him to a straw man of one's apologetics) would be to lose a potential religious teacher, whose different lens on reality uniquely interrupts ways I have subconsciously mistaken my lens on reality for reality.[19]

Again, from a Buddhist perspective all such explorations in theology of religions and comparative theology cannot be divorced from the need to explore critically whether beliefs and practices of religions (Buddhist and non-Buddhist) help cut inner causes of bondage, evoke our best capacities, release us into our deepest ground of freedom. But for such critical inquiry to be well informed, it needs a lot of help—from resources of Buddhist tradition, from current disciplines of investigation and analysis, and also from alternative perspectives that only religious others can provide.

Conclusions

Without compromising my inherited Buddhist focus on specific forms of practice leading to specific results whose fullest realization I understand in Buddhist terms, I view religious others as deeply engaged with the same ultimate reality (the same ultimate ground of experience) that Buddhists engage, potentially realizing some aspects of that reality *more* deeply through their modes of understanding and practice than I have yet as a Buddhist, *because* they are not Buddhist. This would explain the depth dimension of my experience of inter-religious learning – as if Buddhahood were tutoring me *through* the Christian theologian, showing me more possibilities of *Buddhist* understanding than I had previously seen, more

19. The theme of "interruption"—religious others functioning as sources of revelation by interrupting accustomed frameworks of one's own tradition—is informed by the work of Boeve 2003, 163–179. It is also informed by numerous Asian Buddhist stories of masters who interrupt accustomed conceptual frameworks of individuals and institutions by unexpected modes of teaching or action, so the *Dharma* can be re-revealed in that moment in a fresher and fuller way.

than my Buddhist formation alone had permitted. What has been said here about Buddhist learning from Christians is equally applicable to Buddhist learning from all other religious others.

This kind of theology of religions has been called "open inclusivism."[20] The Buddhist open inclusivism articulated here can support Buddhist ways of engaging in comparative theology, in interreligious learning. In such work, we explore what can be learned from elements of another religion, doing so from within the perspective of our own religious worldview. This is done not just to categorize religious others within pre-established, unchanging categories of our own tradition, but to permit new learning from religious others to inform and enlarge the understandings of our tradition. This is done not by turning away from our own tradition but by learning better to keep faith with the deepest ground of that tradition, and through that, to receive more of what it can only teach us through religious others.

Acknowledgements

Previously published in 2011 in *Buddhist-Christian Studies*, Volume 31 (University of Hawai'i Press).

These reflections were informed by discussions with colleagues Paul Knitter, Mark Heim, Catherine Cornille, John Thatamanil, Frank Clooney, Michael Himes, Wendy Farley, Charles Hallisey, Anantanand Rambachan, Perry Schmidt-Leukel, Abraham Vélez de Cea, Loye Ashton, Karen Enriquez, Willa Miller, Leah Weiss, and others, to whom I am grateful.

References

Boeve, Lieven. 2003. *Interrupting Tradition: An Essay on Christian Faith in a Postmodern Context*. Louvain: Peeters.

Chagdud Tulku. 2001. *Gates to Buddhist Practice*. Junction City, CA: Padma.

Chödrön, Pema. 1994. *Start Where You Are*. Boston: Shambhala.

Chökyi Nyima Rinpoche and Shlim, David. 2006. *Medicine and Compassion: A Tibetan Lama's Guidance for Caregivers*. Boston: Wisdom. https://doi.org/10.2310/7060.2005.12416

Cleary, Thomas, transl. 1993. *The Flower Ornament Scripture: A Translation of the Avatamsaka Sūtra*. Boston: Shambhala.

Clooney, Francis X. 2010a. *Comparative Theology: Deep Learning Across Religious Borders* Malden, MA: Wiley-Blackwell. https://doi.org/10.1002/9781444318951

20. On open inclusivism, see Cornille 2008, 197–204.

Clooney, Francis X, ed. 2010b. *The New Comparative Theology: Interreligious Insights from the Next Generation*. New York: T&T Clark.

Conze, Edward., transl. 1979. *The Large Sūtra on Perfect Wisdom*. Delhi: Motilal Banarsidass.

Cornille, Catherine. 2008. *The Im-possibility of Interreligious Dialogue*. New York: Crossroad.

Dilgo Khyentse Rinpoche. 1993. *Enlightened Courage*. Ithaca, NY: Snow Lion.

Fiorenza, Francis Schussler and John Galvin eds. 1991. *Systematic theology: Roman Catholic Perspectives,* Volume 1. Minneapolis, MN: Fortress.

Fredericks, James L. 2004. *Buddhists and Christians: Through Comparative Theology to Solidarity*. Maryknoll, NY: Orbis.

Heim, Mark. 2001. *The Depth of the Riches: A Trinitarian Theology of Religious Ends*. Grand Rapids, MI: Eerdman. https://doi.org/10.1111/1468-0025.00150

Hick, John and Paul F. Knitter, eds. 1987. *The Myth of Christian Uniqueness: Toward a Pluralistic Theology of Religions*. Maryknoll, NY: Orbis.

Himes, Michael J. and Kenneth R. Himes. 1993. *Fullness of Faith: The Public Significances of Theology*. Mahwah, NJ: Paulist.

Jamgon Kongtrul. 1987. *The Great Path of Awakening*, trans. Ken McLeod. Boston: Shambhala.

Kiblinger, Kristen. 2010. "Relating Theology of Religions and Comparative Theology." In *The New Comparative Theology*, edited by Francis X. Clooney, 24–32. New York: T&T Clark.

Knitter, Paul F., ed. 2005. *The Myth of Religious Superiority: A Multifaith Exploration*. Maryknoll, NY: Orbis.

Kung, Hans. 1968. *On Being a Christian*. Garden City, NY: Doubleday.

Lamotte, Etienne transl. 1998. *Suramgamasamadhisutra: The Concentration of Heroic Progress*. London: Curzon.

Macquarrie, John. 1977. *Principles of Christian Theology*. New York: Charles Scribner's.

Makransky, John. 1997. *Buddhahood Embodied.* Albany, NY: State University of New York Press.

———. 2003. "Buddhist Perspectives on Truth in Other Religions: Past and Present." *Theological Studies* 64(2): 334–361. https://doi.org/10.1177/004056390306400205

———. 2004. "Buddhahood and Buddha Bodies." In *Encyclopedia of Buddhism*, Volume 1, edited by Robert Buswell, 76–79. New York: Macmillan.

———. 2005. "Buddha and Christ as Mediators of the Transcendent: A Buddhist Perspective." In *Buddhism and Christianity in Dialogue*, edited by Perry Schmidt-Leukel, 176–199. Norwich, Norfolk England: SCM.

———. 2007. *Awakening through Love*. Boston: Wisdom.

Makransky, John. 2008. "Buddhist Inclusivism: Reflections toward a Contemporary Buddhist Theology of Religions.' In *Buddhist Attitudes to Other Religions*, edited by Perry Schmidt-Leukel, 47–68. St. Ottilien, Germany: EOS.

McMahan, David. 2002. *Empty Vision*. London: RoutledgeCurzon.

Metz, Johann Baptist. 1968. *Poverty of Spirit*. Translated by John Drury. New York: Newman.

Nyoshul Khenpo. 1995. *Natural Great Perfection*. Translated by Lama Surya Das. Ithaca, NY: Snow Lion.

New Interpreter's Bible. 1995. Nashville, TN: Abingdon.

Śāntideva. 1981. *Śikṣā-samuccaya*. Translated by Cecil Bendall and W.H.D. Rouse. Delhi: Motilal Banarsidass.

Sogyal Rinpoche. 2002. *Tibetan book of Living and Dying*. New York: Harper Collins.

Thurman, Robert, transl. 1986. *The Holy Teaching of Vimalakirti*. University Park: Pennsylvania State University Press.

Tillard, J. M. R. 2001. *Flesh of the Church, Flesh of Christ: At the Source of the Ecclesiology of Communion*. Collegeville, MN: Liturgical Press.

Tillich, Paul. 1968. *A History of Christian Thought*. New York: Simon & Schuster.

Traleg Kyabgon. 2007. *The Practice of Lojong*. Boston: Shambhala.

Ward, Keith. 2000. *Christianity: A Short Introduction*. Oxford: Oneworld.

Watson, Burton, transl. 1993. *The Lotus Sūtra*. New York: Columbia University.

11

Suffering and its Relief: A Buddhist Approach to Religious Pluralism

Christopher Ives
Stonehill College

Christopher Ives is a Professor of Religious Studies at Stonehill College. In his scholarship he focuses on ethics in Zen Buddhism, and currently he is working on Buddhist approaches to nature and environmental issues. His publications include *Imperial-Way Zen: Ichikawa Hakugen's Critique and Lingering Questions for Buddhist Ethics* (2009); *Zen Awakening and Society* (1992); *The Emptying God* (co-edited with John B. Cobb, Jr., 1990); *Divine Emptiness and Historical Fullness* (edited volume, 1995); a translation of Nishida Kitarō's *An Inquiry into the Good* (co-translated with Abe Masao, 1990); and a translation of Hisamatsu Shin'ichi's *Critical Sermons of the Zen Tradition* (co-translated with Tokiwa Gishin, 2002).

Introduction

Over the centuries Buddhists have viewed other religious traditions in various ways, but only in recent years have they formulated explicit approaches to religious pluralism. Given the complexity and diversity of Buddhist traditions, making an argument about what should be *the* Buddhist approach to pluralism proves daunting and may not be worthwhile. But one can at least offer *a* Buddhist approach that accords with core facets of Buddhism and promotes ends valued by the tradition. In this essay I will propose such an approach to religious pluralism, focusing on how religious traditions understand and respond to human suffering in various forms.

In making this argument I will be speaking from a particular Buddhist perspective: as a practitioner of Zen Buddhism who at present is only loosely affiliated with specific Zen lineages and institutions. And while aware that Buddhism is not monolithic, for heuristic purposes I will make claims about elements shared by most if not all types of Buddhism. Needless to say, my perspective is socially conditioned – I am also white, male and privileged in certain ways, and as a non-native citizen of the United States I am also a trespasser on native land.

Responses to religious pluralism, whether by Buddhists or those of other religious persuasions, or by agnostics and atheists, can take many forms, but at the very least we can conceive of two main ways of approaching the diversity of religious traditions. The first is a theoretical approach, in which one formulates a conceptual framework to understand religious pluralism or to categorize the many varieties of "religion." The other is a practical approach, in which one engages with diverse religious traditions to gain something from them, to do something with them, or to do something *to* them.

The theoretical approach, in turn, can go in several directions. Some theorists have formulated exclusivistic frameworks, arguing that one religious tradition, usually their own, has an exclusive handle on truth while other traditions are mistaken if not dangerous. Others have placed religions in a hierarchical or evolutionary scheme (as Hegel did in his *Philosophy of History*), ranking them relative to what the theorist judges to be their relative grasp of truth or their ability to facilitate liberation. Other schema have been more genuinely inclusive, construing religions as perceiving and engaging one-and-the-same Reality or Truth in different ways, though in some cases these schema do not include polytheistic or animistic religions, which are deemed less developed if not "primitive," thus belying lingering traces of hierarchy and exclusivism. We see this "many paths up the same mountain" approach in John Hick's *God Has Many Names*, and Hick acknowledges that he is "speaking of what we commonly call the great world faiths, not of primitive religion" (1982, 56). One other inclusive option is to argue that different religions are getting at different ultimates; we see this in John Cobb's framework as informed by the process philosophy of Alfred North Whitehead.

But what might constitute a genuine Buddhist approach to religious pluralism? Faced with an array of Buddhisms – numerous strands of thought and practice in different cultural and historical contexts – we can at least offer up *a* Buddhist approach to pluralism and acknowledge that it may reflect the orientation and commitments of one type of Buddhism or simply one theorist. Cognizant of the risk of succumbing to claims about a purported essence to Buddhism that is found in each and every phenomenon we can legitimately categorize as a type of Buddhism, or of trying to recover an ostensibly original, untainted teaching of the historical Buddha as a touchstone for what is genuinely Buddhist, we can, cautiously, make a claim about elements of commonality across the array of Buddhisms and then on that basis craft a largely pan-Buddhist approach to pluralism. Taking this tack, we can avoid arguing that we have, in congruence with a purported essence of Buddhism, formulated the most authentic Buddhist approach to pluralism and simply make a proposal to which most Buddhists can assent.

But what might that common element be? We could start with Buddhist truth claims, and find therein some shared notion of ultimate reality. From there we could follow the lead of Hick and view Buddhism and other religious traditions as offering different ways of seeing this reality, or different *degrees* of seeing it, or failing to see it. Masao Abe (1915–2006), the main recent Buddhist participant in dialogue with other religions, took such a metaphysical and theological approach in drawing correspondences and contrasts between the Buddhist construct of *śūnyatā* (emptiness) and other religious constructs like God, Yahweh, the godhead and the Trinity; his approach generated a de facto hierarchical scheme, with different religions having different degrees of insight into emptiness, which Abe regarded as the final word on the nature of reality.

Although what Abe formulated does constitute *a* Buddhist approach to pluralism, it expresses a particular modern, Japanese, Zen Buddhist perspective, to which many Buddhists in other places and times would not subscribe. This is not simply a matter of other Buddhists seeing reality as something other than Abe's "emptiness." Rather, most Buddhists have not been interested in metaphysical questions. Lay Buddhists have been more concerned with accruing karmic merit, properly memorializing the dead and securing this-worldly benefits, none of which entail sustained grappling with metaphysical questions and constructs like emptiness. The main concern of monks has been more psychological and ethical or, if functioning as ritual officiants ("priests"), liturgical; here, too, the concern is not metaphysical. Moreover, Buddhists who are more metaphysically inclined do not necessary focus on *śūnyatā* or accept Abe's treatment of the construct. In short, despite the impression one might get from Abe's approach, for most Buddhists metaphysical constructs like emptiness are not a concern, and some Buddhists might even bring in the Buddha's voice and claim that such a focus on metaphysics "does not edify," or at least not as much as other possible foci do.

If we look across the Buddhist landscape, we might find other doctrines, perspectives or commitments that are, compared with *śūnyatā,* shared more widely in Buddhism and deemed more crucial to the Buddhist path. We might lift up *Nirvāṇa* or certain meditative states, or perhaps *karma*. I would argue that the strongest candidate here is suffering (P. *dukkha*, Skt. *duḥkha*), for it appears safe to claim that the Four Noble Truths[1] stand in

1. Suffering, the cause of suffering, the cessation of suffering, and the path to the cessation of suffering.

the background, and sometimes in the foreground, of the multiple strands of Buddhism, and the *ultimate* concern that most unifies Buddhists across denominational, spatial and temporal boundaries is the amelioration if not elimination of suffering. I make this claim fully cognizant of the fact that the more *proximate* concern of many lay Buddhists is generating karmic merit by giving alms and doing other good deeds, or drawing on the ritual prowess and power of priests to ensure effective performance of such rituals as funerals and memorial services or to secure this-worldly benefits.

In other words, I would argue that a more pan-Buddhist and fruitful approach is to step away from viewing the plurality of religious traditions as different ways of getting at the Real or *śūnyatā* (à la Hick and Abe) and take the alternative position of viewing the plurality of religious traditions as different responses to various human existential problems that typically do not lend themselves to scientific explanations and solution.[2]

In taking this position and using the expression "various," I am not positing one common form of suffering, some universal "human condition" or, to reify it with upper-case letters, some core "Human Condition" or "Human Problem" to which all religious traditions are responding. In this respect, parallel to Cobb's notion of multiple ultimates, I want to leave open the possibility that it is *not* the case that different religious traditions are wrestling with one and the same existential problem from different angles. Even though I might be inclined to argue that religious traditions are responding to the fear and insecurity surrounding death and other types of chaos in our world (including unexplainable events, violence, injustice, illness, hunger, material insecurity), I do not want to foreclose the possibility that they may very well be addressing other human problems.

If we focus on suffering in this way, the Four Noble Truths can provide a template for encountering (and perhaps analyzing and categorizing) diverse religious traditions, for theorizing religious pluralism. So, in a Buddhist encounter with religious pluralism, one might ask:

1) *What does this or that religious tradition construe as the basic human problem(s), the condition(s) from which people suffer?* Is it suffering as understood by Buddhists? Is it estrangement from the divine? Living a life of sin? A break in our communion with others? With nature? Other problems? In what respects do religious diagnoses of the problem(s) concur and diverge?

---

2. In part I am thinking of problems like the three "problems of interpretability" that Clifford Geertz flagged in his "Religion as a Cultural System": bafflement, suffering, and evil.

2) *What does the tradition see as the cause of that problem?* Does it derive from craving and ignorance? Disobedience? Not holding up the human end of a covenantal relationship? Some sort of selfishness? Idolatry? A state of impurity? Disharmony with deities, ancestors or natural forces? In what respects do religious analyses of the cause(s) concur and diverge?
3) *What does the tradition see as the condition in which that problem has been solved? Nirvāṇa*? Awakening? Eternal life in heaven or paradise? A just and peaceful Kingdom of God? Blissful union with ultimate reality? Living in fruitful harmony with natural forces?
4) *How does one achieve that condition?* Practising something like the Eightfold Path? Humbly accepting Christ as one's saviour? Another type of faith? Following guidelines given by God? Submission to the one God? Intensive prayer or meditation? Vision quests? Healing the world? Living in a certain way in community? Attuning to natural patterns?

Again, what I am proposing here is that a focus on responses to core human problems, including what Buddhism designates as "suffering," would be a more pan-Buddhist and more genuinely Buddhist approach to pluralism than a focus on metaphysical claims about what true reality (the Real, ultimate reality, the sacred) might be. That is to say, insofar as Buddhism takes a largely pragmatic approach to truth, the core concern is not how religious worldviews get at the same Real (Hick) or correspond with ultimate reality (thinkers like Hegel and Abe) but how religious doctrines, practices, values and institutional arrangements, at the practical level, address human suffering.

Buddhists could on this basis proceed to formulate a typology for further theorizing of religious pluralism. They could group religious doctrines in terms of whether they focus on problems of the individual (for example, the existential problem of death), society (e.g., the existential problem of failing to find fulfilment in a community with fractured and unjust relationships) or the human relationship with "nature" (the existential problem of struggling to survive and flourish). They could also group different analyses of the cause of the problem(s) in, for example, three main categories: detrimental mental states (à la the Buddhist analysis and certain strands of Hinduism), estrangement from the divine, and disharmony with spirits, deities and natural forces.

Or, they can refrain from constructing a typology and simply propose that, from a Buddhist perspective, religious pluralism can be understood as the phenomenon of human beings in different cultures addressing recurring problems in different ways.

At the risk of making sweeping claims about what holds across the Buddhist tradition, I would argue that insofar as the core concern of Buddhism(s) is the alleviation of suffering and the tradition is pragmatically open to different ways of analyzing suffering and responding to it, as seen in the doctrine of skilful means (*upāya*), the Buddhist approach to religious pluralism that I am proposing here is not only theoretical but practical. That is to say, on the basis of the theoretical stance that religious traditions are responding to fundamental problems in human existence, Buddhists can engage those plural responses with an eye toward learning from them and thereby developing and refining Buddhist doctrines and practices.

Reforming the tradition in this way is nothing new. Buddhists have continually been rethinking core elements of their tradition in dialogue with other systems of thought and practice, as seen, for example, in the case of China and the Buddhist encounter with Daoism and Confucianism. In this respect, in their contemporary encounter with religious pluralism, Buddhists can fruitfully engage other traditions by studying their analyses of the problems about which Buddhists are concerned.[3] One of the fruits of this engagement may be the development of Buddhist analyses of and responses to suffering beyond the individual level, an area that many contemporary Buddhists (including Abe Masao) have flagged as needing development.

Talk of "suffering beyond the individual level" prompts the question of the exact connotation and denotation of "suffering" in traditional Buddhism. Different strands of Buddhism have different views of what, exactly, constitutes suffering and what configurations of suffering most merit our attention. The historical Buddha reportedly said, "There are, friend, these three kinds of suffering: the suffering due to pain, the suffering due to formations, and the suffering due to change" (Bhikkhu Bodhi 2000, 1299). The first (P. *dukkhadhukkhatā*) is physical pain and anguish over the challenges that life inevitably brings. The second (*sankhāradukkhatā*) refers to suffering caused by "formations" (*sankhāra*), which refers primarily to our volitional formations or dispositions. The third (*vipariṇā-*

3. Of course, to some extent this has already begun, as seen in Buddhist-Christian dialogue. Reformation of Buddhism has also been happening in the Buddhist encounter with such phenomena as Western psychology, environmentalism, feminist analysis and civil rights movements.

madukkhatā) refers to the suffering we experience when things to which we are attached change.[4] Historically the Buddhist tradition has been most concerned with the second and third, which pertain especially to existential, "religious" suffering as opposed to more physical types of suffering.

This does not mean, however, that the tradition has ignored suffering in the first sense, which consists of what we might term "mundane suffering," ranging from aches and pains all the way up to such forms of socio-political suffering as poverty, discrimination, abuse, oppression and war. The Buddha recognized the need to address this type of suffering. Scriptural passages portray him saying, for example, that hungry people needed to be fed before he preached to them (Jenkins, 2003). As indicated by the *Cakkavatti-Sīhanāda Sutta* (D 26, at D III 58–79), he also made comments about the need to address poverty, for it can lead to theft, violence and other actions contrary to Buddhist ethics. In general, however, Buddhist thinkers have spent little time exploring the relationship between individual existential suffering and socio-political suffering.

With regard to the Second Noble Truth, the cause of suffering, the Buddha lifted up *taṇhā*. This Pāli term literally means "thirst," and we can construe it as the desire or greed seen in craving for things or conditions we don't have and clinging to things or conditions we do have. The discourse on the cause of suffering was elaborated in the doctrine of the Three Poisons (ignorance, greed and ill will) and this constituted one component of a broader theory of detrimental mental states that is central to the moral psychology of Buddhism. With this orientation, Buddhism has looked primarily at psychological causes of suffering in the individual at the expense of developing this analysis through consideration of related external, social causes of suffering. Currently we see this happening in certain Western appropriations of Buddhism that are highly interiorized and individualistic.[5] As a result, Buddhists have often portrayed the Buddhist path to Awakening as in effect happening in a vacuum, divorced from social conditions, even though those conditions can exacerbate or ameliorate suffering, and hinder or support efforts on the path.

4. John Makransky renders these three types of *duhkha* as "obvious suffering," "the suffering of ego-conditioning" and "the suffering of transience" (2007, 161–163).

5. We see this especially in contemporary mindfulness programmes, many of which focus on the individual and his/her stress or scattered awareness with little attention to possible causes of that stress or scatteredness in the external situation of the individual, such as a corporate office where one is expected to work long hours in a frenetic, competitive and tense environment.

Thus, while Buddhism offers rich resources for investigating facets of individual suffering, the existential and psychological anguish from which so many of us suffer, Buddhists should not succumb to the complacency of thinking that they have fully investigated that suffering, or of seeing it as unrelated to social conditions. In the kind of engagement with religious pluralism that I am advocating here, Buddhists can learn from other traditions' analyses of human struggles and the mental states and social conditions behind them. For example, investigation of Christian analyses of sins (such the Seven Deadly Sins) and virtues (theological and moral) can help Buddhists refine their analyses of both the cause of suffering and the nature of human flourishing. Examination of Jewish practices like devoting the ten days between Rosh Hashanah and Yom Kippur to taking stock of the ways in which one's actions have been wide of the mark over the past year can suggest ways in which Buddhists might deepen their own grappling with detrimental mental states and the actions they generate. Exploration of Muslim views of justice can help Buddhists grapple with what Buddhist thinker David Loy has termed the "institutionalization" of the Three Poisons and the ways in which greed, ill will and ignorance writ large in social practices and institutions exacerbate the working of the Poisons in individuals or make extrication from them harder than might be the case under other social conditions. Engagement with indigenous traditions can deepen Buddhist understanding of conditioned arising[6] across the natural world.

Some Buddhists might argue here that the Buddhist moral psychology is highly sophisticated and there is little Buddhists can learn from other traditons about the causes and contours of the existential or religious suffering that has been the central Buddhist concern. But even if for the sake of the argument we allow for this possibility, we have to acknowledge the fact that Buddhism has generally been weaker than other traditions in analyzing social forms of suffering and their causes. This lacuna, coupled with the symbiotic relationship Buddhism has had with rulers and the status quo across Asia through its 2500-year history, has resulted in little critical reflection on social (in)justice (though Buddhists have lifted up *karma* in a deterministic fashion as a kind of retributive and compensatory justice).

Granted, some Buddhist thinkers have recently been giving thought to possible Buddhist responses to "mundane" suffering and its causes. But this reflection is limited mainly to contemporary "engaged" Buddhists and is still in its infancy. For this reason, Buddhist thinkers, and Buddhists in

6. Pāli *paṭicca-samuppāda*, also translated as interrelational arising or interbeing.

general, can benefit, for example, from Christian thinkers like Gustavo Gutierrez, Paul Knitter, Rosemary Ruether, John Cobb, Catherine Keller, James Cone, Sallie McFague and Heather Eaton. These theologians have construed soteriology at levels broader than the salvation of the individual, focusing on socio-political liberation from injustice and environmental degradation. By studying the de facto Four Noble Truths set forth by these thinkers, Buddhists can craft a more systemic analysis that links existential *dukkha* with socio-political *dukkha*. They can learn, for example, from Paul Knitter's "soteriocentric" approach to religious pluralism, which focuses on "the welfare of humanity and this earth, the promotion of life and the removal of that which promotes death" (Knitter 1990a, 37) and lifts up "the 'salvation' or 'well-being' of humans and Earth as the starting point and common ground for our efforts to share and understand our religious experiences and notions of the Ultimately Important" (Knitter 1990b, 17).

In advocating a Buddhist approach to pluralism that focuses on the ways in which different religious traditions address basic human problems, I am not trying to articulate a trans-historical approach to diversity. Despite Buddhist claims about *universal* patterns of suffering, about how the Three Poisons operate in all people at all times, for a Buddhist response to suffering and its causes to be effective or "skilful," Buddhist ethicists and activists must pay careful attention to the *particular* configurations of suffering in their historical situations, both in terms of the forms that suffering takes and the conditioning factors that operate along the lines of dependent arising.

In our historical moment, humanity is facing profound configurations of suffering. I would argue that the two most daunting forms right now are the negative impacts of climate disruption and violence (by state and non-state actors). Though psychological factors involved in these instances of suffering might lend themselves to traditional Buddhist analysis in terms of greed, ill-will and ignorance (as well as ignor-ance), the actual configuration of these problems and the steps needed to ameliorate if not eliminate them call for more than theories of detrimental mental states, however much they play a role in causing the problems. In this respect, a shift from the psychological to the socio-political dimension is essential, and in making this shift Buddhists can benefit from studying how people in other religious traditions have analyzed and responded to these forms of suffering and structures of power behind them.

With this practical approach to pluralism, Buddhists can build on dialogue with other traditions and engage in collaborative action with them in response to problems like the climate crisis and violence. As many people have discovered over the centuries, one way to engage religious pluralism is to make efforts to understand, appreciate, and maybe even achieve concord if not collaboration with other religious traditions, and this can be cultivated not simply through dialogue but through working together on a common project. That is to say, through history religious people have fruitfully engaged religious diversity and in many cases achieved strong relationships with those of other traditions by collaborating in response to a local, national or global problem. As recent examples of this collaboration, we can point to the September 2014 climate march in New York. Or we can point to interreligious efforts by organizations like GreenFaith and the Greater Boston Interfaith Organization.

In short, the theoretical and practical approach to religious pluralism that I am proposing here can help Buddhism develop not only its response to the suffering of Buddhists but also its contribution to the alleviation of human suffering more broadly. Both of these developments fall squarely within the arena of "correct Dharma" (J. *shōbō*) and will in all likelihood deepen it.

References

Bodhi, Bikkhu, trans. 2000. *The Connected Discourses of the Buddha: A Translation of the Saṃyutta Nikāya*. Boston: Wisdom.

Hick, John. 1982. *God Has Many Names*. Philadelphia: Westminster.

Jenkins, Stephen. 2003. "Do Bodhisattvas Relieve Poverty?" In *Action Dharma*, edited by Christopher Queen, Charles Prebish and Damien Keown, 38–49. London: RoutledgeCurzon.

Knitter, Paul F. 1990a. "Interreligious Dialogue: What? Why? How?" In *Death or Dialogue? From the Age of Monologue to the Age of Dialogue*, edited by Leonard Swidler, John B. Cobb, Jr., and Paul F. Knitter, 19–44. Philadelphia: Trinity.

———. 1990b. *Jesus and the Other Names: Christian Mission and Global Responsibility*. Maryknoll NY: Orbis.

Makransky, John. 2007. *Awakening through Love: Unveiling Your Deepest Goodness*. Boston: Wisdom.

12

Religious Diversity and Dialogue: A Buddhist Perspective

Asanga Tikakaratne
University of Colombo

Asanga Tilakaratne is Emeritus Professor of Buddhist Studies at Colombo University. He graduated from Peradeniya University, Sri Lanka, specializing in Buddhist Philosophy. He has published, both in Sinhala and English, more than one hundred papers on Buddhist studies. Of his more recent academic works, *Theravada Buddhism: the View of the Elders* (2012) was published by University of Hawai'i Press. He co-edited with Professor Oliver Abeynayaka *2600 Years of Sambuddhatva: Global Journey of Awakening* (2012), a work covering the history and the current status of global Buddhism of all three traditions. Professor Tilakaratne founded the Sri Lanka Association of Buddhist Studies (SLABS), an academic and professional organization of Buddhist scholars in Sri Lanka.

Introductory remarks

The phenomenon of religious diversity and interreligious dialogue are closely connected. How one perceives religious diversity determines to a large extent one's attitude to interreligious dialogue. Although dialogue has been around for a considerable time, still there are uncertainties as to what it is and why it is, even among those who practise it, let alone those who do not. In the Roman Catholic tradition, interreligious dialogue as a definitive concept and practice was started with Vatican II (1964–1966). Discussions on mission, however, had been carried out among other Christian denominations for some time before this. The World Missionary Conference held in 1910 in Edinburgh is an early example from Protestant churches.[1] It appears that different denominations of Christianity have

1. Fr. Pieris refers to several similar local Sri Lankan efforts: the Anglican priest (later, bishop) Lakdasa de Mel who, about three decades before Vatican II, had pioneered religio-cultural encounters with Buddhists and created indigenous liturgies and liturgical music; the Anglican monk-priest (later priest) Yohan Devananda who was already in the field (1959), creating an ashram-type Christian presence in harmony with the rural Buddhist culture at "Devasarana" in Ibbagamuwa; The Christian Workers' Fellowship started in 1958; and Rev. Lynn de Silva who pioneered an intellectual

their own histories of interreligious activities.[2]

In this discussion, first I will review briefly the current understanding of "dialogue" among its practitioners. In particular, different Roman Catholic perceptions of dialogue that shape the current practices and debates will be reviewed. Then I will look at the state of interreligious dialogue in the local context in Sri Lanka. Thirdly I will try to develop a Buddhist response to dialogue both in theory and practice through an analysis of religious diversity. I will conclude with some observations on the future of interreligious dialogue.[3]

To limit my scope, the focus of this paper is Vatican II and the subsequent developments in the Roman Catholic tradition. My Buddhist reflections basically come from my Sri Lankan experience as a Theravāda Buddhist. My intellectual debts in writing this essay will be clear as it unfolds, and I am in particular grateful to those Christian scholars who have been open-minded and self-critical about a theme that is very close to their religion.

Interreligious dialogue and its internal discontents

One cannot start a discussion on interreligious dialogue as if one is dealing with a concept with a universally agreed content leading to a set of unanimously accepted practices. As Aloysius Pieris S. J. has discussed in detail, the new attitude to other religions and the mission proposed in Vatican II was not the result of a smooth process culminating in unanimity among all participants. According to Pieris, clearly there were two schools of thought, one characterized by openness to other religions and rejection of the old practices of mission in favour of understanding and dialogue, and the other, the conservative Vatican group keen on defending the status quo. The debate was on whether the Vatican council was meant to be about reform or renewal. The distinction between the two perspectives in Peiris's words is as follows:

---

dialogue with Buddhism after he took over the Centre for Religion and Society which is now called "Ecumenical Institute for Study and Dialogue" (Pieris 1995b, 109).

2. See Hettiarachchi 2012 chapters 3 and 4 for a discussion on histories, debates and disputes on dialogue in Catholic and Protestant traditions respectively.

3. A slightly revised version of this paper is scheduled to appear under the title "Religious Diversity and Dialogue: Some Buddhist Reflections" in *Collected Papers of Asanga Tilakaratne: Interreligious Understanding* to be published in Colombo toward the end of 2019.

> there is a vast difference between these two options. **Reform** is a controlled and graduated process of change that keeps the institutional set-up of the church intact. It comes from top to bottom, from the centre to the periphery. Such were Vatican I and Trent. Rome issued decrees and they were followed far away. But **renewal** is exactly the opposite process. It irrupts from below and works its way up to the top volcanically. It is initiated in the periphery where fresh and new ideas flow in more freely than in the center of the establishment. Renewalist currents that begin to whirl in the margin of the church surge into centripetal waves that dash on the fortified ecclesiastical structures. (Pieris 2010, 137)

Then Pieris goes on to describe how this polarization has played a crucial role in determining the subsequent course of interreligious dialogue for the Roman Catholic Church. I will not reproduce that information here leaving room for interested readers to go to the original source.

It appears that even at the highest level of the Catholic Church there are differences of opinion as to what dialogue means and as to what its purpose is. According to one author, the Papal Encyclical *Redemptoris Missio* defends the Church's right to convert people and claims that interreligious dialogue is a "part of the evangelizing mission" (Rajashekar 2011, 239), although it is what most of the pro-dialogue Christians wish to see dialogue as not.[4] While one group of Roman Catholics, represented by such eminent theologians as Aloysius Pieris S. J. in Sri Lanka, thinks in terms of conversion as inner conversion, namely, one converting to true Christianity and to true Buddhism, or to the true God from false gods such as money and power, and supports such conversion wholeheartedly, there are others who think in terms of universal conversion.

After Vatican II even those who were keen on conversion would not talk in terms of conversion or proselytization any more, and would, instead, use such terms as "sharing the faith," "reaching out in love" and "witnessing" (Rajashekar 2011, 233) to communicate what was meant by those terms. Efforts at conversion, therefore, continue unabated with questionable means and questionable results (Premawardhana 2011; Rajashekar 2011). The comments made by Pope John Paul II (in his *Crossing the Threshold of Hope*) on Buddhism, that Buddhist soteriology is negative and hence is indifferent to the world and impedes the development of man and the world,[5] and the aggressive manner in which the Roman Catholic Church

4. In the persistence of this way of inside understanding, it is no wonder that many non-Christian religions perceive dialogue as the same old method of conversion in a new garb.
5. See Pieris 1995a, 62–95 for a comprehensive discussion on this issue which became controversial with the Papal visit to Sri Lanka in 1994.

speaks of "new evangelization," a movement meant to convert the world to Christianity, launched in order to celebrate the 2000th birthday of Christ, have to be seen as powerful expressions of disagreement with Vatican II.

Dialogue and Buddhism in Sri Lanka

In discussing dialogue with Buddhists in Sri Lanka, Pieris identifies three stages of its history: a period of bitterness and suspicion (1950s and 1960s), a period of incipient dialogue and co-operation (1970s), and a period of bitterness and suspicion (1980s and 1990s). In this analysis, Pieris discusses major historical and social factors that shaped the destiny of dialogue in Sri Lanka during these periods. The middle period discussed here is one during which Vatican II took place. According to Pieris,

> thanks to the Second Vatican Council, our local Catholic church began to view the social reality of our country with different eyes and began to re-assess the church's own historical role in the light of the Conciliar teachings. The Council opened up new perspectives with regard to other religions and the social reality in which the Church was to spell out its mission. [...] The late sixties saw many groups of Sri Lankan Catholics enter a new era of dialogue and collaboration with people of other faiths. (1995b, 108)

Discussing this further, Pieris says that these efforts were not sufficient to remove the distrust the Buddhists had toward Christians. It is interesting to note that the efforts at dialogue that Pieris refers to were originating from Christians, and there was no reciprocity on the part of Buddhists in this Christian initiative. In addition to the fact that dialogue was a very new concept for Buddhists, although not interreligious co-existence and co-operation, the breaking down of trust, referred to above, seems to have been a key reason.

In the work of Elizabeth Harris we read that one British missionary, Spence Hardy, complained in 1850 about what he saw as the Buddhist monks' "indolence, indifference, overconfidence in the truth of their own system" (Harris 2006, 195). But being indifferent is not the whole story of the Buddhist monastic attitude to Christianity. There are records of monks who resisted and complained about the missionary activities from a very early period of British rule. At the same time British missionaries themselves recorded how they were welcomed by Buddhist monks at their monasteries and how at times the monks even allowed missionaries to have their public lectures on their religion at the "*Dharma-ṣāla*" of the monastery. According to scholars like Harris, things became unpleasant when the monks found that the trust they placed in the missionaries had been betrayed (Harris 2006, 198–204). From the latter half of the nineteenth century the relationship between the two groups was characterized by mutual suspicion and rivalry, a situation which has continued to the present.

Given the not-so-pleasant memories of the colonial past, it is understandable why, in the early stages, Buddhists were not coming forward for dialogue in Sri Lanka. But why Buddhists are not making efforts at dialogue on their own may not be explained with reference to the above-mentioned historical reasons alone. The fact that dialogue still remains a Christian affair even after fifty years of Vatican II and *Nostra Aetate* requires some further explanation.

Buddhists self-understanding of their own religion and its implications for dialogue

As mentioned above, historical reasons that made Buddhists not enthusiastic about dialogue have been discussed by scholars such as Peiris. Beyond such historical reasons, there must be other doctrinal and philosophical reasons to explain this phenomenon. Perhaps it could be the reasons that Spence Hardy had in his mind when he described the Buddhist monks' attitude as "overconfidence in the truth of their own system" (Harris 2006, 195). In this context it is useful to examine the self-understanding of Buddhists concerning their own system, which probably caused them to be unenthusiastic about dialogue.

What could be the discourses of the Buddha which may have shaped the Buddhist attitude to Christianity, which is a theistic religion? Although reviewing all the relevant instances is out of place here, I will refer only to two instances to establish that the Buddha rejected the concept of God as creator and saviour. The first example I refer to is the *Mahā Titthāyatana Sutta* of the *Aṅguttara-nikāya* (A I 173–174), which identifies three religious views which "when questioned, interrogated, and cross-examined by the wise, and taken to their conclusion, will eventuate in non-doing" (A I 173; translated by Bodhi 2012, 266). They are: the view that all that is experienced, whether pleasurable, unpleasurable or neutral, is due to the deeds committed in the past (*sabbaṁ-pubbekata-hetu*); that all that is experienced [...] is due to the creative activity of God (*issara-nimmāna-hetu*); and that all is experienced [...] is due to no reason and no condition (*ahetu appaccaya*). The Buddha's discontent with these views is that they ultimately lead to non-action, denying thereby the need for human action without which moral responsibility becomes meaningless. According to the *sutta*, any voluntary act is impossible without free will, which, in turn, is impossible within a tradition in which God determines human action. Although this difficulty is not fully articulated in the discourse, the Buddha's position can be regarded as a result of being aware of this philosophical difficulty. Nevertheless, Christianity holds that God has given free will to human beings. But this uneasy marriage between divine ordination and free will causes some well-known philosophical and theological problems that cannot be easily bypassed.

The second example is an empirical argument used by the Buddha to show how the belief in a creator God does not have an experiential basis.[6] In a discussion with a young and learned Brahmin called Kapathika (*Canki Sutta,* M 95; translated by Bodhi 1995, 775–785), the Buddha demonstrates that none of the advocates of the alleged divine tradition has personal experience of its source, none is in a position to say "I see this; I know this." Rather, these brahmins are guided by mere faith, which under these circumstances becomes "groundless" (*amūlika*). In his rebuttal, Kapathika says that Brahmins go not only by faith but also by the tradition. Rejecting faith and tradition (and three other phenomena) as unreliable sources, the Buddha says they could lead to two results, either to truth or to falsehood. What is accepted on faith or tradition could well be false whereas what is not accepted on faith or tradition may well be true. Here the Buddha's statement is not a blanket denial of what is asserted by faith or tradition, but a highlighting of the essential unstableness of them as sources of knowledge. It is relevant to note in this context that the Indian Brahmanic tradition, during and after the Buddha, did not have any hesitation in characterizing the Buddha as "an advocate of destruction," a nihilist (*venayika*),[7] owing to his denial of *atma* (the self), and in including his teaching in the category of negative systems (*nāstika-vāda*), owing to its denial of the divine origin of the Veda. From this, it is clear that non-theism has been a key aspect of the Buddhist self-understanding.

6. This is not to deny the reality of the experiences claimed by believers to have been caused by God. Commenting on the position that I have developed in this paper, Fr. Peiris had this to say (in a private communication): "whosoever starts with the premise that Buddhism is a philosophy and not a religion could find it a waste of time to dialogue with theists. But a soteriology is accepted on the basis of experience. From a soteriological point of view I can be a Buddhist because *Nirvāṇa, alobha, arāga, adosa* and *amoha* [absence of desire, attraction, anger and delusion] as well as *taṇhānirodha* [cessation of craving] as proposed by the Buddha, is also what I struggle to achieve as a Christian. We are all *kiṁkusalagavesino* [inquirers after what is good], despite disagreements about Creator/Creation or rebecoming vs. resurrection. Creation pertains to philosophy – it is a rational conclusion derived by many, for or against."

7. See for example the *Alagaddūpama Sutta,* M 22, (M I 130–142).

Buddhist monks with a fair knowledge of the teaching of the Buddha should be expected to be familiar with the Buddhist critique of the concept of a creator God (*issara-nimmāna-vāda;* the creationist view).[8] Therefore it is understandable if the Sri Lanka Buddhist monks did not find Christianity religiously and intellectually exciting. If this was the intellectual attitude of Buddhist monks of the nineteenth century toward Christianity, I would submit that the intellectual attitude of the present day Buddhist monks remains the same.[9] It is perhaps this understanding that makes them satisfied with their own system and not under any necessity to learn from any other religion, although this by no means provides a justification for such an attitude. In addition, in a situation where the Christians themselves are not unanimous as to what dialogue is and for what purpose it is, it is understandable that Buddhists (or the adherents of any other religion for that matter) are hesitant about interreligious dialogue initiated by the Christian religion.

Buddhism and religious diversity

Pluralism, exclusivism and inclusivism in religion, views opposite to one another, all are premised on diversity of religion, which is a fact about the world. If, according to the *Shorter Oxford English Dictionary*, pluralism means "the toleration or acceptance of a diversity of opinions, values, theories etc." a pluralist can be either an inclusivist or an exclusivist. But according to the *Oxford Concise Dictionary*, pluralism is "a theory or system that recognizes more than one ultimate principle," a pluralist has to be a relativist. There is much debate about the position of the Buddha. In this context it is worth discussing briefly at least Abraham Vélez de Cea, who has done a thorough study of the Buddha's position on religious diversity.[10] I will not make a comprehensive study of Vélez de Cea's well-researched work. I will limit my comments to some key positions he holds.

Vélez de Cea characterizes the Buddha's attitude to other religions as pluralistic inclusivism. He distinguishes his position from what he

8. I do not venture into the debate existing among some Christian scholars to the effect that the Buddha really did not deny the existence of God. Raimundo Panikkar (1989), who held that the Buddha was most faithful to God by refusing to speak of Him in the so-called unanswered questions (*avyākrta-prashna*), is a classic example of this genre of scholars. I have discussed this matter in Tilakaratne 1993, 114.

9. Walpola Rahula, a well-known Buddhist monastic scholar, begins his now famous introductory book on Buddhism, *What the Buddha Taught* (1959) highlighting the non-theistic character of Buddhism.

10. Vélez de Cea (2013) provides a useful reference to a variety of strands of pluralism in the context of Buddhism.

considers "the prevalent Buddhist approach to religious diversity" which is a "sincere inclusivist attitude with an exclusivist view of liberation and the highest stages of holiness" (Vélez de Cea 2013, 1). Vélez de Cea identifies three different meanings of "pluralism" in relation to religion, and seems to consider the Buddha as a pluralist in the following sense: "an attitude that proactively engages other religions through dialogue without necessarily seeking agreement or conversion" (Vélez de Cea 2013, 167). For the pluralist reading of Buddhism that Vélez de Cea supports, it is very important that the Buddha accepted the possibility of liberation outside Buddhism. Vélez de Cea adduces sufficient evidence to prove that it is the case. In my understanding, however, in order for Vélez de Cea's pluralist interpretation to be true about the Buddha's position, one has to specify as to what the Buddha meant by liberation and the path leading to it. As Vélez de Cea himself has shown with reference to many discourses of the Buddha (Vélez de Cea 2013, 84–85), what the Buddha meant by liberation is what one gains within the four noble truth scheme. It is the liberation that the Buddha found, and it is the same that the Buddhas of the past found and the Buddhas of the future will find. According to the Buddha, there is no liberation outside the Four Noble Truths. What Vélez de Cea denies is that these Truths are found only in the Buddha's teaching, which existed in a particular space and time. Vélez de Cea is quite to the point when he says that the Buddha "refuses to claim that liberation is exclusive to his teaching-and-discipline" (Vélez de Cea 2013, 153) and again that "liberation is not exclusive to Buddhism" (Vélez de Cea 2013, 170). But what one needs to be aware of is that what is meant by the path and liberation is not *any* path or *any* liberation but what the Buddha exactly meant by those terms. According to the Buddhist belief, there were, there are and there will be many Buddhas in many world systems (*loka dhātu*) who teach the same truth.

In a well-known discourse, the *Nagara Sutta* (S II 105–106; trans. Bodhi 2000, 603), the Buddha is compared to a pioneer who discovered an ancient abandoned path leading to a lost city and showed the way for others to reach the same. The implication of the simile is quite clear: the path leading to the elimination of suffering, namely, the ancient path, and the goal of elimination of suffering, namely, the ancient city, have been there all the time. What any particular Buddha does is to discover these truths by himself and to teach others. The path and the goal are there to be discovered by anyone at anytime; they are not the monopoly of the Buddha or the Buddhists. The important thing to know is that the path and the city are the same whoever discovers them whenever.

Vélez de Cea discusses the *Cūḷa Hatthipadopama Sutta* (M 27: The lesser discourse on the simile of the elephant's footprint) as a key text supporting his pluralist interpretation, and claims that it has been misunderstood by the tradition. In the discourse, the Buddha advises his disciples not to reach a definitive conclusion about the Buddha, the Dhamma and the *Saṅgha* unless and until one knows for oneself that the Buddha is fully enlightened, the Dhamma is well taught by the Buddha and the *Saṅgha* is practising the path well. In the discourse the Buddha elaborates on the simile of an elephant tracker who does not cease his search for an elephant in the forest, despite much evidence such as large footprints, until he himself sees the elephant. The Buddha says, in a like manner, disciples must continue their search until they know for themselves that the Buddha is fully enlightened, etc. Interpreting this discourse, Vélez de Cea says:

> if something can be inferred from this simile, is that the Buddha would like his disciples to keep an open mind, at least until they attain enlightenment and see by themselves the truth about the Buddha, the Dharma and the *Saṅgha*. This openness requires the cultivation of intellectual humility and inquisitiveness, that is, it requires the abandonment of dogmatic attitudes that claim to know what they actually do not know, i.e., what can and cannot be found in other forests. That is, whether other forests are devoid of big elephants (exclusivism), or whether other forests have elephants exactly like those already found in the Buddha's forest (inclusivism). A true disciple of the Buddha would take the simile of the elephant's footprint more seriously, would avoid dogmatic assumptions, and would actually explore other forests before reaching a precipitated conclusion about the kinds of elephants that can and cannot be found outside one's own Buddhist forest. (2013, 6)

Vélez de Cea's interpretation would have been different had he given due weight to the role of trust (*saddhā*) in the path and the gradually ascending nature of the Buddhist practice. At the stage spoken of in the discourse, the disciple has already passed the stage of looking for other elephants in other forests. It is true that until one establishes "rational faith" (*ākāravatī-saddhā*)[11] in the Buddha to accept him as the teacher, the would-be disciple will have to be open to other possibilities. The best example of being open, inquisitive and intellectually humble is the Buddha's own practice as Siddhartha going from teacher to teacher and experimenting with various methods until he made up his mind to follow his own path.

11. See for instance *Vīmaṁsaka Sutta,* M 47; see Jayatilleke 1963, 386ff for a discussion of this.

We may think that many people who came to listen to the Buddha were in this stage for most of them would have been followers of other religious traditions. But once they listened to the Buddha and settled down to follow him, they could not waver and be inquisitive any longer. The interesting fact about the path [and of course about any procedure] is that one has to act it in order to see the results. At this stage one cannot do so if one does not have trust in the Buddha. Therefore it is trust that makes one proceed in the path. As I have discussed in detail elsewhere (Tilakaratne 1997), without trust one cannot act and without acting one cannot experience the result. The process described in the *sutta* is not a continuation of being open to other systems, being inquisitive or being intellectually humble. It is a gradual progress in the path, seeing/experiencing more and more evidence with increasing strength until one reaches the very end of the journey by seeing the elephant with one's own eyes. It is at this stage that one does not require trust any more for one has conclusive knowledge that the Buddha is fully enlightened. As K.N. Jayatilleke has shown (Jayatilleke 1963, 397), at this stage one's *saddhā* is completely replaced by *paññā* (knowledge). Therefore the whole point of the "elephant-simile" is not about being inquisitive till the end but about the gradual progress of knowledge to its completion.

Elaborating on openness to other traditions, Vélez de Cea characterizes it as "critical (inquisitive), firmly rooted in one's own tradition" (Vélez de Cea 2013, 7). If one is firmly rooted in one's own tradition, I do not see how one can at the same time be open and inquisitive about other systems. These two terms appear to be mutually exclusive and contradictory. One does not need to be open or inquisitive about other religious systems, if one is following one's tradition with confidence. This, however, should not be construed as refusing to be open to other religious systems in the sense of having a healthy attitude towards the other systems, accepting and respecting their right not merely to exist but even to thrive, and being humble enough to learn from them. If one who is open to dialogue is firm on his or her own system, he cannot be inquisitive in the sense of shopping for a better system.

Vélez de Cea thinks that the *Cūḷa Sīhanāda Sutta* (M 11: The shorter discourse on the Lion's Roar), where the Buddha very clearly and emphatically asserts that the four stages of Arhanthood (religious perfection as conceived in the teaching of the Buddha) and those who have reached those stages are found only within the teaching of the Buddha, poses a challenge to his interpretation of Buddhism as pluralism. In this discourse the Buddha asserts:

> here itself is the first *śramaṇa*. Here itself is the second, the third and the fourth *śramaṇa*. The systems of others are devoid of *śramaṇas*: bhikkhus, utter well the lion's roar in this manner. (*Idheva paṭhamo samano, idha dutiyo samano, idha tatiyo samano, idha catuttho samano, suññā parappavādā samanehi aññe ti evam evaṁ bhikkhave sammā sīhanādaṁ nadatha.*)

In this statement the Buddha encourages his followers to utter the "lion's roar" proclaiming this fact. Vélez de Cea makes a concerted effort to interpret the crucial term "*idheva*" (meaning "only here" or "here itself") as not having the meaning usually attributed to it. What is stated in the *Sutta* need not be interpreted as contradicting the Buddha's acceptance of the possibility of one's attaining *Nirvāna* on one's own in the absence of the *Sāsana* (teaching) of a Buddha. The statement should be understood as highlighting the position of his teaching *vis-a-vis* the other contemporary religious traditions. This is an instance of a clear rejection of contemporary systems by the Buddha, but not necessarily condemnation or criticism of them or an attack on them. Vélez de Cea seems to propose this interpretation owing to the (mistaken) understanding that the Buddha did not reject other religious teachings. Had he seen the *Mahā Titthāyatana Sutta* of the *Aṅguttara-nikāya*, discussed above, in which the Buddha rejects three current religious beliefs including the creationist view (*issara nimmāna vāda*), he would not have drawn this conclusion. I could not find any evidence that Vélez de Cea has seen this important discourse.

Vélez de Cea examines many other discourses in the course of his study. In particular he discusses a section of the *Mahāparinibbāna Sutta* (D. II 151), where the Buddha addresses his last disciple and makes a claim similar to the one found in the "Lion's Roar." I will not discuss these instances for want of space.

Implications for dialogue

In the previous section I have argued for a position akin to what Vélez de Cea characterizes as (to repeat) a "sincere inclusivist attitude with an exclusivist view of liberation and the highest stages of holiness." I do not have a problem in calling the Buddha a pluralist in the sense in which Vélez de Cea seems to use the term (to repeat: "an attitude that proactively engages other traditions through dialogue without necessarily seeking agreement or conversion"). But can the Buddha be a pluralist in the regular sense of the term as defined by the *Concise Oxford Dictionary* (to repeat: "a theory or system that recognizes more than one ultimate principle") even disregarding its metaphysical assumptions alien to Buddhism? The foregoing discussion should have shown that the Buddha is not a pluralist in this sense, namely, accepting the validity of more than one ultimate religious goal.

Within orthodox Christianity salvation is always through Jesus and the Church. Some pro-dialogue Christians are of the view that Christianity must think of salvation as coming from God, allowing more openness to other religions, a view not encouraged by the Vatican Curia. But, unlike perhaps other theistic religions, even in this God-centred scheme of salvation, Buddhists who deny the existence of a creator God who saves but advocate a definitive ethical path leading to cessation of suffering do not seem to have much hope. It is because the four-noble-truth-scheme and the concept of a saviour God are mutually exclusive, each making the other redundant.

For the pre-Vatican II Christians with an exclusivist view that salvation is only through Jesus Christ there is no question of being open to other systems. Even for the post-Vatican II proponents of dialogue, being open is to be open to other systems to see whether they can be accommodated within the salvific scheme of God.[12] Viewed from outside, for a religion which has been exclusivist in its outlook and which wields power in the arena of world religions, this is being magnanimous. It is also true that those who extend this magnanimity have had to reinterpret their tradition even at the risk of their own integrity being misunderstood in their organization. But the crux of the problem, whether one is open to dialogue or not, is that salvation in Christianity is always through God. Jose Kuttianimattathil, who is pro dialogue and who wrote a voluminous dissertation on dialogue concludes his essay in the following words:

> in dialogue, we come to the realization that the saving action of God, the origin and Goal of all, is reaching out to all peoples in ways mysterious to us. We confess that the Word, who became flesh, enlightens all those who come into the world and is the savior of all. We affirm that the Spirit is ever at work in the hearts and traditions of peoples drawing all to God. We accept the different religious traditions as God's gift to humankind. These traditions and their saints help in the divine-human encounter of their followers. The sincere adherents of these religions are members of God's Kingdom. As members of the Church, which is at the service of the Kingdom of God, we reach out to them in dialogue for mutual understanding, enrichment and cooperation in building the Kingdom and walking together with them towards the Infinite. (1995, 635)

This is to justify religious dialogue essentially on Christian grounds. Whether or not this means much for any other religion, in particular, to

12. For this view see Amaladoss 1985, 2 *passim* and 1992, 56 *passim*.

a non-theistic religion, remains a question. In so far as this justification remains applicable to Christianity it is an internal matter. Other religious traditions too will develop their own justifications for accepting religious diversity, resulting in peace and cooperation among the adherents of different religions while themselves remaining in their own conceptual universes. This is both realistic and desirable.

A problem arises when the Christian religious position is given as the universally applicable basis for interreligious dialogue. It has in it the problematic belief that all participants in dialogue have to share the same ultimate reality or the same salvific scheme. Underlying this position is the assumption that interreligious dialogue is impossible in the presence of differences. Buddhism questions this assumption, and holds that organizational religions can co-exist and cooperate while acknowledging their differences.

Contrary to the widely held belief, exclusivist claims are not always the result of being arrogant or being not ready or not open to learn.[13] Furthermore asserting differences is not necessarily being rude to others provided it is done with a proper attitude. Being inquisitive at one stage and being certain at another, as we find in Buddhist practice, are not mutually contradictory states in religious practice. I think the time has come to abandon the programme to create a theology encompassing all religions as precondition for interreligious dialogue. As the Dalai Lama emphatically says: "there *are* differences" (Roloff and Weisse 2015, 19). But interreligious dialogue for peace, understanding, harmony, co-existence and co-operation has to continue.

References

Amaldoss, S. J. Michael. 1985. *Faith, Culture and Interreligious Dialogue*. New Delhi: Indian Social Institute.

———. 1992. *Walking Together: The Practice of Interreligious Dialogue*. Anand, Gujarat: Gijarat Sahitya Prakash.

Aṅguttara-nikāya. I: 1961; II: 1976; Richard Morris. III: 1976. IV & V: 1958; E. Hardy. VI: 1960. Mabel Hunt. London: Pali Text Society.

Bodhi, Bhikkhu, trans. 2000. *The Connected Discourses of the Buddha: A Translation of the Saṃyutta Nikāya*. Boston: Wisdom.

———. 2012. *The Numerical Discourses of the Buddha: A Translation of the Aṅguttara Nikāya*. Boston: Wisdom.

13. Since I do not have space to discuss what Buddhism can learn from the West and Western religion, let me refer to the insightful discussion of Sally B. King on what Buddhism has to offer and what it can learn from the West, in Roloff and Weisse 2015.

Dhammajoti, Kuala Lampur, Asanga Tilakaratne and Kapila Abhayawansa, eds. 1997. *Recent Researches in Buddhist Studies: Essays in Honour of Professor Y. Karunadasa*. Colombo: Y. Karunadasa Felicitation Committee.

Fernando, Marshal and Robert Crusz, eds. 2011. *Theology Beyond Neutrality: Essays in Honour of Wesley Ariarajah*. Colombo: The Ecumenical Institute for Study and Dialogue.

Harris, Elizabeth J. 2006. *Theravāda Buddhism and the British Encounter: Religious, missionary and colonial experience in nineteenth century Sri Lanka*. Abingdon: Routledge. https://doi.org/10.4324/9780203098776

Hettiarachchi, Shanthikumar. 2012. *Faithing the Native Soil: Dilemmas and aspirations of post-colonial Buddhists and Christians in Sri Lanka*. Colombo: Self-published.

Jayatilleke, K.N. 1963. *Early Buddhist Theory of Knowledge*. London: George Allen and Unwin.

King Sally B. 2015. "Buddhism in Dialogue with the West: What it offers and what it learns." In *Dialogue and Ethics in Buddhism and Hinduism*, edited by Carola Roloff and Wolfram Weisse, 31–44. Münster: Waxmann.

Kuttianimattathil, Jose, SDB. 1995. *Practice and Theology of Interreligious Dialogue*. Bangalore: Kristu Jyoti.

Majjhima-nikāya. 1974. Volume IV. Translated by Mrs. Rhys Davids. London: Pali Text Society.

———. 1977. Volumes II and III. Translated by Robert Chalmers. London: Pali Text Society.

———. 1979. Volume 1. Translated by V. Trenckner. London: Pali Text Society.

Panikkar, Raimundo. 1989. *The Silence of God: The Answer of the Buddha*. New York: Orbis.

Pieris, Aloysius. 1995a. "The Christian and Buddhist Responses to the Pope's Chapter on Buddhism." *Dialogue* XXII: 62–95. Colombo: The Ecumenical Institute for Study and Dialogue.

———. 1995b. "Dialogue and Distrust Between Buddhists and Christians." *Dialogue* XXII: 104–121. Colombo: The Ecumenical Institute for Study and Dialogue.

———. 2010. *Give Vatican II a Chance: Yes to Incessant Renewal and No to Reform of the Reforms*. Kelaniya: Tulana Media Unit.

Premawardhana, S. 2011. "Towards a Deeper Understanding of Conversion: The Next Set of Questions for Churches." In *Theology Beyond Neutrality: Essays to Honour Wesley Ariarajah*, edited by Marshal Fernando and Robert Crusz, 257–271. Colombo, Sri Lanka: Ecumenical Institute.

Rajasekar, P. 2011. "Proselytism in an Age of Pluralism." In *Theology Beyond Neutrality: Essays to Honour Wesley Ariarajah*, edited by Marshal Fernando and Robert Crusz, 231–242. Colombo, Sri Lanka: Ecumenical Institute.

Roloff, Carola and Wolfram Weisse, eds. 2015. *Dialogue and Ethics in Buddhism and Hinduism*. Münster: Waxmann.

Samyutta-nikāya. 1973. Volume I; Volume II: 1970; Volume III: 1975; Volume IV: 1973; Volume V: 1976; Volume VI: 1960; edited by M. Leon Feer. London: Pali Text Society.

Schmidt-Leukel, Perry, ed. 2008. *Buddhist Attitudes to Other Religions*. Germany: EOS.

Tilakaratne, Asanga. 1993. *Nirvana and Ineffability: A Study of the Buddhist Theory of Reality and Language*. Colombo: Postgraduate Institute of Pali and Buddhist Studies.

Tilakaratne, Asanga. 1997. "*Saddha*: A Prerequisite of Religious Action." In *Recent Researches in Buddhist Studies: Essays in Honour of Professor Y. Karunadasa*, edited by Bikkhu Kuala Lumpur Dhammajoti, Asanga Tilakaratne, and Kapila Abhayawansa, 593–611. Hong Kong: Chi Ying Foundation.

Vélez de Cea, Abraham. 2013. *The Buddha and Religious Diversity*. Abingdon: Routledge. https://doi.org/10.4324/9780203072639

13

Finding the Right Questions about Religious Diversity: What Buddhists Could Contribute to Discussions of Religious Diversity

Rita M. Gross

University of Wisconsin

Rita M. Gross (1943–2015) was Professor Emerita of Comparative Studies of Religion at the University of Wisconsin-Eau Claire. A past president of the Society for Buddhist-Christian Studies, she participated in many forums for interreligious exchange. Gross was the author of many books and articles. Her major works include *Buddhism after Patriarchy: A Feminist History, Analysis, and Reconstruction of Buddhism* (1993); *Soaring and Settling: Buddhist Perspectives on Contemporary Social and Religious Issues* (1998); *Religious Feminism and the Future of the Planet: A Buddhist-Christian Conversation* (with Rosemary Radford-Ruether; Continuum 2001); *A Garland of Feminist Reflections* (University of California Press, 2009); *Religious Diversity What's the Problem: Buddhist Advice for Flourishing with Religious Diversity* (Cascade Books 2014). With Terry Muck, she edited two books of articles from the journal *Buddhist-Christian Studies: Buddhists Talk about Jesus, Christian Talk about the Buddha* (Continuum 2000); *Christians Talk about Buddhist Meditation, Buddhists talk about Christian Prayer* (Continuum 2003). In addition to her academic work, she taught meditation and Buddhism at many Buddhist centres in North America.

Introduction

Promoting more cogent thinking about religious diversity has been central to me for my entire life, even though I am better known for my work on Buddhism and gender. I have now evened the score with the publication of *Religious Diversity – What's the Problem? Buddhist Advice for Flourishing with Religious Diversity* (Gross 2014). That book title implies what I would argue is the key issue about religious diversity. Why do we regard religious diversity as a problem or an issue? Why do so many people think that religious diversity is a theological mistake or that the world would be a better place if only everyone would just agree to follow the best religion – "ours" of course. I have never been able to figure out how intelligent, morally responsible people could imagine that all the world's people could be equally satisfied by the same religion, despite how different people are from one another, especially intellectually and spiritually. Yet many of the world's religions have sought a religious monopoly for themselves and this position is still very common. A popular opinion, voiced to me by many Westerners, both religious and non-religious, is that everyone thinks their own religion is "the best," not only for themselves but for everyone else. The problem with this claim is that it simply doesn't hold up worldwide. There are at least four modes of religious belonging, only one of which involves the claim that "my" religion is "truest" and best for everyone (Gross 2014, Chapter One).

One of my claims is that Western theologians of religions, dominated mainly by Christianity, have been asking the wrong questions, concerning themselves primarily, with an emphasis on the "truth" of religions and asking if other religions can compete with "ours" in their "truthiness," to use Stephen Colbert's coined word. It seems to me that, as theologians of religion, we need to start at the other end of the puzzle, conceding from the get-go that religious diversity is here to stay, is inevitable, normal, natural, and is not a theological mistake, problem or issue. Perhaps, when the world's major religions were more isolated and less able to interact with each other, people could imagine that one of the religions was "superior" to the others. But it is difficult for me to imagine grounds for holding such a view, given current conditions. In other publications, I have argued that it simply is not religiously cogent to imagine that any one of the world's current religions could or should become the sole surviving religion on the planet or could meet the spiritual and religious needs of everyone on the planet, any more than everyone would or should adopt the same language, the same culture or the same diet. I do not want to repeat those arguments here (Gross 2004; Gross 2014, 118–135).

If we do not concede that religious diversity is inevitable and not theologically problematic, we wind up with the same kinds of hierarchical dualisms that result in racism, sexism, nationalism and the suffering that results when one group of people claims superiority over those who are different. It is hard to understand the urge to rank alternatives hierarchically into true/false, better/worse dichotomies whenever differences are perceived. But, given that oppositional dualism seems to be a default mode for human consciousness, such alleged dichotomies are common. It is very sad that such thinking has been so pervasive regarding religious diversity. Then it becomes clear that the important questions are not about *them*, the others who are different from us, but about *us*. The relevant question becomes, "Why do we dislike diversity so much?" Why the almost knee-jerk response to differences of ranking the different options hierarchically? An important question then becomes, "How can we cure our own discomfort with diversity?" The question is not whether religious others are enough "like us" that we should decide that they also possess some measure of truth or are deeply similar. In fact, I will claim that regarding religions, the central questions are not about the truth of religious propositions but about whether they work to provide meaningful ethical transformation and accomplishment in their adherents. That is another reason why I claim theologians of religions have been asking the wrong questions. But the primary question remains: how can my religion accommodate the fact of religious diversity without stress or anxiety, overcoming any lingering dislike of diversity?

These are my conclusions and my questions as a Buddhist deeply influenced by the modern comparative study of religions. This starting point is the same for all contemporary theologians of all religions, whose situations are essentially the same. I do not see any alternative except accepting that religious diversity will be a fact for the foreseeable future, and I would posit forever, given what we know about religions globally. Theologians of each religion need to present what their tradition can offer for living peacefully and gratefully with religious diversity. That is my job as a Buddhist constructive and critical thinker. I am not especially concerned with claims about Buddhism's past record, or even with troubling present situations regarding Buddhism and other religions, nor for that matter with the records of other religions but with what they presently offer and propose as methods to cope creatively and peacefully with religious diversity.

In my book, I discussed many points and practices that would promote flourishing with religious diversity, all of which are compatible with Buddhist practices and values, and which I learned primarily from Buddhist contemplation and practice, though they are more generally applicable and not limited to Buddhism in their relevance. Because in my book I discussed so many ideas and practices that would promote flourishing with religious diversity, it is difficult to condense them into a brief chapter. At this point, I would want to start with the non-dual, non-conceptual state of awareness that is so valued in Buddhist sensibilities. Both non-duality and non-conceptuality are not well-known or well-understood in much academic theology and are exceedingly difficult to present in sound-bite form. Non-duality counters the oppositional duality I have already discussed as a major problem that makes it difficult to flourish with religious diversity. Especially important is to think more clearly about the assumed independent existence of self and other, subject and object, a topic to which I devoted many pages in my book. Non-conceptuality counters the fixation on doctrinal correctness that has fuelled so much inter-religious hostility and conflict.

This brief chapter will focus more on non-conceptuality than on non-duality. Non-conceptuality is connected with one of the many Buddhist sensibilities that I claim could greatly benefit discussions of religious diversity, namely Buddhism's suspicion that verbal and conceptual propositions cannot be trusted to be reliable absolute truths, or to be "most certainly true," as I was taught to regard them as a child. There are many examples of how Buddhists have fallen short of taking these sensibilities seriously, including a disappointing history of intra-Buddhist sectarianism. Nevertheless, these Buddhist teachings are both central to *Buddhist* sensibilities and could be extremely helpful in a religiously diverse world if they were deeply internalized by religious leaders and practitioners.

This suspicion is often expressed in an analogy that is extremely common in Zen Buddhism, of the moon and a finger pointing to the moon. This analogy is of someone pointing at the moon, while an onlooker focusses on the tip of the finger, ignoring the moon to which the person is pointing. The point of this analogy is to emphasize the difference between theoretical teachings and insight into the (non-conceptual) meaning of teachings, in keeping with frequent Buddhist advice regarding how to take teachings: rely on the meaning not the words. The point is not that there is nothing to "know" but that that knowledge cannot be captured in words and concepts, much as Western apophatic theology points out - God is always beyond our theologies. Instead, we must pursue the disciplines, the skilful means of teachings and practices that put us in touch with the "god beyond god" to quote Paul Tillich, disciplines that also give us the strength to be comfortable with uncertainty, to rest in the state of "not knowing." This relationship between words or concepts and deep understanding is pointed out in the words of a great twentieth century meditation master, Thrangu Rinpoche:

> when you rest in this experience of the mind, which is beyond extremes or elaborations, what is the experience of that like? It is characterized by a profound state of ease, which means an absence of agitation or discomfort. Therefore, the experience is comfortable and pleasant. The term comfortable does not indicate pleasure in the sense of something you're attached to, or the pleasure of acting out an attachment or passion. It's simply the absence of any kind of discomfort or imperfection in the nature of the mind itself. Therefore, the experience of that nature is characterized by comfy blissfulness. This is as close as we can come in words to what you

> experience when you look at your mind. You can't actually communicate what you experience. It's beyond expression [...].[it] is inexpressible, indescribable and even inconceivable. (2002, 90)

Conceding what words and concepts can do as well as their limits would really go far to promote flourishing with religious diversity because it would significantly limit the tendency towards "competitive theology," which is often expressed in looking for an underlying similarity between their religion and ours, a method of dealing with religious diversity that does not really concede that religions are diverse and that difference is not necessarily a problem and need not promote negative comparison, as it so often does.

Conceding that all theologies or conceptual systems encounter the same limits regarding their verbal formulations puts them on a level playing field, which fosters flourishing with religious diversity. One of the problems, in my view, is that many theologians and religious thinkers seem confused about the inevitable nature of religious language. They tend to talk as if the language of their own religious tradition is unmediated, directly from a non-human and non-natural source, as if the deity speaks only Hebrew or Arabic, or whichever language they prefer. But if one understands interdependence and emptiness, one would not suppose that one's own language is unmediated (though some Tibetans seem to think that of Tibetan!) Both Buddhism and the modern comparative study of religion would agree that because phenomena are conditioned, unconditioned religious language is impossible. I would not claim that in general Buddhists recognize this fact more readily than adherents of other religions.

Religious and theological language, if one is honest about it, is speculative, metaphysical and/or mythological, not empirical and often not rational. I am not one who thinks this is a problem unless one insists that religious claims are of some other order, but not speculative, metaphysical, mythological and therefore metaphorical in the long run. Such language is conditioned by its cultural matrix, a fact recognized more thoroughly by comparative studies in religion than by most Buddhists or by most theologians of other traditions. Nevertheless, because of the limits and nature of speculative, metaphysical or mythological language, it is important not to become attached to views, concepts and teachings, and to make a sharp distinction between words and meaning when de-ciphering religious texts and teachings. The major problem here is a post-enlightenment tendency to mistake the nature of religious language and claims, to take them as facts rather than as symbols, analogies or metaphors. This is a very serious problem, both in popular religion and in formal theology these days.

Problems that occur with undue or inappropriate reliance on words and concepts are consistent in Buddhist commentaries with the four main attachments to which people are easily subject. To understand why attachment to words and concepts is so dangerous, clear understanding of the way that Buddhists understand the role of attachment or grasping (*tṛṣṇā*) in causing human suffering is required. These teachings are at the heart of Buddhism. As is well-known, the first truth of the Noble Ones is that suffering is inevitable in conventional ways of living and the second truth of the Noble Ones is that suffering is caused by attachment, which is desperately wanting what we cannot have or wanting things to be different than they are. These teachings on suffering and attachment are at the core of Buddhist teachings. In turn, when explaining the Second Truth, teachings on conditioned genesis (*pratītyasamutpāda*), the twelve *nidāna*s or on interdependence develop these teachings further. These twelve links (*nidāna*s) trace out the conditioning links that connect all phenomena, which means that all phenomena are interdependent but none of them is independent. In a single word, they are "empty" of inherent or independent existence.

Important texts represent the Buddha as teaching "Bhikkhus, there are these four kinds of clinging. What four? Clinging to sensual pleasures, clinging to views, clinging to rules and observances, and clinging to a doctrine of self" (*Cūḷasīhanāda Sutta* M. I 66; Ñāṇamoli and Bodhi 1995, 161). Clinging to views, including religious views, is one of the four major things to which we habitually cling. Thus, rather than being a virtue, holding religious views strongly, which could be defined as being too convinced of one's own religious views, is an impediment, a problem. The link between suffering and clinging to religious views is important to explore. Most, if not all wars and persecutions stem from too much conviction in the rightness and correctness of one's own views, as well as self-centredness. Few people reflect seriously on the aggression inherent in ideology, a.k.a. holding views strongly. Holding one's own views strongly often results in aggression and disrespect towards those with whom one disagrees. One also experiences the suffering of one's own anger, one of the most painful of all emotions. Religions often encourage their followers to adhere to the religion's doctrines with unquestioning, unreflective allegiance. The more fiercely people adhere to the religious doctrines of their sect, the more they are praised for "having true faith."

In politics, anyone who thinks through a situation or an issue and changes his or her mind is derogatively called a "flip-flopper." Just reflect on how much more pleasant life could be if peoples' beliefs about many things, including religion and politics, were held less dogmatically, with less attachment. Think how much personal and family discord is caused when close friends and family members, who do not know how to flourish with diversity and discord in their midst, argue with their relatives and friends about religion or politics, even "unfriending" those who refuse to change their views until they accord with those of the one with strong views.

No wonder so many spiritual teachers regard opionionatedness or rigid conviction of the correctness of one's own views, religious and otherwise, as one of the greatest obstacles on the spiritual path. Religions often decry self-centredness and attachment to sensual pleasure as great obstacles for realizing deep spirituality, but few realize that attachment to one's own version of religious truth is just as big an obstacle to spiritual attainment. It completely destroys the equanimity and evenness of mind so prized by Buddhists, which bring so much peace and which make religious diversity and religious co-existence unproblematic. It is very interesting and insightful to realize that attachment to views could be as unhelpful as attachment to sensual pleasures or self-centredness. I would argue that this is one of the most important contributions Buddhists could make to discussions of religious diversity and co-existence.

People who are very attached to their own opinions are often under the illusion that the world would be a better place and everyone would be happier, if only everyone else would adopt their opinions, not realizing that such a vision is no more realistic than the dream of a universally comprehensible language, which is a much more practical and desirable outcome than universally accepted religious or political/social systems. One of the most insightful comments about the aggression inherent in such conviction and opionatedness is that of Chögyam Trungpa:

> while everyone has a responsibility to help the world, we can create additional chaos if we try to impose our ideas or our help upon others. Many people have theories about what the world needs. Some people think that the world needs communism: some people think that the world needs democracy; some people think that technology will save the world; some people think that technology will destroy the world. The Shambhala teachings [or any non-oppressive vision] is not based on converting the world to another theory. (1998, 29)

The operative word here is "theory," as in "converting the world to another theory." The *problem is never with one's views, but with the desire to universalize or absolutize them*, to think they could or should be relevant for everyone. As I stated over and over throughout my book, the problem with universalized religious truth claims, such as that Jesus is the "only universal saviour of the world" or that the Four Truths are superior to other truth claims is not the belief itself but how it is held, with attachment and dogmatically. Those to whom such a belief is dear would not be harmed in any way if they changed the way those beliefs were held. A belief that is not universalized or absolutized is not less meaningful if it is held in a more flexible and relaxed manner. It is the same with most of the "hot button" social issues. Those who advocate for marriage equality never claim that everyone should enter same sex unions, whereas those who oppose marriage equality often claim that only the form of marriage they prefer, heterosexual unions, should be allowed. Why the arrogance and aggression of thinking everyone else should adopt one's views and preferences, for Jesus, for Christianity, for Buddhism or for heterosexuality? Given that, regarding religion, I prefer diversity and co-existence to intolerance and universal truth claims, I am sometimes asked if such preferences are not "intolerant" of those who prefer universalism to valuing diversity or of those who advocate stridently for their own religion out of intense conviction that it is the only worthwhile religion on the planet? I answer "No" because a situation in which many religious views flourish does not diminish any specific view unless it claims that it is worthy of being absolutized and universalized, and I would claim that no view rises to that standard.

There are many Buddhist images for the inadvisability of clinging to religious views, even the Buddhist teachings themselves. Two of the most relevant similes compare "truth" or *Dharma* held with grasping and fixation to a snake grabbed by the wrong end and to a raft that has already served its purpose of getting one across a body of water but which one still wants to carry around. The snake simile is better known for its later use by Nāgārjuna in explaining how teachings on emptiness are totally misunderstood and become damaging if they are taken literally or nihilistically, but it is also used in Pāli texts. The statement attributed to the Buddha says: "suppose a man needing a snake, seeking a snake, wandering in search of a snake, saw a large snake and grasped its coils or its tail. It would turn back on him and bite his hand or his arm or one of his limbs, and because of that he would come to death or deadly suffering" (*Alagaddūpama Sutta,* M 22, at M I 133–134; Ñāṇamoli and Bodhi 1995, 227). In the much quoted raft parable, found in the same collection of *sutta*s, the Buddha talks of a man who, on a dangerous shore of a body of water, sees the peaceful and pleasant other shore and decides to build a raft out of grass and branches, with which he paddles himself to the other shore using his hands and his feet. He then thinks that because the raft was so useful, he should continue to carry it around on dry land. The

Buddha says of that plan, "Bhikkhus, when you know the Dhamma to be similar to a raft, you should abandon even the teachings, how much more so things contrary to the teachings" (*Alagaddūpama Sutta,* M 22 at M I 135; Ñāṇamoli and Bodhi 1995, 229).

This principle is stated even more forcefully by the contemporary Tibetan teacher Dzongsar Khyentse, Rinpoche, who says, "At the point of total realization, you must abandon Buddhism. The path is a temporary solution, a placebo to be used until you understand emptiness" (Khyentse 2007, 77–78). Later in the same book, he writes, "If you still define yourself as a Buddhist, you are not a Buddha yet" (Khyentse 2007, 106). By no means do most or all Buddhists meet this standard, and Buddhist sectarianism, especially intra-Buddhist sectarianism, is rife. Nevertheless, that high standard is part of the Buddhist view, taught more frequently than it is adhered to.

The analogy of religious teachings as a raft locates the purpose of the raft in getting us to the other shore. But it does not describe the raft; rafts that work could presumably be of different shapes and colours. This is in keeping with not fixating on the conceptual content of religious teachings, which need only one quality. They must be seaworthy and not fail us midstream, before we get to the other shore, dumping us disastrously into the water. Therefore, it is a good idea to evaluate the seaworthiness of a raft before entrusting ourselves to it. Those of us who evaluate religious diversity as normal and valuable, and refuse to rank religions against one another or regard it as foolhardy to attempt to assess the truth value of religious claims are often accused of being "relativists" and are asked if we have no standards for evaluating religions. But, even if it is problematic and dangerous to be too attached to the truth of our religious claims, rafts do need to be tested and found seaworthy. How? By what criteria?

I have already stated that I do not think religions are about "truth." But they should work. They should do something. What? They cannot provide certain answers to questions about which only speculation is possible. But they should "get us to the other shore" to use the raft analogy. In other words, their job or function is to be a skilful means for transformation, to transform those who follow them from self-centredness towards greater kindness and flexibility. There is no reason to suppose that there is only one tool or skilful means for meaningful transformation, which nicely answers the question about how to think about the multiplicity of religions. The question we need to ask of other religions is not "Are they true or "more true," whatever that might mean?" but, "Do they work? Are their believers kind to women, animals, the unfortunate and nature? Are they kinder and more flexible, less rigid and dogmatic than they were formerly?" I would contend that this question about the practicality of religion, about how effective they are as skilful means for relevant ethical transformation, is the question about religious diversity that should be uppermost but is most often unasked and overlooked, because so many commentators are far too concerned with questions of truth in religion.

In my work, I have consistently claimed that the effectiveness of religious teachings and practices in promoting meaningful transformation is much more relevant than questions of the "truth" of religious claims, something that is impossible to determine. That effectiveness is what Buddhists sometimes call "skilful means," the ability of religious practices and teachings to promote meaningful and auspicious transformation. Flourishing with religious diversity is much more likely to occur if people are more concerned with the utility and effectiveness of religions, that is to say their track record as skilful means, than with their truth.[1] My suggestions for evaluating the diverse religious teachings and practices as skilful means, methods for spiritual transformation, is Buddhist-inspired rather than purely Buddhist. The concept of skilful means is authentically Buddhist and is part of a complex of teachings involved in the common pairing of wisdom (*prajñā*), gendered feminine, and skilful means (*upāya*), gendered masculine, especially common in Vajrayāna Buddhism. They are paired because the one without the other is relatively useless. In other words, having answers or "truth" without knowing how to work with the situation at hand is useless, even ineffective. One also has to have enough skill to put knowledge or information into effect, to get practical results. Knowledge is only meaningful when paired with appropriate skills. Contemplating that pairing led me to conclude that teachings or ideas are, in fact, more in the realm of *upāya* than the realm of *prajñā*, which initially strikes even many Western Buddhists as counter-intuitive.

The emphases on focusing on the practicality of religions, rather than their truth fits well with or could be considered another aspect of trusting non-conceptuality. Just as non-conceptuality does not mean there is nothing to know, so the claim that words and concepts cannot communicate completely what is to be known, mistrust of words, does not mean that words are useless. They are very useful if we do not overestimate what they can do. Nor will evaluating religions as skilful methods for relevant transformation solve all the problems than can arise with religious diversity. Disagreements will still occur. Disagreement need not be a problem and is much less troubling to one if one is much less attached to one's own views. Also, if one is not so attached to one's own views and is therefore

1. For my full discussion of this point, see chapter five in Gross 2014, 118–135.

less troubled by the disagreement of others with oneself, one is much less angry and aggressive in the face of disagreement. Disagreement itself is to be expected and is therefore not especially a problem. The aggression and self-righteousness that so many people fall into when someone disagrees with them are the problem. We are back to the problems that go with holding one's views too tightly, with too much attachment. To use an old slogan, we must cultivate disagreement without being disagreeable.

Short of overcoming our own discomfort with diversity, there seem to be few viable options. Many of the other solutions that have been tried – ethnic cleansing or holocaust, aggressive proselytizing, economic and political penalties for belonging to a disapproved religion, even hostility or indifference to religion in general – are deeply immoral and/or unsatisfying. Instead, we need to develop a theology, a spiritual/religious worldview, which finds theological, not just historical or sociological justification, for prioritizing diversity and difference over unity and sameness. Even more importantly, we need to practise the spiritual disciplines that help us overcome our egocentric preferences for a world in which everyone else would be just like us and can, instead, live comfortable in a world that accommodates vast differences.

References

Bhikkhu Ñāṇamoli and Bhikkhu Bodhi, trans. 1995. *The Middle Length Discourse of the Buddha: A Translation of the Majjhima Nikāya.* Boston: Wisdom.

Chögyam Trungpa. 1998. *Shambhala: The Sacred Path of the Warrior.* Boston: Shambhala.

Gross, Rita M. 2004. "Excuse Me but What's the Question? Isn't Religious Diversity Normal?" In *The Myth of Religious Superiority*, edited by Paul Knitter, 75–87. Maryknoll, NY: Orbis.

———. 2014. *Religious Diversity, What's the Problem? Buddhist Advice for Flourishing with Religious Diversity.* Eugene, OR: Wipf & Stock.

Khyentse, Dzongsar Jamyang. 2007. *What Makes You Not a Buddhist?* Boston: Shambhala.

Thrangu Rinpoche. 2002. *Pointing Out the Dharmakaya.* Crestone, CO: Namo Buddha.

Index

A

Abe, Masao, 125, 189–192

Abeysekara, Ananda, 99, 103, 106

Abhidhamma Piṭaka, 17, 48n5

Abhidharmakośabhāṣya, 72n8

Abrahamic religions, 64, 70, 80, 172

Ādhipateyya *Sutta*, 87

Advaita Vedānta, 132

Aggañña Sutta, 100

Ajita Kesakambala, 7, 27–28, 31

Alagaddūpama Sutta, 202n7, 219–220

Ālāra Kālāma, 25

al-Biruni, 74n14

American Buddhism, 121–122, 125

Anagārika Dharmapāla, 108

Anālayo, Bhikkhu, 82, 85

analogies. *See* metaphors

Ānanda, 13–14

Aṅguttara Nikāya, 14, 32, 48n4, 201, 207

Anurādhapura, 107–108

Apadāna, 19

apologetics, 89, 183

appreciation, 5, 46–47, 58–59, 63, 81, 124, 159, 160, 161; defined, 46

Arahants, 15n9, 17, 28, 37, 49, 50; (im)possibility of non-Buddhist, 7–10, 12–13, 16, 52, 206

Ariyapariyesanā Sutta, 48, 66

Ariyawansha, Niranjala, 103–106, 111

art or images: Bhadrakālī, 97; Buddha, 103, 109; mandalas, 176n11

ascetics, 101; non-Buddhist, 10, 12–14, 18, 27, 30, 40–41; four kinds of (Subhadda passage), 7–8, 11, 25, 28–29, 31–33, 35, 37–39, 51–52; *Paccekabuddhas* as, 18–20, 35. *See also* brahmins: ascetics and/or

attachment, 40, 215; aversion and, 118, 123, 124; freedom from, 73, 118; to pleasure, 218; to religion, 89, 118, 159, 218; to rules and ceremonies, 32, 42; suffering caused by, 217; to tenet systems, 118, 124; to views, 29–30, 218–219, 222; to words and concepts, 217

Atthasālinī, 43n10

attitudes, 2, 69n4, 75, 87, 102, 111, 143; views or claims vs., 68–69, 69n4, 100, 143, 151

Avataṃsaka Sūtra, 171–172

awakening. *See* enlightenment

Ayya Khema, 56n17

B

Bahudhātuka Sutta, 52

Barth, Karl, 53n13

bhikkhunīs. *See* nuns

bodhi. *See* enlightenment

Bodhi, Bhikkhu, 5, 23–26, 30, 32, 34–35, 37, 40–41, 44, 48n5, 76

bodhicitta, 179

Bodhisatta/Bodhisattva, 20, 138, 139, 176–177; path or vow of, 138, 175–176, 178

Bön, 117

Brahmajāla Sutta, 33n5

brahmavihāras, 21, 72, 84

brahmins, 21, 100, 202; ascetics and/or, 12–13, 27, 32, 38–39, 51, 101

C

colonialism, 4, 173; exclusivism and, 107, 109, 111; intellectual, 3; in Sri Lanka, 107, 109–111, 201

compassion (*karuṇā*), 6, 69, 72–74, 82; for all beings, 64, 83–84, 170; of Buddha, 52, 182; in Bodhisattva path, 177, 178; Dalai Lama on, 5, 88, 155, 157–158, 162, 164; in four immeasurables, 21; Nyingma perspective on, 174–175; in *tong-len* meditation, 178–179; as virtue, 3, 21; as universal value, 5, 21

conditioned genesis. *See* dependent origination

Cone, James, 195

confidence (*saddhā*), 57, 205–206

contemplation (*samādhi*), 6, 18, 74, 131n3, 178, 214; Christian modes of, 181; morality, wisdom, and, 55, 56

conventional truth, 72, 79–81, 86, 90, 145

conversion: to Buddhism, 35; to Christianity, 109, 199–200; eschewed, 5, 89, 159, 204, 207, 218; interreligious dialogue and, 163

Cornille, Catherine, 168, 184n20

corruptions, 12, 14

cosmologies, Buddhist, 37, 98; Buddha's uniqueness in, 35, 37, 43–44; early, 6, 8–9; science and, 43–44, 152n13; tolerance of, 21; planes of existence in, 20–21

craving, 7–8, 10, 13, 32, 42, 191, 193, 202n6

Critical Buddhism, 149

Cūḷa Hatthipadopama Sutta, 205

Cūḷaniddesa, 17n14, 18–19

Cūḷa Sīhanāda Sutta, 12, 51n12, 65–66, 206–207, 217

D

Dalai Lama XIV, 3, 5, 72, 122, 209; on compassion, 5, 88, 155, 157–158, 162, 164; on core characteristics of religion, 87–88, 157–158; exclusivism and, 77–78, 150, 152–153, 156, 159–165; on faith and respect, 161; Geluk school of, 164–165; Great Perfection and, 152; nonsectarianism and, 86, 116, 119–120, 124, 152, 153; opposition to, 123, 152; on other religious paths, 77–79, 81, 89, 125, 155–164; as pluralist or pluralistic attitude of, 77, 86, 90, 156–157, 159–164; on skilful means, 77–78, 158; on Two Truths, 79–80

dam tsig (*samaya*), 175

Dambulla, 109–111; Buddhist exclusivism in, 98–99, 107, 110–111; Buddhist temple in (*see* Rangiri Dambulu Vihāraya); as Buddhist sacred space, 97–98; Hindu temple in, 97, 99; history of, 102–103; Kandalama protest in, 103–104, 106–107; mosque in, 98–99, 105–107, 109–112; mosque attack in, 98–99, 102, 105–107; nuns' ordination in, 104

Daoism, 192

dasa sil mātās, 104, 104nn9–10. *See also* nuns

defilements, 11, 49, 164

Deleuze, Gilles, 135

delusion, 174, 179, 202n6; greed, hatred, and, 34, 41, 49. *See also* ignorance

Denys Rinpoche, 121

dependent origination (conditioned genesis; dependent arising;

pratītyasamutpāda), 13, 15, 18–19, 34, 39–40, 42, 44, 195, 217

Deshung Rinpoche, 119–120

de Silva, Lily, 55, 60

dge lugs, 130, 143. *See also* Geluk school

dhamma (factors of existence), 12

Dhamma/*Dharma*, 13, 17, 48, 84, 123, 176, 183n19; Buddhism vs., 25–27, 35; clinging to, 219; correct (*shōbō*), 196; cosmology and, 44; in "*dhammavinaya*," 7, 23, 25–26, 28–29; doctrines of, 39, 41; essentialist view of, 36; followers of, 42; forgotten, 53; inclusivist view of, 41n7, 52; interpretations of, 6, 35–36; liberation and, 23, 25; non-Buddhist, 35–36; public teachings of, 75; as raft, 220; Right Method (*ñāya*) of, 37–38; schools incompatible with, 24, 31; spreading of, 87; taught by historical Buddha, 7–8, 11, 20, 23, 25–27, 29, 31, 32, 43, 170, 172, 205; taught by other Buddhas, 8–9, 49, 55, 171; threatened, 102, 109, 120, 123; transcendent reality or God as, 57–58; whole vs. partial, 49. *See also* Three Jewels

Dhammapada, 12, 51

Dhammapada-aṭṭhakathā, 20n17

Dhammavisuddhi, Yatadolawatte, 55–56

dharmakāya, 171, 175, 176, 179–180

Dharmakīrti, 148

dialogue, interreligious, 2–3, 27, 72, 87–89, 135, 195; academic discourse on, 64, 89; Buddhist-Christian, 180, 189, 192; Christian-initiated, 2, 124, 197–201, 203, 209; Dalai Lama and, 78, 120, 126, 155–157, 160, 163; scholarship on, 2, 208; three categories of (*see* tripolar typology); types of, 67, 155–156

dialogue, intra-Buddhist, 2, 27

Dīgha Nikāya, 51, 100–101; rival teachers in, 7n2, 31–32. *See also* names of individual *sutta*s

Dilgo Khyentsé Rinpoche, 119, 121, 178n13

diversity: acceptance of, 69, 82, 156, 159–160, 162–163, 165, 203, 214, 220; appreciation vs. tolerance for, 46, 58–59; Buddha's response to, 27, 89, 203–204; of Buddhist schools, 116, 137, 149, 187–188, 216; celebration or welcoming of, 64, 67–68, 159; as challenge or problem (or not), 2, 82, 212–214, 216; Christian discussions of, 125, 147; Dalai Lama on, 155–157, 161–165; of *Dhamma*, 27, 36; dialogue and, 197–198, 209; discomfort with, 214, 222; due to different spiritual levels, 58–59; Ferrer on, 132–133, 136, 139; flourishing with, 214, 216, 218–219, 221; historical views of, 3; implicitly unbiased response to, 121; Nāgārjuna's tetralemma and, 142; nonsectarian response to, 116, 119, 124, 149–150; popular vs. traditional views of, 3; practical vs. theoretical approach to, 188, 195–196; salvation and, 147; of spiritual paths, 5–6; theological response to, 124–126; unity in, 72

Divyāvadāna, 20n18

dṛṣṭi, 69n4, 144n3. *See also* views

Duckworth, Douglas S., 1, 129, 142

Dzongsar Khyentse Rinpoche, 220

idheva, 7, 8, 29–30, 207

ignorance, 67, 84; craving and, 7, 8, 10, 13, 191; dependent origination and, 40; exclusivist views and, 78; greed, ill will, and, 193–195

images. *See* art or images

impermanence: of conditioned things, 1, 146; of existence, 7, 22; of eye, etc., 42; meditation on, 14; suffering, no-self, and, 18, 19, 40, 132

inclusivism: Buddha's (lack of), 41n7, 65–66, 100, 203–205, 207; Buddhist, 47n1, 67, 99–100, 107–108, 111, 137, 138n8, 150; as cross-cultural category, 3; defined, 50, 64, 99n5, 156; hierarchical, 134, 144n4; Jayatilleke's, 54–55; nonsectarianism and, 117, 130; of Pāli Canon, 65–66, 100; pluralism overlaps with, 66–67; skilful means and, 78; Sri Lankan, 98, 108, 111; strategies of, 100–102; subordination and, 100–102, 110; Theravāda, 50, 52, 54–56, 58–59; Tibetan, 75, 77, 86, 89, 130, 137, 149; tolerance and, 66. *See also* meta-inclusivism; open inclusivism; pluralis(tic) inclusivism

Indian Buddhism, 4, 68, 70, 76, 86, 101, 117; schools of, 79. *See also* Early Buddhism; Madhyamaka

insight. *See* wisdom

interreligious dialogue. *See* dialogue, interreligious

Isigala Sutta, 17

Islam, 56, 57, 68, 74n14, 151, 194; Dalai Lama on, 155, 156. *See also* Sri Lanka: Muslims in

Itivuttaka, 47

Ito, Tomoni, 56n18

J

Jackson, Peter, 56n18, 58

Jainism, 16

Jambukola Vihāra. *See* Rangiri Dambulu Vihāraya

Jamyang Khyentsé Wangpo, 117, 118, 121

Japanese Buddhism, 4, 70, 149, 189

*Jātaka*s, 20, 49n8

Jayatilleke, Kalatissa Nanda, 33, 54–55, 205n11, 206

Jesus Christ, 53n13, 55, 99n5, 150, 156, 175, 177–179, 182, 191, 208; as a Buddha, 57

*jhāna*s, 11, 21

Jonang Tāranātha, 121

Jonang tradition, 121

joy, altruistic or sympathetic (*muditā*), 21, 64, 72, 73, 75, 84, 175, 176n11

Judaism, 151, 155, 175, 194

K

Kagyü school, 86, 120n1, 130, 149; Karma Kagyu, 123

Kalu Rinpoche, 121

Kangyur, 70

Kantians, 136–137, 144

karma/kamma, 119, 147, 151, 189; rebirth and, 11, 20–21, 163; spreading Buddhism as positive, 87

Karunadasa, Y., 33

Kassapa, 101

Keller, Catherine, 195

Kevaddha Sutta, 100–101

Khaggavisāṇa Sutta, 17–18

Khentrul Rinpoche, 121

Kiblinger, Kristin Beise, 47n1, 66–67, 99–101, 125, 137, 169

Klein, Anne, 145
Knitter, Paul, 64n1, 70, 125, 171n5, 195
Kongtrül, Jamgön, 117–119, 124–125, 130, 149; lineage of, 121, 123
Korean Buddhism, 4, 70
Küng, Hans, 149
Küster, Volker, 64, 67
Kūṭadanta Sutta, 100
Kuttianimattathil, Jose, 208
Kyabje Tashi Norbu Rinpoche, 121

L

language, 67, 69, 133–134, 215, 216
LGBTIQ, 84, 219
liberation: of all sentient beings, 85; of *Arahant*s, 10; conventional truth as means to, 90; from ego, 41, 58; *Nibbāna* and, 47–48; as OTMIX, 69; of *Paccekabuddha*s, 16–19, 35–36; via Buddha's teachings, 6, 14, 23, 29, 40, 50–51, 163, 170–172; via Eightfold Path, 8, 23, 25, 51, 56; exclusivist view of, 163–164, 204, 207; via non-Buddhist paths, 10–11, 18–20, 23–25, 32–33, 35–36, 40, 41, 43, 47, 50, 55–57, 59, 77, 116, 171, 204; via Prāsaṅgika-Madhyamaka only, 143, 150, 163–164; via *Sammā-sambuddha*s' teachings, 8–9, 13, 15–16, 22; socio-political, 195. *See also* enlightenment; *Nirvāṇa/Nibbāna*; ultimate goal(s)
Lochen Dharmaśrī, 131n3
Lokottaravādins, 19–20
Longchenpa, 117, 146, 147
love, 3, 64, 69, 73, 74, 84, 88, 157–158, 162, 164, 174, 175, 176n11, 199; of God and neighbor, 175; *tong-len* meditation and, 178–179
loving-kindness (*mettā/maitrī*), 21, 55, 73, 84–85, 157
Loy, David, 194
lta ba, 69n4. *See also* views

M

Madhyamaka, 129–131, 137, 143, 164; Two Truths view of, 79–81, 86. *See also* Prāsaṅgika Madhyamaka
Madhyamakāvatāra, 80
Mahā Titthāyatana Sutta, 201, 207
Mahāgovinda Sutta, 52–53, 55
Mahāmudrā, 121, 151
Mahānidāna Sutta, 13
Mahāparinibbāna Sutta, 7–9, 12, 27–31, 37, 51, 52, 207
Mahāsāṃghikas, 20
Mahāsīhanāda Sutta, 101
Mahāvagga, 10n6, 47n3
Mahāvastu, 19–20
Mahāyāna Buddhism, 56, 59, 76, 176; "anonymous Buddhists" in, 150–151; Buddhas in, 43, 176n11; inclusiveness vs. exclusiveness of, 26; inclusivism of, 149; Prāsaṅgika-Madhyamaka as pinnacle of, 131n3; scriptures in, 171–172, 176n11; Theravāda view of, 54, 54n14
Majjhima Nikāya, 38–39, 48. *See also* names of individual *sutta*s
Makhādeva Sutta, 74n13
Makkhali Gosāla, 7n2, 27–28, 31
Makransky, J., 76, 138n8, 144n5, 167, 193n4
marginalization strategy, 130, 144n4, 148
McCagney, N., 69
McFague, Sallie, 195

meditation, 11, 13, 74, 131n3, 146n6, 189, 191; as category of demarcation, 147–148, 152; on four immeasurables, 75, 82; insight, 14, 19; Mipam on, 145–146; non-Buddhist, 21; non-dual, 181, 214; serenity, 14, 19; secular mindfulness, 75; in Tibetan Buddhism, 74; tranquility, 14; undirected, 147

meditative equipoise, 145–146

meta-inclusivism, 64, 67

metaphors: blind men and elephant, 51; elephant tracker, 205–206; finger pointing to moon, 67, 133, 215; glow worms, 51–52; multiple rivers, 157; path to lost city, 204; raft, 219–220; snake, 219

metaphysics, 81, 129, 137, 160–162, 165; as aspect of religion, 87, 157–158; criteria of ethics vs., 67, 69, 135–136, 164

Milindapañha, 47–48, 53

mindfulness, 11, 14, 193n5

Mipam, 117, 131, 145–146, 147n8

missionaries, 102, 108–109, 173, 197, 198–200

moral psychology, 193–194

morality, 11, 19, 21, 49, 55, 56, 101, 164, 201, 212

Mūlamadhyamakakārikā, 80, 137n7

Myanmar (Burma), 3, 54n14, 70, 104n9

N

Nagara Sutta, 204

Nāgārjuna, 69, 80, 137, 142–143, 148, 153, 219

Nanda, 32

New Kadampa Tradition, 123

Ngawang, Geshe Thubten, 75

Nibbāna. See Nirvāṇa/Nibbāna

Nigaṇṭha Nāthaputta, 7, 27–28, 31

Nikāyas: diversity in, 36; on Eightfold Path, 8–9, 11–12, 15, 41; on other schools or paths, 5–6, 22, 23, 26, 40–41; on *Paccekabuddhas*, 16–17, 34–36; phrase *idheva* in, 29; phrase *ito bahiddhā* in, 12, 37–39; on stream-enterers, 41–43

*nirmanak*āya, 176

Nirvāṇa/Nibbāna, 22, 47–50, 134, 189, 191, 202n6; Buddhists attain, 2, 6, 7, 9, 16, 50; deathless, 9, 43, 47–49; enlightenment or liberation and, 47–48, 170; Geluk or Dalai Lama's view of, 130, 144, 150, 164; happiness of, 75, 78; inner inclination towards, 49–50, 58; as mental state, 47, 48n5, 58; Nāgārjuna on, 80; non-Buddhists attain, 50, 78, 207; non-Buddhists' partial progress toward, 50, 55; *saṃsāra* vs., 47; as transcendent reality, 47–48, 48n5, 50, 50, 57–58, 66

non-conceptuality, 131n2, 214–215, 221

non-duality, 6, 214–215

non-returners, 8, 13

nonsectarianism, 136, 139; alternatives to, 132, 138; as attitude, 117–118, 120, 122–124; defined, 149–150; of events, 122; of historical Buddha, 116, 148; as movement, 117, 119–122, 125, 130, 143, 149, 151; pluralism and, 138, 139, 152n12, 153; scriptures on, 124; sects or sectarianism of, 130, 150; in Tibet or Tibetan Buddhism, 3, 79, 86, 88, 115–125, 130–133, 138, 143, 148–153, 220. *See also* rimé tradition

Noriaki, Hakamaya, 149

polemics, 31, 65, 84, 89, 102
practice, 57, 65, 69, 69n4
prajñāpāramitā literature, 69
Prakrit, 70
Prāsaṅgika Madhyamaka, 64, 130–131, 143, 150, 163
pratītyasamutpāda. *See* dependent origination
Protestant Buddhism, 109–110
Puggala-paññatti, 17, 19
Pūraṇa Kassapa, 7n2, 27, 31

R

Race, Alan, 64n1, 68, 99
Rahner, Karl, 150
Rahula, Walpola, 54, 203n9
Rangiri Dambulu Vihāraya (Golden Temple; Jambukola Vihāra): background and history, 99, 102–103, 105; leadership of, 98, 98n3, 103; media affiliated with, 102, 106; reputation of, 104–105
Rangjung Dorjé, 117
rebirth, 7, 13, 53, 59, 163; good, 6, 20–22, 85; liberation from (*see* liberation)
reformers: Buddhist, 56, 84, 192; Catholic, 198–199
refuge: objects of, 15, 75; taking of, 71, 73, 147–148, 174
relativism, 24, 132–134, 136, 138, 149, 220; pluralism and, 133, 151, 156, 162, 203
Religious Dialogue in Modern Society (ReDi) project, 72, 74n15, 78n20
religious diversity. *See* diversity
religious experience, 132–133, 156, 170, 182, 195, 202
rigpa, 179. *See also* dharmakāya
Rimay Gyalten Sogdzin Rinpoche, 120–121
rimé tradition (*ris med* tradition), 79, 115–116, 123, 129, 143, 149, 151; contemporary, 119–120; historical, 116–119; events, 199, 122; lineages, masters, or centres, 117, 119–123; literature, 123–124. *See also* nonsectarianism
Roberts, Michael, 103, 110
Roloff, Carola [Bhikṣuṇī Jampa Tsedroen], 63
Roman Catholicism, 103, 185, 197–200
Ruegg, David Seyfort, 101–102
Ruether, Rosemary, 195
rūpakāya, 176

S

saddhā. *See* confidence
Sakya school, 86, 149
Sallekha Sutta, 170
samādhi, 21, 55
Sāmaññaphala Sutta, 31
sambhogakāya, 176
Sāṃkhya, 18
*Sammā-sambuddha*s, 8–9, 12, 16–19, 22, 49, 52
Saṃyutta Nikāya, 9, 12–13, 26, 39, 42
Sandaka Sutta, 54
Saṅgha/Saṃgha, 9, 50, 52, 53, 105, 122, 172; Buddha, *Dhamma/Dharma* and (*see* Three Jewels); non-exclusivist meaning of, 57; *Paccekabuddha*s and, 18, 49, 55; in Sri Lanka, 98n3, 105, 110; in Thailand, 84; uniqueness of, 53, 56–57
Saṅgīti Sutta, 76, 84n24
Sañjaya Belaṭṭhaputta, 7, 27–31

trust. *See* confidence (*saddhā*)
truth. *See* conventional truth; Two Truths; ultimate truth
Tsongkhapa, 117, 143, 145, 146n6, 149
Tulku, Ringu, 116–117, 124–125
Two Truths, 57, 72, 79–82, 86, 90–91. *See also* conventional truth; ultimate truth

U

Udāna, 17, 47, 51–52
Uddaka Rāmaputta, 25
ultimate goal(s), 11, 47, 50n10, 188, 208; Buddhahood, 137, 176; Eightfold Path and, 7–9; suffering's end or amelioration as, 77, 190; exclusivist view of, 8, 15, 20, 24, 26, 40–41, 163–165; in nonsectarian movement, 79; "one vehicle" and, 137–138; pluralist view of, 9; *Paccekabuddhas* and, 18; *paṭiññā* as, 27; plurality of, 135; provisional goals vs., 5–6, 20–22, 54; supreme happiness as, 75. *See also* enlightenment; liberation; *Nirvāṇa/Nibbāna*
ultimate reality, 24, 209; Buddhahood as, 180–181; God as, 138, 180–181; empty, 144; language about, 133; *Nibbāna* as, 48–49; as OTMIX, 69; religious other's, 64, 91; theological views of, 171, 180–183, 188–191; undetermined, 133–135, 137, 138, 139, 142–144
ultimate truth, 57, 63, 87, 133, 135, 151; Dalai Lama or Geluk school on, 144, 152, 158, 163–165; determinate, 139, 152; different views of, 79, 81, 86, 130–132, 144; emptiness or *śūnyatā* as, 79, 129–130, 142–145; Mipam on, 131; Nāgārjuna on, 80; in non-Buddhist religions, 80–81, 90–91, 100, 132; openness and, 63, 70, 72, 79; in (Prāsaṅgika) Madhymaka, 86, 129–131. *See also* Two Truths
Upanishads, 18
Upāyakauśalya Sūtra, 77
upāyakauśalya/*upāyakosalla*. *See* skilful means
upekkhā/upekṣā. *See* equanimity

V

Vasubandhu, 72n8
Vatican II, 197–201, 208
Vedic/Brahmanical religion, 100, 101, 202
Vélez de Cea, Abraham, 23, 59n22, 125, 139n9, 155, 203n10; on attitudes vs. views, 68–69, 69n4, 100, 102, 116, 143; on Buddha or Early Buddhism, 8, 14, 89, 100, 116, 203–207; on Dalai Lama, 77; on Theravāda pluralism, 47n1, 50n9; on *Paccekabuddhas*, 18; on pluralist(ic) inclusivism, 67, 100, 100n6, 116, 203; on tripolar typology, 64n1, 68–69
Vibhaṅga, 15n9
Vietnamese Buddhism, 70, 74n13
views, 52, 69n4, 144n3; attachment or clinging to, 29–30, 216–219, 221–222; attitudes vs. (*see under* attitudes); differing, 78, 81, 86, 88, 90, 101, 130, 134; dissenting, 76; false or perverse, 52, 75; hierarchies of (*see under* hierarchies); non-action from three, 201; non-Buddhist, 78, 150; relinquishing all, 137n7; sixty-two, 32–33; of suffering, 147, 192
Vigrahavyāvartanī, 137n7

W

Z

www.ingramcontent.com/pod-product-compliance
Lightning Source LLC
Chambersburg PA
CBHW070403270326
41926CB00014B/2679
9781781799055